CENTURY PSYCHOLOGY SERIES

Richard M. Elliott, Editor
Kenneth MacCorquodale, Assistant Editor

TECHNIQUES OF
ATTITUDE SCALE CONSTRUCTION

Techniques of
Attitude Scale Construction

by

ALLEN L. *Louis* EDWARDS

Professor of Psychology
The University of Washington

New York
APPLETON-CENTURY-CROFTS, INC.

Library of Congress Catalog No.
56-11542

To

Louis Leon Thurstone

1887—1955

Preface

The impetus given to research involving social attitudes by the writings of L. L. Thurstone in the 1920's has maintained itself for over a quarter of a century. During this time there has been a continued interest upon the part of psychologists, political scientists, sociologists, and educationists in the use of scales for measuring attitudes.

This book is concerned with techniques for the construction of attitude scales. Once a set of attitude statements has been collected, there are two general methods that have been used in the development of attitude scales. One of these methods involves the use of a judging group. The judging group is not asked to respond to the statements in terms of their own agreement or disagreement with them, but rather to judge the degree of favorableness or unfavorableness expressed by each statement. These judgments are then used as a basis for determining scale values of the statements upon a psychological continuum. Once the scale values of the statements are known, subjects can then be asked to express their agreement or disagreement with the individual statements. Attitude scores for these subjects can then be obtained based upon the prior knowledge of the scale values of the statements.

The judgment methods for constructing attitude scales differ only in the manner in which the judgments and scale values of the statements are obtained. They include the method of paired comparisons, the method of equal-appearing intervals, and the method of successive intervals. These methods are described in Chapters 2 through 5.

A second method of developing attitude scales is based upon direct responses of agreement or disagreement with attitude statements. Since the response methods do not require prior knowledge of the scale values of the statements in any exact sense, a judging group is not necessary. It is sufficient for the response methods if one can assume that the response "agree" to a statement indicates a more favorable attitude than the response "disagree," or vice versa. The response methods for constructing attitude scales include the method of summated ratings and scalogram analysis. These methods are presented in Chapters 6 and 7.

Another method for constructing an attitude scale that makes use of both judgments and responses is described in Chapter 8. This method is termed the scale-discrimination technique. It is an early effort upon the part of Kilpatrick and myself at a synthesis of a scaling and a response method for developing an attitude scale.

H-technique, as described in Chapter 9, is also a response method. It has as its objective the improvement of a cumulative scale—a kind of scale about which more will be said in the text. In this chapter I have also described another effort at a synthesis of scaling and response methods which, for want of a better name, I have called W-technique.

This, in brief, represents the content of this book. It is intended for those who may desire to measure attitudes toward something in which they are interested, but who fail to find an appropriate scale available. It is my hope that the methods presented here may be of some assistance to such persons in developing their own attitude scales suitable for their own particular purposes.

This book is not intended as an exhaustive treatise of psychological scaling methods. For this reason, I have not included discussions of the unfolding technique of Coombs, the latent structure model of Lazarsfeld, nor developments in the field of multidimensional scaling. These models are relatively recent in origin and have not been applied to any great extent in the development of attitude scales. Nor have I included any discussion of rating methods and indirect techniques of assessing attitudes.

And now a word about how this book may be used. The independent reader can follow the worked-out examples in the text. If the book is used as a classroom text, the instructor can make use of the problems and questions at the end of each chapter as laboratory exercises to be carried out by the students. I would suggest that in such cases the students, through discussion, decide upon some institution, object, group, issue, or thing of interest. Each student could then be responsible for obtaining a part of the initial set of attitude statements relating to this object of interest. Through co-operative effort, the data collections suggested in the various problems would not demand excessive work upon the part of any one student. The data thus collected co-operatively can be used by each student in carrying out subsequent assignments. Thus, if used as a classroom text, this book may serve as a kind of laboratory manual which students will be expected to use, rather than just passively read. It is, after all, an old principle of psychology that we learn by doing.

I am indebted to Professor Sir Ronald A. Fisher, Cambridge, and to Messrs. Oliver and Boyd Ltd., Edinburgh for permission to reprint Table III from their book, *Statistical Methods for Research Workers*. C. I. Bliss's table of the angular transformation for percentages is reproduced by the kind permission of both Dr. Bliss and Dr. Snedecor from Dr. Snedecor's book, *Statistical Methods*, published by the Iowa State College Press.

For permission to use portions of articles published previously, with Katherine C. Kenney and F. P. Kilpatrick as coauthors, I am indebted to both of these individuals and to the publishers of the *Journal of Applied Psychology* and *Psychometrika* in which the articles originally appeared.

My greatest debt, of course, is to those research workers who have contributed to the field of attitude measurement. It is their research that made this book possible, and acknowledgment of their contributions is made at appropriate places in the text.

A.L.E.

Seattle, Washington

Contents

TECHNIQUES OF
ATTITUDE SCALE CONSTRUCTION

"The concept of attitude is probably the most distinctive and indispensable concept in contemporary American social psychology. No other term appears more frequently in experimental and theoretical literature."

Gordon W. Allport—1935

1

Introduction

There is a vast literature in the journals of psychology, sociology, education, and political science dealing with attitudes. Some of these articles have had as their concern the comparison of attitudes of members of different groups. Others have reported upon the way in which attitudes are developed in young children. The interest of some writers has been in the theory and nature of attitudes and in the way in which attitudes are defined. Others have investigated and reported upon the problem of attitude change — the manner in which new experiences modify existing attitudes. Still others report upon the relationship between attitudes and other variables such as personality traits and level of intelligence. The influence of attitudes upon such psychological processes as learning and remembering, perception, reasoning and thinking, has also been investigated in some detail. Another major area of interest in attitudes concerns the methods by which attitudes might be measured.

This book is also concerned with the measurement of attitudes. Attitude scales, used in the measurement of attitudes, have proved to be useful in a variety of research problems. When a research worker is interested in measuring the attitudes of a large number of individuals, he may find that there is no available scale suitable for his purpose. It thus becomes necessary for him to construct his own

1

scale. The purpose of this book is to describe the various methods that have been used in the construction of attitude scales.

DEFINITION OF ATTITUDE

When you ask someone about his attitude toward something, say his job, what is it that you are interested in finding out? If you are primarily interested in how he *feels* about his job and, in particular, whether he *likes* or *dislikes* his job, then you are using the concept of attitude in much the same way that it will be used in this book.[1]

We shall, following Thurstone (1946), define an attitude as *the degree of positive or negative affect associated with some psychological object*.[2] By a psychological object, Thurstone means any symbol, phrase, slogan, person, institution, ideal, or idea toward which people can differ with respect to positive or negative affect. A particular job, for example, may be a psychological object. The United Nations, a political party, the title of a book, a minority group, a nation, labor unions, and a particular food are still other examples of psychological objects.

In the literature of psychology, the terms *affect* and *feeling* are used interchangeably. An individual who has associated *positive* affect or feeling with some psychological object is said to *like* that object or to have a *favorable* attitude toward the object. An individual who has associated *negative* affect with the same psychological object would be said to *dislike* that object or to have an *unfavorable* attitude toward the object.

---

[1] For a historical survey of the concept of attitude, see Allport (1935).

[2] References are cited by author and by date in the text and are listed at the end of each chapter.

THE METHOD OF DIRECT QUESTIONING

It might seem logical to assume that if we want to know how individuals feel about some particular psychological object, the best procedure would be to ask them. Direct questioning may, indeed, be satisfactory for some purposes. By means of direct questions we might be able to classify individuals into three groups: those with favorable attitudes, those with unfavorable attitudes, and those who say that they are doubtful or undecided about their attitudes toward the object. If you have ever been interviewed about your attitude toward a political party by one of the national public opinion polls, you will recall that the interviewer was apparently trying to determine whether to classify you as one of those who liked or had a favorable attitude toward the party or as one of those who disliked or had an unfavorable attitude toward the party. If you were reluctant about expressing how you felt about the party, then you were probably classified by the interviewer in the "don't know" category.

The reluctance of many individuals to give public expression to their feelings or attitudes on controversial issues is, of course, a disadvantage of the method of direct questioning. During wartime when rationing is in effect, many individuals with negative attitudes toward rationing might not care to express these attitudes publicly because of fear of social disapproval. Only when the social atmosphere is free from felt or actual pressures toward conformity might we expect to obtain evidence about a person's attitudes by means of direct questioning.[3]

In an unpublished study by Edwards, college students

---

[3] See, for example, the various studies related to this point cited in Cantril (1944).

interviewed residents of Seattle, Washington, about their attitudes toward a proposed state legislative bill intended to provide a cash bonus to war veterans. Half of the individuals interviewed were asked directly about their attitudes toward the bill. The others were given a sheet marked "Secret Ballot" and a pencil and were asked to check whether they were in favor of or against the bill. The ballot was then folded by the individual and inserted by him into a box plainly labeled "Secret Ballot Box." It was found that many more "don't know" responses were obtained by direct questioning than by the use of the secret ballot and that the proportion of individuals saying that they had unfavorable attitudes toward the bill was much higher for the secret-ballot group than for the direct-question group. Some weeks later, when the actual election vote of Seattle residents on the bill was obtained, it was found that the proportions obtained from the secret ballot were much more in accord with the actual vote than those from the direct interview. The apparent reason for the discrepancies between the two methods was that most of the interviewers were themselves war veterans and many of the individuals with unfavorable attitudes toward the proposed bill did not choose to express this attitude openly to the interviewers.

There are other objections to the method of direct questioning. According to the findings of clinical psychologists and psychiatrists, some individuals may not be aware of their feelings toward a given psychological object. Early in a clinical interview, a parent may profess the greatest love and concern for his children. Later, in the course of therapy designed to provide new insights into his feelings, the same individual may confess to highly ambivalent feelings about his offspring or perhaps even to extreme dislike of them. In other cases, the clinical psychologists and psychiatrists tell us that some individuals who profess great dislike of something may, in fact, be reacting against unconscious impulses of the opposite nature. Thus, the man who abhors liquor and is constantly protesting against its use in any form may, perhaps, be reacting against his own fondness for the bottle. The young male teenager who "hates" girls may, perhaps, also be reacting against his fondness for them.

It is also true that sometimes our feelings about a psychological object are so mixed and confused that it is difficult for us to evaluate how we feel by introspective methods. We may, for example, have both positive and negative affect associated with the same psychological object. How, then, are we to weigh and evaluate the strength or intensity of the two opposed affects and to decide whether we like or dislike the object? Such evaluations may demand more objectivity and insight than some individuals are capable of giving, and certainly upon the spur of the moment and in response to a direct question.

Additional problems involved in asking people direct questions about their attitudes are discussed in some detail by Payne (1951) in his book, *The Art of Asking Questions,* and also by Maccoby and Maccoby (1954), Cantril (1944), Parten (1950), Kornhauser (1951), and Remmers (1954).

DIRECT OBSERVATION OF BEHAVIOR

Another approach to the problem of investigating attitudes has been to observe the behavior of individuals with respect to a psychological object, rather than to ask direct questions about how they feel about the object. There are limitations to this approach also. A research worker interested in the attitudes of a large number of individuals toward some object may not have the opportunity to observe in detail the behavior of all of the individuals in whom he is interested. For example, if he were interested in the attitudes of individuals toward the Negro, he might spend considerable time waiting for the desired behavioral interactions between the individuals and Negroes to occur.

If the behavior with respect to the object does eventually occur, it, of course, may also fail to reveal the feelings of the individual. In many cases behavior is designed to conceal feelings. We are all aware of situations in which we have acted contrary to the way in which we felt because of various reasons. If a man dislikes fish — that is, has an unfavorable attitude toward fish — he might not choose to express this attitude at a dinner party at which fish is served because of his desire not to offend his hostess.

Another individual may have a great fondness for steak (a favorable attitude toward this psychological object), yet if we observe his behavior in the local meat market, we may note that he passes up the display of filets mignons and selects for purchase two pounds of wieners. This bit of behavior, of course, does not necessarily express either his attitude toward steak or toward wieners. The price of steak may be more than he cares to pay. The wieners may be purchased, not for his own personal consumption, but for a picnic at which his children will be the chief consumers.

An elderly gentleman may be observed in attendance at the performance of the local symphony each week. The casual observer might infer that this behavior indicates that the gentleman has a very favorable attitude toward symphonic music. Direct questioning, on the other hand, might indicate that he detests symphonic music, but that he loves his wife very much. It is his wife, not he, who has the favorable attitude, and it is his wife who is responsible for his attendance at the concerts.

A man may purchase a local newspaper, not because he agrees with its editorial policies, but because it has the most complete stock market coverage of any of those papers available to him, or because his wife depends upon the paper in making up her week-end shopping list, or because his children take delight in the comic page.

Nor does a man necessarily quit his job simply because he may have an unfavorable attitude toward it. Whether he quits or not will depend upon the availability of other means of employment and a number of other possible factors. A housewife does not stop washing dishes merely because she has an unfavorable attitude toward this task. The dishes must be washed. She may prevail upon her children or, in their absence, her husband to do this chore. She may also make it plain to all concerned, by her verbal behavior, how she feels about washing dishes. It seems likely, however, that if family finances permit, she will sooner or later obtain the assistance of a maid or an electric dishwasher, in order to avoid what she considers an unpleasant task.

These examples illustrate that there is no necessary one-to-one correspondence between overt behavior and attitudes. Attitudes, as factors influencing or determining behavior, may be one of many such, and not necessarily the most prepotent. If we expect to predict behavior from feelings or attitudes, then these other factors must be taken into account. And similarly, if we expect to infer attitudes or feelings from direct observations of behavior, we must always consider the possibility that our inference will be incorrect simply because the behavior may be determined by factors other than the individual's feelings.

It would seem that, despite the limitations of the method of direct questioning, verbal behavior, under many circumstances, would provide a better, that is, more accurate, indication of the feelings or attitudes of individuals than observations of their non-verbal behavior. This, as we have pointed out earlier, is most apt to be the case when the social atmosphere is free from pressure so that feelings can be verbally expressed without fear of social disapproval. Some assurance of anonymity, as provided for in secret ballots, may result in individuals giving verbal expression to attitudes that they might otherwise deny or attempt to conceal.

It may be noted that in the definition of attitude given earlier we stressed the notion of *degree* of positive or negative affect associated with a psychological object. It is a disadvantage of both the method of direct questioning and the observation of behavior that they do not conveniently lend themselves to an assessment of the degree of affect individuals may associate with a psychological object. These methods instead result in a rather crude classification of attitudes. They may enable us, at best, for example, to classify individuals as favorable or unfavorable or undecided. Within the group of favorable individuals, it does not necessarily follow that they are all *equally* favorable. The members of this class may be quite heterogeneous with respect to the strength or intensity of their attitudes. This may be true also of the individuals classified as unfavorable.

To be able to assign individuals with respect to some variable to one of three classes may at times be satisfactory and useful. For some purposes, for example, it may be useful to know whether an individual belongs in the below average, the average, or the above average class with respect to height, weight, intelligence, or some other variable.

But for research purposes, where we are most often interested in relating one variable to another variable, we would like a greater degree of refinement in our system of classification. It would be advantageous, for example, to know an individual's height in terms of inches, his weight in terms of pounds, or his intelligence level in terms of his IQ, rather than merely that he was above average, below average, or average with respect to these variables. When we use a refined system of classification we can always obtain a cruder system by combining classes, if that is our desire.

ATTITUDE STATEMENTS

Most of us have encountered psychological tests of one variety or another. These tests consist of items to which we are asked to respond in some specified way. In general, these tests contain items that have been carefully edited and selected in accordance with some criteria. The tests are usually administered under controlled conditions and with standardized instructions. Since psychological tests can, in many instances, be given to large groups of individuals at one time, tests provide quick and convenient measures of variables of interest. The usefulness of psychological tests in education, industry, and research has been amply demonstrated. It has been a similar desire for a quick and convenient measure of attitudes that could be used with large groups that has led to the development of *attitude scales*. Attitude scales also provide us with one means of obtaining an assessment of the degree of affect that individuals may associate with some psychological object.

A well-constructed attitude scale consists of a number of items that have been just as carefully edited and selected in accordance with certain criteria as the items contained in any standardized psychological test. The items making up an attitude scale are called *statements*. A statement may be defined as anything that is said about a psychological object. The class of all possible statements that could be made about a given psychological object is often called a *universe of content* or simply a *universe*.

As in the construction of standardized psychological tests, the first step in the construction of an attitude scale is to obtain items, that is, statements, that will represent in a particular test the universe of interest. We may be able to write some of these statements ourselves. Additional statements can be obtained from newspaper editorials and magazine articles dealing with the psychological object or from books written about the object. Still other statements may be obtained by asking individuals to write short descriptions of their feelings about the psychological object.

The universe of statements about a given psychological object may be classified in various ways. But, before considering some of the subclasses making up a universe, we should perhaps first define another psychological concept, that of *belief*. By a person's beliefs about a psychological object we shall mean all of those statements relating to the object that he agrees with or accepts. By a person's disbeliefs about a psychological object we mean all of those statements about the object that he disagrees with or rejects. There remains the possibility that there is a third group of statements that a given person may neither accept nor reject. These are statements that he does not believe and that he does not disbelieve, but about which he is undecided or doubtful.

One of the major assumptions involved in the construction of attitude scales is that there will be differences in the belief and disbelief systems of those with favorable attitudes toward some psychological object and those with unfavorable attitudes.[4] It is not assumed that this will be true for each and every statement in the universe relating to the psychological object, but only with respect to certain subclasses of the statements. Consider, for example, a subclass of statements about a psychological object such that we might agree that each statement in the subclass is a factual statement. If we further assume that the factual knowledge represented by each statement is equally available to both those with favorable and unfavorable attitudes, then we might expect the probability of acceptance of a given statement to be the same for those with favorable and those with unfavorable attitudes. We can only say that, in general, we might expect this to be true, and that it will not necessarily be true for each and every factual statement.[5] It may be, for example, that individuals with favorable attitudes toward the psychological object are in a better position to have become acquainted with a particular factual statement than those with unfavorable attitudes, or vice versa. It may be true also that the particular kinds of facts that one learns about a psychological object are related to the particular attitude that one has toward the object.[6]

The point remains, however, that if a given statement is equally likely to be endorsed or accepted by those with favorable and by those with unfavorable attitudes, then this

[4] For a psychological analysis of belief and disbelief systems, see the article by Rokeach (1954).

[5] Campbell (1950), in his review of indirect measures of attitude, has described several techniques that depend upon reactions to factual statements as a basis for assessing attitude.

[6] The studies by Bartlett (1932), Watson and Hartmann (1939), Levine and Murphy (1943), Edwards (1941), Zillig (1928), and Seeleman (1940) bear upon this point.

statement will not be useful in differentiating between those with favorable and those with unfavorable attitudes. And this possibility always exists with respect to a factual statement unless we have prior knowledge that those with favorable attitudes are more or less likely to accept the statement than those with unfavorable attitudes.

It seems reasonable, as a first approximation, that the kinds of statements about a psychological object that are more likely to be endorsed or accepted by those with favorable attitudes than by those with unfavorable attitudes are those statements that are nonfactual but that are judged as expressing favorable feelings about the object. On the other hand, statements that are nonfactual but that are judged as expressing unfavorable feelings about a psychological object are more likely to be endorsed by those with unfavorable attitudes toward the object than by those with favorable attitudes. Our expectation is that individuals are much more likely to respond to statements of these two subclasses upon the basis of their attitudes or how they feel about the object than in terms of what they may regard as the factual truth or falsity of the statements. As a first step in developing an attitude scale, therefore, we eliminate from consideration all statements about the psychological object that are factual or that might be interpreted as factual.

We should also try to eliminate statements that might be considered ambiguous. For the moment we may define an ambiguous statement as one that can be interpreted in more than one way. When individuals are asked to judge the degree of favorableness or unfavorableness of such statements, we may expect their judgments to be influenced by the particular interpretation they give the statement. For example, the statement "There should be an international scientific holiday" might be interpreted by some individuals as being a favorable statement about science and by others as an unfavorable statement because of the ambiguity of the meaning of *scientific holiday*. If *scientific holiday* is interpreted as meaning a day on which science is to be honored, then the statement is likely to be regarded as favorable. On the other hand, if *scientific holiday* is interpreted as meaning a period during which the world is to enjoy a breather from further scientific discovery, the statement would probably be judged as being an unfavorable statement about science.

One of the best procedures in the preliminary evaluation of statements is to have several individuals respond to the statements as they would if they had favorable attitudes toward the object under consideration. The same individuals may then be asked to respond to the statements as they would if they had unfavorable attitudes. If it is possible for them to give similar responses of acceptance or rejection when they assume different attitudes, then such statements are not likely to be of value in an attitude scale. Preliminary evaluation of statements in the manner described can thus serve to eliminate many ambiguous as well as factual statements.

INFORMAL CRITERIA FOR ATTITUDE STATEMENTS

Wang (1932), Thurstone and Chave (1929), Likert (1932), Bird (1940), and Edwards and Kilpatrick (1948) have suggested various informal criteria for editing statements to be used in the construction of attitude scales. Their suggestions are summarized below:

1. Avoid statements that refer to the past rather than to the present.
2. Avoid statements that are factual or capable of being interpreted as factual.

3. Avoid statements that may be interpreted in more than one way.

4. Avoid statements that are irrelevant to the psychological object under consideration.

5. Avoid statements that are likely to be endorsed by almost everyone or by almost no one.

6. Select statements that are believed to cover the entire range of the affective scale of interest.

7. Keep the language of the statements simple, clear, and direct.

8. Statements should be short, rarely exceeding 20 words.

9. Each statement should contain only one complete thought.

10. Statements containing universals such as *all, always, none,* and *never* often introduce ambiguity and should be avoided.

11. Words such as *only, just, merely,* and others of a similar nature should be used with care and moderation in writing statements.

12. Whenever possible, statements should be in the form of simple sentences rather than in the form of compound or complex sentences.

13. Avoid the use of words that may not be understood by those who are to be given the completed scale.

14. Avoid the use of double negatives.

In addition to the above suggestions, Payne (1951) has provided a checklist of things to be considered in preparing single questions for public opinion surveys. Many of the items in his list are also applicable to the phrasing of statements for attitude scales.

QUESTIONS AND PROBLEMS

1. Select some psychological object of interest and write five statements that you believe represent varying degrees of favorableness toward the object. Write also five statements about the same object that you believe represent varying degrees of unfavorableness. Get several individuals to rank the favorable statements from most to least favorable. Have them also rank the unfavorable statements from most to least unfavorable. Do these rankings tend to agree with

the rankings you assigned the statements? If not, what factors might account for the differences in the ranks assigned?

2. The following statements have been selected from various sources. Evaluate each statement in terms of the informal criteria that have been suggested for writing attitude statements.

Attitude Toward a College Education (Bird, 1940).

   a. A college education is financially expensive.

   b. A college education is valuable because it offers training in thinking and increases the opportunities for securing a good position after graduation.

Attitude Toward Censorship (Rosander and Thurstone, 1931).

   a. Whether censorship is good or bad depends to a large extent upon the censor.

   b. It is a shame that so many fine books and plays have been suppressed by censors.

   c. Censorship can never make people moral.

Attitude Toward the Church (Thurstone and Chave, 1929).

   a. I believe that if young people are not interested in the church, it is the fault of either their parents or the church leaders.

   b. Neither science nor religion will explain the riddle of man's existence.

   c. I believe the church is doing good, but it should be more modern in its point of view.

Attitude Toward Capital Punishment (Peterson, 1931).

   a. It is unfortunate that we have no efficient substitute for capital punishment.

   b. I don't believe in capital punishment but I'm not sure it isn't necessary.

   c. I think the return of the whipping post would be more effective than capital punishment.

Attitude Toward War (Bird, 1940).

   a. Wars are hard to eradicate because they are rooted in human nature.

3. Evaluate each of the following statements in terms of the informal criteria suggested for writing attitude statements.

Psychological Object	*Statement*
a. Russia	It was fortunate that Russia was our ally during World War II.

b. Motion Pictures	Hollywood produces more and better motion pictures than any other film capital in the world.
c. American communists	All American communists should be executed immediately and without trial.
d. United Nations	There is too much distrust of each other by the countries belonging to the United Nations.
e. Scientific method	It doesn't matter to me whether the scientific method is taught in the schools or not.
f. Psychology	Most people would find the study of psychology of interest.

4. Talk with several people and bring up the subject of attitudes. Ask each individual to define what he means by the concept. Compare the various definitions. Are they similar to the definition proposed in the chapter?

5. What are some of the difficulties involved in direct questioning of individuals about their attitudes?

6. What are some of the difficulties involved in inferring attitudes from observed behavior?

7. What are some of the reasons why factual statements may not be of value in assessing attitudes?

8. What are some of the reasons why ambiguous statements may not be of value in assessing attitudes? What are some of the things that might contribute to the ambiguity of an attitude statement?

REFERENCES AND SUGGESTED READINGS

(References following each chapter that are marked with an asterisk are suggested as supplementary reading assignments.)

*ALLPORT, G. W. Attitudes. In C. Murchison (Ed.), *A handbook of social psychology*. Worcester, Mass.: Clark Univ. Press, 1935. Pp. 798-844.

BARTLETT, F. C. *Remembering: a study in experimental and social psychology*. Cambridge, England: Cambridge Univ. Press, 1932.

BIRD, C. *Social psychology*. New York: Appleton-Century-Crofts, 1940.

CAMPBELL, D. T. The indirect assessment of social attitudes. *Psychol. Bull.*, 1950, 47, 15-38.

CANTRIL, H. *Gauging public opinion*. Princeton, N. J.: Princeton Univ. Press, 1944.

EDWARDS, A. L. Political frames of reference as a factor influencing recognition. *J. abnorm. soc. Psychol.*, 1941, 36, 34-50.

——— and KILPATRICK, F. P. A technique for the construction of attitude scales. *J. appl. Psychol.*, 1948, 32, 374-384.

*KORNHAUSER, A. Constructing questionnaires and interview schedules. In Jahoda, Marie, Deutsch, M., and Cook, S. W. (Eds.), *Research methods in social relations*. New York: Dryden Press, 1951. Pp. 423-462.

LEVINE, J. M., and MURPHY, G. The learning and forgetting of controversial material. *J. abnorm. soc. Psychol.*, 1943, 38, 507-517.

LIKERT, R. A technique for the measurement of attitudes. *Arch. Psychol.*, 1932, No. 140.

*MACCOBY, ELEANOR E., and MACCOBY, N. The interview: a tool of social science. In G. Lindzey (Ed.), *Handbook of social psychology*. Cambridge, Mass.: Addison-Wesley, 1954. Pp. 449-487.

PARTEN, MILDRED B. *Surveys, polls and samples*. New York: Harper, 1950.

PAYNE, S. L. *The art of asking questions*. Princeton, N. J.: Princeton Univ. Press, 1951.

PETERSON, RUTH C. *Scale for the measurement of attitude toward capital punishment*. Chicago: Univ. of Chicago Press, 1931.

REMMERS, H. H. *An introduction to opinion and attitude measurement*. New York: Harper, 1954.

*ROKEACH, M. The nature and meaning of dogmatism. *Psychol. Rev.*, 1954, 61, 194-204.

ROSANDER, A. C., and THURSTONE, L. L. *Scale for the measurement of attitude toward censorship*. Chicago: Univ. Chicago Press, 1931.

SEELEMAN, VIRGINIA. The influence of attitude upon the remembering of pictorial material. *Arch. Psychol.*, 1940, No. 258.

*THURSTONE, L. L. Comment. *Amer. J. Sociol.*, 1946, 52, 39-50.

—— and CHAVE, E. J. *The measurement of attitude*. Chicago: Univ. Chicago Press, 1929.

*WANG, K. A. Suggested criteria for writing attitude statements. *J. soc. Psychol.*, 1932, 3, 367-373.

WATSON, W. S., and HARTMANN, G. W. Rigidity of a basic attitudinal frame. *J. abnorm. soc. Psychol.*, 1939, 34, 314-336.

ZILLIG, MARIE. Einstellung und Aussage. *Z. Psychol.*, 1928, 106, 58-106.

2

The Method of Paired Comparisons

Let us suppose that we have 10 objects of the same size but of differing weights and that we wish to arrange the objects from the lightest to the heaviest. We could easily place each object on a scale, read the pointer on a dial, and record the measured weight. On the basis of our observations, the objects could then be arranged in order from the lightest to the heaviest. But suppose that a scale for weighing the objects is not available. Instead of weighing the objects, we present them to individuals and ask them to make judgments about the respective weights of the objects. We could, for example, ask each individual to arrange the objects from the lightest to the heaviest. Or we could present the objects in all possible pairs and ask each individual to judge which member of each pair was the heavier. Regardless of the particular method of obtaining the judgments, we could also order the objects from the lightest to the heaviest upon the basis of the average judgments of a large group of individuals.

The scale that we use in weighing objects we call a physical scale, and the ordering of the objects in terms of their measured weights is said to be on a *physical continuum*. The ordering of the objects upon the basis of judgments is said to be on a *psychological continuum*. In the early laboratory days of psychology, many investigations were made of the relationship between the ordering of objects or stimuli on a known physical continuum and the ordering of the same objects on a psychological continuum established by the judgments of individuals. The methods used in studying these relationships were known as *psychophysical methods*.

THURSTONE'S CONTRIBUTION

In the 1920's, Thurstone (1927*a*,1927*b*) published two important articles in which he developed his *law of comparative judgment*. The statement of the law of comparative judgment was important because it provided a rationale for the ordering of stimuli along a psychological continuum, even in those cases where there is no known physical continuum to which the values of the stimuli on the psychological continuum might be related. The law of comparative judgment thus made possible the quantitative investigation of all kinds of values and subjective experiences. Since Thurstone's original contribution, new methods for the scaling of stimuli have been developed, and Thurstone himself remained an important contributor to these methods and to their application to psychological problems. These methods are now generally known as *psychological scaling methods*, rather than psychophysical methods, since the interest is no longer in relating scale values of stimuli on a psychological continuum to those on a physical continuum, but rather in the psychological scale values themselves.

Given any set of *n* stimuli, we may postulate that these each possess in varying but unknown degree some attribute in which we are interested. The problem of psychological scaling is then to determine whether the *n* stimuli can be ordered on a psychological continuum with respect to the degree of the attribute each possesses. Psychological scaling methods do not, however, guarantee that the end result will be successful, that is, that a psychological continuum will be found for each and every attribute. It may also be pointed out that any given set of stimuli may be ordered in various ways, that is, that they may differ with respect to more than one attribute and that their ordering may not be the same on the various psychological continua corresponding to the attributes. This is a problem that we shall want to consider in greater detail in later discussions.

The law of comparative judgment assumes that for a given Stimulus i there is associated a most frequently aroused or *modal discriminal process* on a psychological continuum. A discriminal process, designated by S_i, is a theoretical concept and represents the experience or reaction of an individual when confronted with Stimulus i and asked to make a judgment of some attribute.[1] It is, as Thurstone (1927a) states, whatever it is that goes on when we make a discrimination or response involving a judgment of some attribute. It is not assumed that any given stimulus always evokes the same discriminal process. Since discriminal processes other than the modal one will occur for Stimulus i, it is necessary to make some assumption concerning the distribution of these discriminal processes. Thurstone makes the plausible assumption that the distribution of all discriminal processes aroused by Stimulus i is normal about the modal discriminal process. This distribution is illustrated in Figure 2.1.[2]

We know, from elementary statistical considerations, that any normal distribution, such as shown in Figure 2.1, can

---

[1] S_1 is used to designate a discriminal process associated with Stimulus 1 or, in general, S_i corresponds to a discriminal process associated with Stimulus i.

[2] Figures are numbered serially by chapters for convenient reference. Thus Figure 2.1 means the first figure in Chapter 2.

be described in terms of two parameters. These two parameters are the arithmetic mean of the distribution and the standard deviation of the distribution. We also know

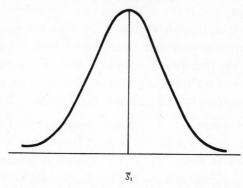

$$\overline{S}_i$$

Psychological Continuum

FIG. 2.1—Theoretical normal distribution of discriminal processes evoked by Stimulus i about the modal discriminal process $\overline{S}_i$.

that for any normal distribution the mean, median, and mode all have exactly the same value. Therefore, the modal discriminal process will also be the same as the mean or median of the distribution shown in Figure 2.1. The mean or median discriminal process associated with Stimulus i is taken as the *scale value* of the stimulus and is designated by $\overline{S}_i$. The standard deviation of the distribution of discriminal processes Thurstone refers to as the *discriminal dispersion* or dispersion of the discriminal processes for Stimulus i. The symbol used to designate the discriminal dispersion for Stimulus i is σ_i.

We have already pointed out that a given stimulus may vary with respect to more than one attribute. The modal discriminal process and discriminal dispersion for any given stimulus will, therefore, depend upon the particular attribute that is being judged. Let us, however, hold the attribute constant and introduce a second stimulus, say Stimulus j. Stimulus j, in other words, is also to be judged with respect to the same attribute that Stimulus i was judged. We again assume that Stimulus j has associated with it a modal discriminal process for this attribute and that the distribution of discriminal processes S_j is also normally distributed about the modal discriminal process $\overline{S_j}$ with its characteristic discriminal dispersion or standard deviation σ_j. For the same attribute, then, two stimuli, i and j, may differ with respect to their modal discriminal processes, that is, their scale values $\overline{S_i}$ and $\overline{S_j}$, and also with respect to their discriminal dispersions, σ_i and σ_j.

Assume, for example, that i and j are two statements about some psychological object. We ask a large group of subjects to make comparative judgments as to whether i or j is the more favorable statement and we find that .500 of the subjects say that i is more favorable than j and .500 say that j is more favorable than i.[3] On the basis of this finding, we might argue that Stimulus i and Stimulus j are exactly equal with respect to the attribute we are trying to scale. For, if the modal discriminal processes aroused by the two stimuli are exactly the same, that is, if $\overline{S_i} = \overline{S_j}$, then the discrimination or judgment i greater than j would, in fact, be expected to occur equally frequently with the judgment i less than j, if judgments of i equal to j are not permitted.

On the other hand, if we find that more than .500 of the subjects say that i is more favorable than j, then we might argue that i has a higher modal discriminal process than j on the psychological continuum ranging from least to most favorable. If it is true, for example, that $\overline{S_i} > \overline{S_j}$, then we

---

[3] Judgments of i equal to j are not permitted.

would expect to find more than .500 of the subjects saying that i is more favorable than j.[4] Similarly, if we find that less than .500 of the subjects say that i is more favorable than j, this result would be consistent with the notion that $\overline{S}_i < \overline{S}_j$. The scale separation of the modal discriminal processes, $\overline{S}_i$ and $\overline{S}_j$, on the psychological continuum should, in other words, be some function of the proportion of judgments i greater than j.

By getting comparative judgments of the kind described above, we can obtain an empirical frequency corresponding to the number of times that i is judged to be more favorable than j. We let

$$f_{ij} = i > j \qquad (2.1)$$

where f_{ij} is the frequency with which i is judged greater than j. We can express this frequency as a proportion by dividing by the total number of judgments obtained. We let N represent the total number of judgments so that

$$p_{ij} = f_{ij}/N \qquad (2.2)$$

where p_{ij} is the proportion of times that i is judged greater than j.[5]

The values of p_{ij} can be expressed as unit normal deviates z_{ij} by means of Table I in the appendix. The marginal entries of Table I show the proportions p_{ij} and the cell entries give the values of z_{ij} corresponding to the proportions. It may be observed, for example, that when $p_{ij} = .500$, then $z_{ij} = .000$, and this would be in accord with

---

[4] The symbol $>$ means "is greater than" and $<$ means "is less than." $\overline{S}_i > \overline{S}_j$ is read "S bar i is greater than S bar j" and $\overline{S}_i < \overline{S}_j$ is read "S bar i is less than S bar j."

[5] Formulas and tables, like figures, are numbered serially by chapters for convenient reference. Thus a reference to formula (2.1) would mean the first formula in Chapter 2, and Table 2.1 means the first table in Chapter 2.

what we might expect when $\overline{S}_i = \overline{S}_j$. When the proportion of comparative judgments p_{ij} is greater than .500, we assume that i has a higher modal discriminal process than j, and the value of z_{ij} will be positive in sign. Table I shows, for example, that if $p_{ij} = .842$, then $z_{ij} = 1.003$. If the proportion of comparative judgments p_{ij} is less than .500, then we assume that i has a lower modal discriminal process than j, and z_{ij} will be negative in sign. Table I shows, for example, that if $p_{ij} = .182$, then $z_{ij} = -.908$. The relations between p_{ij} and z_{ij} for the cases described are shown graphically in Figure 2.2.

We have assumed that the distributions of discriminal processes for two stimuli, i and j, are normal. In elementary statistics, it is shown that the difference between two normally distributed variables is also normally distributed with standard deviation equal to

$$\sigma_{i\;-\;j} = \sqrt{\sigma_i{}^2 + \sigma_j{}^2 - 2r_{ij}\sigma_i\sigma_j} \qquad (2.3)$$

where $\sigma_{i\;-\;j} =$ the standard deviation of the differences, $S_i - S_j$

$\qquad \sigma_i =$ the standard deviation of the discriminal processes S_i

$\qquad \sigma_j =$ the standard deviation of the discriminal processes S_j

$\qquad r_{ij} =$ the correlation between S_i and S_j

Thurstone (1927a) expresses the scale separation between the two modal discriminal processes, $\overline{S}_i$ and $\overline{S}_j$, in terms of formula (2.3) and the value of the normal deviate z_{ij} corresponding to the proportion of comparative judgments p_{ij}. Thus

$$\overline{S}_i - \overline{S}_j = z_{ij}\,\sqrt{\sigma_i{}^2 + \sigma_j{}^2 - 2r_{ij}\sigma_i\sigma_j} \qquad (2.4)$$

The values of z_{ij} are found by entering Table I in the

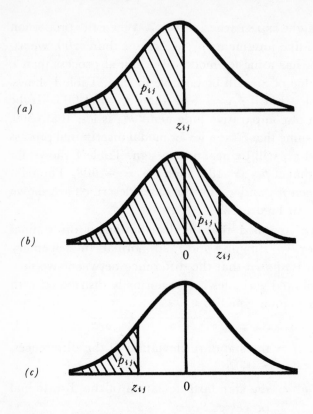

FIG. 2.2—The unit normal deviate transformation for p_{ij}. When $p_{ij} = p_{ji}$ as in (*a*), then z_{ij} will correspond to the origin or zero point on the abscissa. When $p_{ij} > p_{ji}$ as in (*b*), then z_{ij} will fall to the right of the zero point on the abscissa and be positive in sign. When $p_{ij} < p_{ji}$ as in (*c*), then z_{ij} will fall to the left of the zero point on the abscissa and be negative in sign. Measurements on the abscissa are in units of one standard deviation.

appendix with the empirically determined values of p_{ij}. Writing formula (2.4) in terms of the known z_{ij} values, we have

$$z_{ij} = (\bar{S}_i - \bar{S}_j) / \sqrt{\sigma_i{}^2 + \sigma_j{}^2 - 2r_{ij}\sigma_i\sigma_j} \qquad (2.5)$$

If we have n statements and each statement is paired with every other statement, then the total number of pairs will be given by

$$_nC_2 = \frac{n(n-1)}{2} \tag{2.6}$$

where $_nC_2$ is the number of combinations of n things taken 2 at a time. Assume, for example, that we have 4 statements and that they are presented in all possible pairs. We would then have $4(4-1)/2 = 6$ equations of the kind given by formula (2.5), or one for each of the pairs.

Formula (2.5) indicates, however, that the proportion of comparative judgments p_{ij}, or rather the normal deviate z_{ij} corresponding to this proportion, is not only a function of the scale separation, $\overline{S}_i - \overline{S}_j$, but also a function of the standard deviations, σ_i and σ_j, and the correlation coefficient r_{ij}. For our 4 stimuli we would have the 6 equations given by formula (2.5), but these 6 equations would involve 14 unknowns, that is, the 4 scale values, the 4 standard deviations, and the 6 intercorrelations. Since we would have only 6 known values, the z_{ij}'s, the solution of this system of equations is not possible.

As a first approximation to a solution for the scale separations of the propositions, let us assume that the standard deviations are all equal. If, in general, $\sigma_i = \sigma_j = \sigma$, then we have

$$\begin{aligned} z_{ij} &= (\overline{S}_i - \overline{S}_j)/ \sqrt{\sigma_i^2 + \sigma_j - 2r_{ij}\sigma_i\sigma_j} \\ &= (\overline{S}_i - \overline{S}_j)/ \sqrt{2\sigma^2 - 2r_{ij}\sigma^2} \\ &= (\overline{S}_i - \overline{S}_j)/ \sqrt{2\sigma^2(1 - r_{ij})} \end{aligned} \tag{2.7}$$

where we have dropped the subscripts for the standard deviations since we have assumed that they are equal to one another.

If we write our 6 equations in terms of formula (2.7), we would still have more unknowns than knowns, because of the 6 intercorrelations. Let us further assume, therefore, that the intercorrelations are all equal to one another so that we may write formula (2.7) as

$$z_{ij} = (\overline{S}_i - \overline{S}_j)/ \sqrt{2\sigma^2(1 - r)} \qquad (2.8)$$

where we have now dropped the subscript for r since we have assumed that the intercorrelations are all equal to one another.

Then, under the assumptions we have made, $\sqrt{2\sigma^2(1 - r)}$ will be a constant and is the common unit of measurement of the scale separations of the various pairs of stimuli. Without any loss of generality, we can let this common unit of measurement be equal to 1.00, so that we have

$$z_{ij} = \overline{S}_i - \overline{S}_j \qquad (2.9)$$

Formula (2.9), with the assumptions involved in its derivation, is commonly referred to as Case V of the law of comparative judgment.

Writing the 6 equations for 4 stimuli in terms of formula (2.9), we would have 6 equations with only 4 unknowns, the 4 scale values. It is common statistical practice when we have more equations than unknowns to use a least-squares solution for the equations. Mosteller (1951) has shown that the procedure to be described for finding the scale values of the stimuli is a least-squares solution.

SCHEMATIC REPRESENTATION OF PAIRED COMPARISON DATA

The F Matrix

If we give $n(n - 1)/2$ pairs of statements to a group of 50 to 100 individuals and ask them to make comparative judgments as to which member of each pair is the more favorable, our original data will consist of the frequencies corresponding to the number of times that each stimulus or statement is judged more favorable than every other statement. Table 2.1 shows the schematic arrangement of the frequencies in which the cell entries correspond to the frequency with which the column stimulus is judged more favorable than the row stimulus. Thus the cell entry f_{13} means the frequency with which Stimulus 1 was judged more favorable than Stimulus 3 or, in general, f_{ij} means the frequency with which the ith stimulus is judged more favorable than the jth stimulus. We shall always write f_{ij} in such a way that the first subscript corresponds to the column stimulus and the second subscript to the row stimulus.[6]

TABLE 2.1

Schematic representation for the F matrix giving the frequency with which the column stimulus is judged more favorable than the row stimulus

STIMULI	1	2	3	.	i	.	n
1	f_{11}	f_{21}	f_{31}	.	f_{i1}	.	f_{n1}
2	f_{12}	f_{22}	f_{32}	.	f_{i2}	.	f_{n2}
3	f_{13}	f_{23}	f_{33}	.	f_{i3}	.	f_{n3}
.	.	.	.	.	.	.	.
j	f_{1j}	f_{2j}	f_{3j}	.	f_{ij}	.	f_{nj}
.	.	.	.	.	.	.	.
n	f_{1n}	f_{2n}	f_{3n}	.	f_{in}	.	f_{nn}

If we let N be the total number of individuals doing the judging, then, although we do not obtain comparative judg-

---

[6] It is customary in matrix notation to give the row subscript first and the column subscript second. It is more convenient, however, in scaling, if we reverse the order of the subscripts. We shall use the first subscript to represent the column and the second the row.

ments for each stimulus with itself, we may assume that if such judgments had been obtained, f_{ii} would be equal to $\mathcal{N}/2$. It may also be observed that the cell entry f_{31} must be equal to $\mathcal{N} - f_{13}$ or, in general, $f_{ji} = \mathcal{N} - f_{ij}$.

The P Matrix

If each of the cell entries of Table 2.1 is divided by $\mathcal{N}$, this will give the p_{ij} entries shown in Table 2.2. The cell entries in this table give the proportion of times that the column stimulus is judged more favorable than the row stimulus. These entries may be obtained most conveniently by multiplying the cell entries of Table 2.1 by the reciprocal of $\mathcal{N}$. Thus

$$p_{ij} = \frac{1}{\mathcal{N}} f_{ij} \qquad (2.10)$$

It also follows that

$$p_{ji} = \frac{1}{\mathcal{N}} f_{ji}$$

$$= \frac{1}{\mathcal{N}} (\mathcal{N} - f_{ij})$$

$$= 1 - p_{ij} \qquad (2.11)$$

The Z Matrix

By means of Table I, in the appendix, we can obtain a table of the z_{ij} entries corresponding to the p_{ij} entries of Table 2.2. The schematic representation of these values is shown in Table 2.3. It may be emphasized, however, that corresponding entries above and below the diagonal elements of Table 2.3 do not represent independent values. We have already shown, for example, that $f_{ji} = \mathcal{N} - f_{ij}$ and that

$p_{ji} = 1 - p_{ij}$. It is also true that if z_{12} is the normal deviate corresponding to the proportion of times that Stimulus 1 was judged more favorable than Stimulus 2, or the scale

TABLE 2.2

Schematic representation of the P matrix giving the proportion of times that the column stimulus is judged more favorable than the row stimulus

STIMULI	1	2	3	.	i	.	n
1	p_{11}	p_{21}	p_{31}	.	p_{i1}	.	p_{n1}
2	p_{12}	p_{22}	p_{32}	.	p_{i2}	.	p_{n2}
3	p_{13}	p_{23}	p_{33}	.	p_{i3}	.	p_{n3}
.	.	.	.	.	.	.	.
j	p_{1j}	p_{2j}	p_{3j}	.	p_{ij}	.	p_{nj}
.	.	.	.	.	.	.	.
n	p_{1n}	p_{2n}	p_{3n}	.	p_{in}	.	p_{nn}
Sums	$\sum p_1.$	$\sum p_2.$	$\sum p_3.$	.	$\sum p_i.$	.	$\sum p_n.$

separation, $\overline{S}_1 - \overline{S}_2$, then z_{21} gives the scale separation, $\overline{S}_2 - \overline{S}_1$, and this value must be equal to z_{12}, but opposite in sign. Thus the entries in the first row of Table 2.3 could be obtained from those in the first column. As a matter of convenience in our calculations of the scale values for the various stimuli, we write the entries above the diagonal as well as those below. That is why we have also included the diagonal entries.

CASE V: COMPLETE DATA

To illustrate the calculation of scale values, we make use of data provided by Hill (1953). At the time of the Korean war, Hill asked 94 individuals to make comparative judgments of the relative degree of favorableness of 7 statements relating to the participation of the United States in the Ko-

TABLE 2.3

Schematic representation of the Z matrix giving the normal deviates corresponding to the proportions of Table 2.2

STIMULI	1	2	3	.	i	.	n
1	z_{11}	z_{21}	z_{31}	.	z_{i1}	.	z_{n1}
2	z_{12}	z_{22}	z_{32}	.	z_{i2}	.	z_{n2}
3	z_{13}	z_{23}	z_{33}	.	z_{i3}	.	z_{n3}
.	.	.	.	.	.	.	.
j	z_{1j}	z_{2j}	z_{3j}	.	z_{ij}	.	z_{nj}
.	.	.	.	.	.	.	.
n	z_{1n}	z_{2n}	z_{3n}	.	z_{in}	.	z_{nn}
Sums	$\sum z_{1\cdot}$	$\sum z_{2\cdot}$	$\sum z_{3\cdot}$	.	$\sum z_{i\cdot}$	.	$\sum z_{n\cdot}$
Means	$\bar{z}_{1\cdot}$	$\bar{z}_{2\cdot}$	$\bar{z}_{3\cdot}$	.	$\bar{z}_{i\cdot}$	.	$\bar{z}_{n\cdot}$

rean war. The 7 statements were presented in all possible pairs so that each individual made $7(7-1)/2 = 21$ comparative judgments. The 7 statements were as follows:

1. I suppose the United States has no choice but to continue the Korean war.
2. We should be willing to give our allies in Korea more money if they need it.
3. Withdrawing our troops from Korea at this time would only make matters worse.
4. The Korean war might not be the best way to stop communism, but it was the only thing we could do.
5. Winning the Korean war is absolutely necessary whatever the cost.
6. We are protecting the United States by fighting in Korea.
7. The reason we are in Korea is to defend freedom.

We might agree, after examination of these 7 statements, that, in general, a person who believed these statements probably had a more favorable attitude toward the participation of the United States in the Korean war than an individual who disagreed with the statements. We might also postulate that the 7 statements represent or express varying degrees of favorableness about the participation of the United States in the war. We have no physical continuum for determining the degree of favorableness expressed by each of the statements, but we can see whether or not they will scale along a psychological continuum ranging from least to most favorable.

TABLE 2.4

The F matrix for 7 statements judged by 94 individuals*

STATEMENTS	1	2	3	4	5	6	7
1	47	65	75	80	75	86	88
2	29	47	51	54	62	68	81
3	19	43	47	49	59	60	63
4	14	40	45	47	49	63	67
5	19	32	35	45	47	51	55
6	8	26	34	31	43	47	57
7	6	13	31	27	39	37	47

*Original data provided by R. J. Hill (1953).

Table 2.4 gives the F matrix or the frequency with which each column stimulus was judged more favorable than the row stimulus. The diagonal entries involving a comparison of each statement with itself are assumed to be equal to $N/2$. The total number of comparative judgments for each pair of statements is 94, the number of individuals making the judgments. The reciprocal of N is $1/94 = .010638$. Multiplying the cell entries of Table 2.4 by this reciprocal, the p_{ij} entries shown in Table 2.5 are obtained.

The numbers used in identifying each of the statements or stimuli in a given set of n are, of course, arbitrary. It is convenient, however, to rearrange the stimuli or statements in rank order of the column sums of the P matrix with the stimulus with the smallest column sum at the left and that with the highest at the right. In interchanging any pair of columns, we must remember to make the corresponding interchange of the pair of rows. This means, for example, that if we interchange the column entries for Stimulus 5 and Stimulus 1, we must also interchange the row entries for Stimulus 5 and Stimulus 1.

No rearrangement of the rows and columns in Table 2.5 is necessary because the stimulus numbers originally assigned to the statements were based upon a guess as to the rank order of the stimuli, with the least favorable-seeming stimulus being assigned the number 1 and the most

TABLE 2.5

The P matrix corresponding to the F matrix of Table 2.4

STATEMENTS	1	2	3	4	5	6	7
1	.500	.691	.798	.851	.798	.915	.936
2	.309	.500	.543	.574	.660	.723	.862
3	.202	.457	.500	.521	.628	.638	.670
4	.149	.426	.479	.500	.521	.670	.713
5	.202	.340	.372	.479	.500	.543	.585
6	.085	.277	.362	.330	.457	.500	.606
7	.064	.138	.330	.287	.415	.394	.500
Sums	1.011	2.329	2.884	3.042	3.479	3.883	4.372

favorable-seeming the number 7. It turns out that this guessed ordering is in accord with the ordering based upon the column sums of the P matrix.

Obtaining the Scale Values

Using Table I, in the appendix, we find the z_{ij} values for the p_{ij} entries of Table 2.5. The z_{ij} values are shown in

Table 2.6. It may be observed from formula (2.9) that the

TABLE 2.6

The Z matrix corresponding to the P matrix of Table 2.5

STATEMENTS	1	2	3	4	5	6	7
1	.000	.499	.834	1.041	.834	1.372	1.522
2	− .499	.000	.108	.187	.412	.592	1.089
3	− .834	− .108	.000	.053	.327	.353	.440
4	−1.041	− .187	− .053	.000	.053	.440	.562
5	− .834	− .412	− .327	− .053	.000	.108	.215
6	−1.372	− .592	− .353	− .440	− .108	.000	.269
7	−1.522	−1.089	− .440	− .562	− .215	− .269	.000
(1) *Sums*	−6.102	−1.889	− .231	.226	1.303	2.596	4.097
(2) *Means*	− .872	− .270	− .033	.032	.186	.371	.585
(3) *Means* +.872	.000	.602	.839	.904	1.058	1.243	1.457

cell entries of Table 2.6 correspond to the scale separations $\overline{S}_i$ and $\overline{S}_j$. For example, taking the entries in the first column, we have

$$z_{11} = \overline{S}_1 - \overline{S}_1$$
$$z_{12} = \overline{S}_1 - \overline{S}_2$$
$$z_{13} = \overline{S}_1 - \overline{S}_3$$
$$z_{14} = \overline{S}_1 - \overline{S}_4$$
$$z_{15} = \overline{S}_1 - \overline{S}_5$$
$$z_{16} = \overline{S}_1 - \overline{S}_6$$
$$z_{17} = \overline{S}_1 - \overline{S}_7$$

or, in general,

$$z_{1j} = \overline{S}_1 - \overline{S}_j \qquad (2.12)$$

where j can take values from 1 to n.

If we now sum the entries in column (1) of Table 2.6, $\overline{S}_1$ will be a constant in this summation and therefore

$$\sum_{j=1}^{n} z_{1j} = n\overline{S}_1 - \sum_{j=1}^{n} \overline{S}_j \qquad (2.13)$$

where $\sum_{j=1}^{n} z_{1j}$ means that column (1) is held constant and the summation is over the n rows of the table. The first term on the right is n times the scale value of Stimulus 1 and the second term is the sum of the scale values of all n stimuli on the psychological continuum. If we divide both sides of formula (2.13) by n, the number of stimuli, we have

$$\bar{z}_{1.} = \overline{S}_1 - \overline{S}$$

or, in general

$$\bar{z}_{i.} = \overline{S}_i - \overline{S} \qquad (2.14)$$

where $\bar{z}_{i.}$ = the arithmetic mean of the entries in the ith column of the Z matrix

$\overline{S}_i$ = the scale value of Stimulus i

$\overline{S}$ = the arithmetic mean of the n scale values

Thus we see that the mean of the z values in column (1) of Table 2.6 expresses the scale value of Stimulus 1 in terms of its deviation from the mean of all of the scale values. Similarly, if we sum the entries in column (2) and divide by n to find the mean, this will give the scale value of Stimulus 2 in terms of its deviation from the mean of all of the scale values. In the same way we obtain the scale values of the other stimuli in terms of their deviations from the mean scale value of all of the stimuli. These values are shown in row (2) at the bottom of Table 2.6. As a check upon our calculations, the sum of the scale values in deviation form may be obtained and this sum should be equal to zero.[7]

Statements with negative scale values are thus judged to be less favorable than the average of the scale values of all statements and those with positive scale values are judged to be more favorable than the average. Since our origin, taken as the mean of the scale values of the statements on

---

[7] It is a general theorem of elementary statistics that the sum of the deviations from the arithmetic mean is equal to zero.

the psychological continuum, is arbitrary, we can add a constant to the deviation scale values to make them all positive. This will not change the distance between any of the scale values nor the relative location of them on the psychological continuum. A convenient constant to add is the absolute scale value of the stimulus with the largest negative deviation. This will make the scale value for this stimulus zero and all of the others will be positive in sign. We have added .872 to the deviation values in row (2) of Table 2.6 to obtain the scale values with origin at $\bar{S}_1$. These are shown in row (3) at the bottom of Table 2.6.

THE INTERNAL CONSISTENCY CHECK

Having obtained the scale values of the 7 statements on a least to most favorable psychological continuum, an internal consistency check may be applied. This check involves determining how well our observed or empirical proportions p_{ij} agree with those to be expected in terms of our derived

TABLE 2.7

Theoretical normal deviates z_{ij}' corresponding to the scale distances between the statements of Table 2.6

STATEMENTS		1	2	3	4	5	6	7
	SCALE VALUES	.000	.602	.839	.904	1.058	1.243	1.457
1	.000							
2	.602	− .602						
3	.839	− .839	− .237					
4	.904	− .904	− .302	− .065				
5	1.058	−1.058	− .456	− .219	− .154			
6	1.243	−1.243	− .641	− .404	− .339	− .185		
7	1.457	−1.457	− .855	− .618	− .553	− .399	− .214	

scale values. The first step is to obtain a matrix Z' of theoretical normal deviates corresponding to the scale separations of the statements.   We set up a table such as Table 2.7 where the rows and columns are bounded by the scale values. If we subtract, in order, the entries at the left of the table from the scale value for Stimulus 1 at the top of column (1), we obtain the theoretical normal deviates z_{ij}' entered in the first column of the table. We obtain these z_{ij}' values only for the $n(n - 1)/2$ entries below the diagonal. These will be the theoretical z_{ij}' values corresponding to the $n(n - 1)/2$ independent z_{ij} values of Table 2.6. For the first column we have

$$z_{12}' = \overline{S}_1 - \overline{S}_2 = .000 - .602 = -.602$$
$$z_{13}' = \overline{S}_1 - \overline{S}_3 = .000 - .839 = -.839$$

and so on. Similarly, if we subtract the entries at the left of the table from the scale value for Stimulus 2 at the top of column (2), we obtain the theoretical normal deviates below the diagonal for column (2). Thus

$$z_{23} = \overline{S}_2 - \overline{S}_3 = .602 - .839 = -.237$$
$$z_{24} = \overline{S}_2 - \overline{S}_4 = .602 - .904 = -.302$$

and so on. The other entries in Table 2.7 are obtained in the same manner.

We can now enter Table I, in the appendix, with the z_{ij}' values of Table 2.7 and obtain the corresponding $n(n - 1)/2$ theoretical proportions p_{ij}'. For example, for $z_{12}' = -.602$, we find that $p_{12}' = .274$. The other values of p_{ij}' are found in the same way and are shown in Table 2.8.

If we subtract the entries in the P' matrix from the corresponding entries in the P matrix, that is, subtract the entries of Table 2.8 from the corresponding independent entries of Table 2.5, we will obtain the discrepancies between our empirical proportions with which we started and our

TABLE 2.8

Theoretical proportions p_{ij}' corresponding to the theoretical normal deviates z_{ij}' of Table 2.7

STATEMENTS	1	2	3	4	5	6	7
1	—						
2	.274	—					
3	.201	.406	—				
4	.183	.381	.474	—			
5	.145	.324	.413	.439	—		
6	.107	.261	.343	.367	.427	—	
7	.073	.196	.268	.290	.345	.415	—

TABLE 2.9

Discrepancies between the theoretical proportions p_{ij}' of Table 2.8 and the observed proportions p_{ij} of Table 2.5

STATEMENTS	1	2	3	4	5	6	7
1	—						
2	.035	—					
3	.001	.051	—				
4	−.034	.045	.005	—			
5	.057	.016	−.041	.040	—		
6	−.022	.016	.019	−.037	.030	—	
7	−.009	−.058	.062	−.003	.070	−.021	—
$|\Sigma|$	.158	.186	.127	.080	.100	.021	

theoretical proportions. These discrepancies for our $n(n-1)/2$ independent comparisons are shown in Table 2.9. Taking the sum of the absolute values and dividing by the number of discrepancies, we have the absolute average discrepancy. Thus

$$AD = \frac{\Sigma \, |p_{ij} - p_{ij}'|}{\dfrac{n(n-1)}{2}} \qquad (2.15)$$

$$= \frac{.672}{21}$$

$$= .032$$

The absolute average discrepancy of .032 for the 7 stimuli is slightly larger than the values usually reported when stimuli are scaled by the method of paired comparisons.[8]

CASE V: INCOMPLETE DATA

In the illustrative example of the previous section, we had no p_{ij} value of 1.00 or .00 . If p_{ij} is 1.00, then this means that Stimulus i was judged more favorable than j by all of the individuals doing the judging. If p_{ij} is 1.00, we may have great confidence that Stimulus i has a higher modal discriminal process on the psychological continuum than j, but unfortunately a p_{ij} of 1.00 does not provide any estimate of the scale separation of $\overline{S}_i$ and $\overline{S}_j$. This would be equally true of a p_{ij} equal to .00 . When the distributions of discriminal processes for two stimuli fail to overlap, we should always expect to find p_{ij} equal to 1.00 or .00, and

---

[8] Hevner (1930) for example, reports an average error of .024 for 20 stimuli, and Saffir (1937) a value of .031 for 25 stimuli, scaled by the method of paired comparisons.

for such values z_{ij} is indeterminate.[9] Non-overlapping distributions of discriminal processes may sometimes occur when comparative judgments are obtained for stimuli falling at opposite ends of the psychological continuum.

In general, it can be said that most individuals working with scaling methods prefer to ignore not only comparative judgments for which p_{ij} is 1.00 or .00, but also whenever p_{ij} is equal to or greater than .99 or equal to or less than .01. The major reason for this is that the difference between the two z values corresponding to the difference between two proportions is much greater at the extremes of a normal distribution than the difference between two z values corresponding to the same proportional difference in the central areas of a normal distribution. For example, moving from p_{ij} equal to .98 to .99, we have the corresponding increase in z_{ij} from 2.054 to 2.326, a distance in normal deviate units of .272, whereas moving from p_{ij} equal to .50 to .51, we have an increase in z_{ij} from .000 to .025, a distance of only .025 normal deviate units.

If the number of judges is large, say 200 or more, then we might use p_{ij} values of .99 and .01, but with less than 200 judges, it is probably better to disregard all comparative judgments for which p_{ij} is greater than .98 or less than

---

[9] A principle enunciated by Fullerton and Cattell (1892) is that "equally often noticed differences are equal, unless always or never noticed." Thus, if p_{12} is .60 and p_{23} is also .60, we assume that the distance between Stimulus 1 and Stimulus 2 is equal to the distance between Stimulus 2 and Stimulus 3 providing, as Thurstone (1927d) later pointed out, the discriminal dispersions of the stimuli are equal. But if the differences between Stimulus 1 and Stimulus 2 and between Stimulus 2 and Stimulus 3 are always noticed so that p_{12} is 1.00 and p_{23} is also 1.00, then the assumption that the distance between Stimulus 1 and Stimulus 2 is equal to the distance between Stimulus 2 and Stimulus 3 on the psychological continuum is not justified.

.02.[10] If such extreme values of p_{ij} are observed, and we ignore them, then we shall have some missing entries in the Z matrix, and a somewhat different procedure than that described in the previous section must be used in solving for the scale values of the stimuli.

Consider, for example, the P matrix for 9 stimuli shown in Table 2.10. There we have a number of p_{ij} values greater than .98 and less than .02, involving, primarily, com-

TABLE 2.10

The P matrix for 9 statements giving the proportion of times the column statement was judged more favorable than the row statement by 78 judges*

Statements	1	2	3	4	5	6	7	8	9
1	.500	.923	.923	.949	.987	.987	1.000	.949	1.000
2	.077	.500	.526	.731	.872	.987	.949	.846	.962
3	.077	.474	.500	.615	.910	.923	.936	.872	.962
4	.051	.269	.385	.500	.859	.897	.910	.833	.936
5	.013	.128	.090	.141	.500	.769	.782	.756	.859
6	.013	.013	.077	.103	.231	.500	.564	.705	.833
7	.000	.051	.064	.090	.218	.436	.500	.654	.667
8	.051	.154	.128	.167	.244	.295	.346	.500	.397
9	.000	.038	.038	.064	.141	.167	.333	.603	.500
Sums	.782	2.050	2.231	2.860	4.462	5.461	5.820	6.218	6.616

*Original data provided by R. J. Hill (1953).

parisons between Stimulus 1 and Stimuli 5, 6, 7, 8, and 9. In Table 2.11 we give the z_{ij} values corresponding to the p_{ij} values of Table 2.10. We have left the cells blank for values of p_{ij} greater than .98 and less than .02.

Let us assume, for the moment, that the Z matrix is complete, that is, that we have an entry in every cell. If we now

[10] Various other standards are sometimes suggested. Guilford (1954, p. 163), for example, recommends not using z_{ij} values more extreme than 2.0 and -2.0 corresponding to proportions of .977 and .023, respectively.

TABLE 2.11

The Z matrix for the P matrix of Table 2.10 eliminating values of p_{ij} greater than .98 and less than .02

STATEMENTS	1	2	3	4	5	6	7	8	9
1	.000	1.426	1.426	1.635				1.635	
2	−1.426	.000	.065	.616	1.136		1.635	1.019	1.774
3	−1.426	− .065	.000	.292	1.341	1.426	1.522	1.136	1.774
4	−1.635	− .616	− .292	.000	1.076	1.265	1.341	.966	1.522
5		−1.136	−1.341	−1.076	.000	.736	.779	.693	1.076
6			−1.426	−1.265	− .736	.000	.161	.539	.966
7		−1.635	−1.522	−1.341	− .779	− .161	.000	.396	.432
8	−1.635	−1.019	−1.136	− .966	− .693	− .539	− .396	.000	− .261
9		−1.774	−1.774	−1.522	−1.076	− .966	− .432	.261	.000

subtract the entries in column (1) from the corresponding entries in column (2), we would have, according to formula (2.9), the following equations:

$$z_{21} - z_{11} = (\overline{S}_2 - \overline{S}_1) - (\overline{S}_1 - \overline{S}_1) = \overline{S}_2 - \overline{S}_1$$
$$z_{22} - z_{12} = (\overline{S}_2 - \overline{S}_2) - (\overline{S}_1 - \overline{S}_2) = \overline{S}_2 - \overline{S}_1$$
$$z_{23} - z_{13} = (\overline{S}_2 - \overline{S}_3) - (\overline{S}_1 - \overline{S}_3) = \overline{S}_2 - \overline{S}_1$$

$$\cdot \qquad \cdot \qquad \cdot \qquad \cdot \qquad \cdot$$
$$\cdot \qquad \cdot \qquad \cdot \qquad \cdot \qquad \cdot$$
$$\cdot \qquad \cdot \qquad \cdot \qquad \cdot \qquad \cdot$$

$$z_{2n} - z_{1n} = (\overline{S}_2 - \overline{S}_n) - (\overline{S}_1 - \overline{S}_n) = \overline{S}_2 - \overline{S}_1$$

or, in general,

$$z_{2j} - z_{1j} = (\overline{S}_2 - \overline{S}_j) - (\overline{S}_1 - \overline{S}_j) = \overline{S}_2 - \overline{S}_1$$

$$(2.16)$$

A similar set of equations could be written for the entries in column (3) minus the entries in column (2), and for those in column (4) minus those in column (3), and so on. Summing the above equations for the entries in column (2) minus those in column (1) we have

$$\sum_{j=1}^{n} (z_{2j} - z_{1j}) = n\overline{S}_2 - n\overline{S}_1 \qquad (2.17)$$

and dividing by n, the number of equations, we get

$$\frac{\sum_{j=1}^{n} (z_{2j} - z_{1j})}{n} = \overline{S}_2 - \overline{S}_1 \qquad (2.18)$$

As a matter of convenience we let

$$\frac{\sum_{j=1}^{n} (z_{2j} - z_{1j})}{n} = D_{21} \qquad (2.19)$$

Then

$$\overline{S}_2 - \overline{S}_1 = D_{21}$$
$$\overline{S}_3 - \overline{S}_2 = D_{32}$$
$$\overline{S}_4 - \overline{S}_3 = D_{43}$$

or, in general

$$\overline{S}_i - \overline{S}_{(i-1)} = D_{i(i-1)} \qquad (2.20)$$

Since our origin on the psychological continuum is arbitrary, we may take the scale value $\overline{S}_1$ as the origin. Setting $\overline{S}_1$ equal to zero, we have

$$\overline{S}_2 = D_{21} \qquad (2.21)$$

To find $\overline{S}_3$, we take $\overline{S}_3 - \overline{S}_2 = D_{32}$ and add $\overline{S}_2$ to the left-hand side and D_{21} to the right-hand side. Thus

$$\overline{S}_3 - \overline{S}_2 + \overline{S}_2 = D_{32} + D_{21} = \overline{S}_3 \qquad (2.22)$$

Proceeding the same way and solving for $\overline{S}_4$, we get

$$\overline{S}_4 - \overline{S}_3 + \overline{S}_3 = D_{43} + D_{32} + D_{21} = \overline{S}_4 \qquad (2.23)$$

We could then use the results of (2.23) to solve for $\overline{S}_5$, and so on, until we have $\overline{S}_n$.

When the $\mathcal{Z}$ matrix is incomplete, some of the equations as given by formula (2.16) estimating the scale separation between two stimuli cannot be written. This will be true when we do not have z values in the same row of the two adjacent columns. For example, in Table 2.12 we show the differences between the z values of adjacent columns of Table

TABLE 2.12

Matrix of successive differences of the column entries of Table 2.11

STATEMENTS	COLUMN DIFFERENCES							
	$2-1$	$3-2$	$4-3$	$5-4$	$6-5$	$7-6$	$8-7$	$9-8$
1	1.426	.000	.209					
2	1.426	.065	.551	.520			− .616	.755
3	1.361	.065	.292	1.049	.085	.096	− .386	.638
4	1.019	.324	.292	1.076	.189	.076	− .375	.556
5		− .205	.265	1.076	.736	.043	− .086	.383
6			.161	.529	.736	.161	.378	.427
7		.113	.181	.562	.618	.161	.396	.036
8	.616	− .117	.170	.273	.154	,143	.396	− .261
9		.000	.252	.446	.110	.534	.693	− .261
(1) Sums	5.848	.245	2.373	5.531	2.628	1.214	.400	2.273
(2) n	5	8	9	8	7	7	8	8
(3) Means	1.170	.031	.264	.691	.375	.173	.050	.284

SCALE VALUES								
$\overline{S}_1$	$\overline{S}_2$	$\overline{S}_3$	$\overline{S}_4$	$\overline{S}_5$	$\overline{S}_6$	$\overline{S}_7$	$\overline{S}_8$	$\overline{S}_9$
.000	1.170	1.201	1.465	2.156	2.531	2.704	2.754	3.038

2.11. The blank entries indicate the missing equations of formula (2.16). The sums of the differences are given at the bottom of the table in row (1), and directly under the sums, in row (2), we enter the number of equations involved in each column sum. Dividing these sums by the corresponding number of equations contributing to the sum, we obtain the values of $D_i(_{i\ -\ 1}) = \bar{S}_i - \bar{S}(_{i\ -\ 1})$ of formula (2.20) shown in row (3) at the bottom of the table. Setting $\bar{S}_1$ equal to zero, we have $\bar{S}_2 = 1.170$. Solving for the scale values of the other stimuli, we obtain the values shown in the last row of the table. It may be noted, from formula (2.21) and formula (2.22), that the scale values are obtained by merely cumulatively adding the $D_i(_{i\ -\ 1})$ values as we have done at the bottom of Table 2.12. Thus

$$\bar{S}_1 = .000$$
$$\bar{S}_2 = .000 + 1.170 = 1.170$$
$$\bar{S}_3 = 1.170 + .031 = 1.201$$
$$\bar{S}_4 = 1.201 + .264 = 1.465$$
$$\bar{S}_5 = 1.465 + .691 = 2.156$$

and so on.

For the case of a complete Z matrix, the procedure described will result in exactly the same relative scale values for the stimuli as the method described in the previous section. The only difference would be that the present method would give the scale separations of adjacent stimuli, whereas in the previous case, the scale values were expressed in terms of their deviations from the mean of all of the scale values. Since our origin in either method is arbitrary, we have, in both procedures, taken $\bar{S}_1$ as the zero value on the psychological continuum, where $\bar{S}_1$ is the scale value of the statement with the lowest scale value.

ATTITUDE SCALES

Having obtained scale values for a set of statements, how can we use these statements and their scale values to obtain estimates of the attitudes of individuals? So far we have not been concerned with measuring the degree of affect that individuals associate with a psychological object, but rather with the judged degree of affect represented by the state - ments. But we might argue that the manner in which an individual responds to these statements, that is, the particular statements that he accepts or rejects would, in turn, enable us to infer something about his location on the same psychological continuum as the one on which the statements have been scaled.

Assume that we have a set of statements relating to some psychological object and that these statements have been scaled on a psychological continuum from least to most favorable. These statements are now presented in some random order to individuals with instructions to indicate whether they agree or disagree with each one. It is assumed that these agree and disagree responses are a function of the degree of affect associated with the psychological object by the subjects. An individual who has a highly favorable attitude toward the psychological object, in other words, is believed to be more likely to agree with statements that have highly favorable scale values than he is with statements that do not. And, similarly, individuals who have the least favorable attitudes toward the psychological object are believed to be more likely to endorse or agree with statements that are scaled near their own positions than they are with statements that have highly favorable scale values.

An attitude score for each individual can be obtained by finding the median of the scale values of the statements with which he agrees. This score is assumed to be an indication of the individual's location on the same psychological continuum as that represented by the scaled statements. For example, if an individual has agreed with statements with scale values of 2.4, 2.9, and 3.3, his attitude score would be taken as 2.9, the median or middle-scale value of the three statements. If he has agreed with four statements with scale values of 2.2, 2.4, 2.8, and 3.3, then his attitude score would be taken as the midpoint of the interval between the two middle-scale values, that is, 2.6. This method of obtaining attitude scores, based upon reactions to scaled statements, has been widely used with statements that have been scaled by the method of paired comparisons or one of the other scaling methods to be discussed later.

Certain variations in the procedure described above for obtaining attitude scores have been suggested. For example, after a subject has checked all of the statements with which he agrees, he might then be asked to indicate the one state-ment that best expresses how he feels about the psychological object. The scale value of this single statement might then be taken as the attitude score of the subject. A major disadvantage of this method would be that the scores would be determined by single scale values and therefore would probably not be as reliable as those obtained by the median method of scoring. A better procedure would be to ask subjects to check the three statements that best express how they feel about the psychological object. Scores could then be taken as the median or middle-scale value of these three statements.

Another procedure has been introduced by Edwards (1956) that departs considerably from the median method of scoring. He obtained scale values for a number of state-ments relating to attitude toward psychology. He then selected 9 statements whose scale values were fairly equally spaced along the psychological continuum. Each of the 9 statements was then paired with every other statement to give $9(9 - 1)/2 = 36$ pairs. For each pair of statements, one statement had a higher or more favorable scale value than the other. The statement with the higher scale value he designated as A and the one with the lower scale value as B. These pairs of statements comprised the items in the attitude scale.

The attitude scale was given to students in introductory psychology classes at the University of Washington. Each student was asked to choose the statement, A or B, in each pair that best expressed how he felt about psychology. An attitude score for each student was obtained by counting the number of times he chose the A or more favorable statement in the 36 pairs.

Kuder-Richardson (1937) estimates of reliability were obtained from two samples of 175 and 174 students For the first sample, the reliability coefficient was .87 and for the second it was .88. These reliability coefficients are comparable to those usually reported for attitude scales scored by the median method.

When the median method of scoring is used, a test-retest reliability coefficient can be obtained by having the same group of subjects indicate their agreement or disagreement with the statements twice, with a time interval separating the two administrations of the scale. Scores obtained at the time of the first administration can then be correlated with those obtained at the second. It may also be possible, under certain circumstances, to obtain two sets of statements with respect to the same psychological object such that the statements in each set have approximately the same scale values.

These two sets of statements might then be regarded as comparable forms of the same attitude scale. If the two forms of the scale are given to the same group of subjects, two scores can be obtained, one on each form. By correlating the scores on the two forms, an estimate of the reliability of the scales can be obtained.

As in all attempts to measure attitudes by means of scales, the subject's position on the attitude continuum is unknown and must be estimated from his responses to the statements contained in the scale. In the case of the median method of scoring, the attitude score gives the position of the subject on the psychological continuum on which the statements themselves have been scaled. In the procedure used by Edwards, this is not the case. The score obtained by this method is regarded as a linear transformation of the subject's position on the psychological continuum on which the original statements were scaled.

QUESTIONS AND PROBLEMS

1. What is the stated objective of a psychological scaling method?

2. In Chapter 1 you were asked to write 10 attitude statements relating to some psychological object of interest. Obtain paired comparison judgments for these statements from as many judges as you can, preferably at least 100. Find the scale values for these statements.

3. Having found scale values for the 10 statements, apply the internal consistency check to determine how well you can reproduce the original proportions. How does the average error you obtain compare with typical values reported in the chapter?

4. What does Thurstone mean by discriminal process and discriminal dispersion?

5. On what basis can we argue that the scale distance between two stimuli is related to the proportion of comparative judgments i greater than j?

6. What is meant by the statement that "equally often noticed differences are equal, unless always or never noticed?"

7. What assumptions are made in obtaining scale values by means of the Case V model?

8. How would one determine the reliability of scores on an attitude scale constructed by the method of paired comparisons?

9. What procedures might be used to evaluate the reliability of the scale values of statements scaled by the method of paired comparisons?

REFERENCES AND SUGGESTED READINGS

EDWARDS, A. L. A technique for increasing the reproducibility of cumulative attitude scales. *J. appl. Psychol.*, 1956, 40, 263-265.

FULLERTON, G. S., and CATTELL, J. McK. On the perception of small differences. *Publ. Univ. Penn., Phil. Series*, 1892, No. 2.

GUILFORD, J. P. The method of paired comparisons as a psychometric method. *Psychol. Rev.*, 1928, 35, 494-506.

———*Psychometric methods.* (2nd ed.) New York: McGraw-Hill, 1954.

*GULLIKSEN, H. Paired comparisons and the logic of measurement. *Psychol. Rev.*, 1946, 53, 199-213.

HEVNER, KATE. An empirical study of three psychophysical methods. *J. gen. Psychol.*, 1930, 4, 191-212.

HILL, R. J. A note on inconsistency in paired comparison judgments. *Amer. soc. Rev.*, 1953, 18, 564-566.

KUDER, G. F., and RICHARDSON, M. W. The theory of the estimation of test reliability. *Psychometrika*, 1937, 2, 151-160.

*MOSTELLER, F. Remarks on the method of paired comparisons: I. The least squares solution assuming equal standard deviations and equal correlations. *Psychometrika*, 1951, 16, 3-9.

SAFFIR, M. A. A comparative study of scales constructed by three psycho-physical methods. *Psychometrika*, 1937, 2, 179-198.

*THURSTONE, L. L. A law of comparative judgment. *Psychol. Rev.*, 1927a, 34, 273-286.

*——— Psychophysical analysis. *Amer. J. Psychol.*, 1927b, 38, 368-389.

——— The method of paired comparisons for social values. *J. abnorm. soc. Psychol.*, 1927c, 21, 384-400.

——— Equally often noticed differences. *J. educ. Psychol.*, 1927d, 18, 289-293.

*———— The measurement of opinion. J. *abnorm. soc. Psychol.*, 1928, 22, 415-430.

*———— Theory of attitude measurement. *Psychol. Rev.*, 1929, 36, 222-241.

*———— The measurement of values. *Psychol. Rev.*, 1954, 61, 47-58.

3

Significance Tests for Paired Comparison Judgments

Mosteller (1951*b*) has developed a χ^2 test of significance for the discrepancies between the observed and theoretical proportions obtained with Case V of the method of paired comparisons. In essence, the test of significance is a means of determining whether the assumptions involved in the Case V model are tenable for a given set of data. In particular, the Case V model assumes additivity along a single dimension or psychological continuum.

When we have a single dimension or continuum, then distances marked off along the continuum are additive. Measurements of length, for example, fall along a single dimension and distances between objects on the length continuum can be added. Consider three objects with lengths of 2, 5, and 9 inches, respectively. The distance between the first and second object is 3 inches and the distance between the second and third object is 4 inches. The distance between the first and the third object is, therefore, the sum of the two distances just found or 7 inches.

Similarly, we might have three stimuli with scale values $\overline{S}_1 < \overline{S}_2 < \overline{S}_3$, and with equal discriminal dispersions. We have assumed that the scale values correspond to the positions of the stimuli on the psychological continuum. If the property of additivity holds for this continuum, and if D_{21}

is the distance between $\bar{S}_2$ and $\bar{S}_1$, and D_{32} is the distance between $\bar{S}_3$ and $\bar{S}_2$, then the distance between $\bar{S}_3$ and $\bar{S}_1$ should be equal to the sum of D_{21} and D_{23}. If the psychological continuum is not unidimensional, then, as Mosteller (1951*b*, p. 208) has noted, "this additive property will usually not hold."

If we apply the χ^2 test to data obtained by Case V of the method of paired comparisons, the null hypothesis we shall be testing is that the assumptions involved in this model are tenable. The alternative to the null hypothesis is, as Mosteller states, quite general. It is merely that the null hypothesis is incorrect. The Case V model assumes, for example, normality of distribution of the discriminal processes, unidimensionality of the psychological continuum, and equality of the various values of the standard deviations of the differences as given by formula 2.3. Theoretically, if the test of significance results in the rejection of the null hypothesis, this might be because of any one or any combination of these assumptions is violated. In practice, however, the test of significance is relatively insensitive to lack of normality and primarily sensitive to lack of unidimensionality.[1] Inequalities in the standard deviations of the differences may under certain circumstances result in an increased value of χ^2, thus making more likely the rejection of the null hypothesis, but not necessarily in all cases. Mosteller, for example, is able to show that if only one of the stimuli has an unusual or aberrant discriminal dispersion and if the scale value for this stimulus is near the mean of all of the scale values, then the χ^2 test is not likely to detect this failure of the Case V model.

[1]Mosteller (1951*b*, p. 216) states: "Failure of normality is not important to the method of paired comparisons, as we shall show elsewhere. It is just as well then that the present test will be very poor at detecting deviations from normality. The normality assumption is more in the nature of a computational device than anything else."

TEST OF SIGNIFICANCE FOR THE CASE V MODEL

The χ^2 test to determine whether the observed p_{ij} and theoretical p_{ij}' values are in accord with each other is based upon a transformation of both the theoretical and observed proportions. The transformation is the inverse sine transformation developed by Fisher (1922), tabled by Bliss (1937), and made generally available by Snedecor (1956). For any proportion p we can find

$$\theta = \text{arc sin } \sqrt{p} \tag{3.1}$$

and θ is approximately normally distributed with variance equal to

$$\sigma_\theta^2 = \frac{821}{N} \tag{3.2}$$

where N is the number of judgments upon which p is based. Values of θ corresponding to values of p are given in Table II in the appendix.

In Table 3.1 we give the values of θ corresponding to the $n(n-1)/2$ empirical proportions p_{ij} obtained for the 7

TABLE 3.1

Values of θ corresponding to the $n(n-1)/2$ empirical proportions p_{ij} of Table 2.5

STATEMENTS	1	2	3	4	5	6	7
1							
2	33.77						
3	26.71	42.53					
4	22.71	40.74	43.80				
5	26.71	35.67	37.58	43.80			
6	16.95	31.76	36.99	35.06	42.53		
7	14.65	21.81	35.06	32.39	40.11	38.88	

statements discussed in the last chapter. Table 3.2 gives the values of θ' corresponding to the theoretical proportions

TABLE 3.2

Values of θ' corresponding to the $n(n-1)/2$ theoretical proportions p_{ij}' of Table 2.8

STATEMENTS	1	2	3	4	5	6	7
1							
2	31.56						
3	26.64	39.58					
4	25.33	38.12	43.51				
5	22.38	34.70	39.99	41.50			
6	19.09	30.72	35.85	37.29	40.80		
7	15.68	26.28	31.18	32.58	35.97	40.11	

p_{ij}' for the same statements. If we now take each discrepancy, $\theta - \theta'$, square it, and sum over the $n(n-1)/2$ values, this sum, divided by $821/N$, will be a value of χ^2. Thus

$$\chi^2 = \frac{\Sigma(\theta - \theta')^2}{821/N} \qquad (3.3)$$

The value of χ^2 obtained from formula (3.3) can be evaluated by reference to the table of χ^2, Table III in the appendix, with degrees of freedom given by

$$df = \frac{(n-1)(n-2)}{2} \qquad (3.4)$$

where n is the number of stimuli.

Table 3.3 gives the discrepancies between the θ values of Table 3.1 and the θ' values of Table 3.2. Squaring and summing these discrepancies, we obtain

TABLE 3.3

Values of $\theta - \theta$ for the entries in Table 3.1 and 3.2

STATEMENTS	1	2	3	4	5	6	7
1							
2	2.21						
3	.07	2.95					
4	−2.62	2.62	.29				
5	4.33	.97	−2.41	2.30			
6	−2.14	1.04	1.14	−2.23	1.73		
7	−1.03	−4.47	3.88	− .19	4.14	−1.23	

$$\Sigma(\theta - \theta')^2 = (2.21)^2 + (.07)^2 + \cdots + (-1.23)^2$$
$$= 127.9037$$

We have $N = 94$ judges and from formula (3.2) we find that $\sigma_\theta^2 = 821/94 = 8.73$. Then, substituting in formula (3.3) we get

$$\chi^2 = \frac{127.9037}{8.73} = 14.64$$

Since we have 7 stimuli, we have $(7 - 1)(7 - 2)/2 = 15$ degrees of freedom for evaluating our obtained χ^2 equal to 14.64. By reference to the table of χ^2 in the appendix, we see that when we have 15 degrees of freedom, the probability P of obtaining a value of χ^2 equal to or greater than 14.64 is between .30 and .50, when the null hypothesis is true. If we regard as significant those values of χ^2 that have a probability of .05 or less, then our observed value would have to be 24.996 or larger. The fact that our observed value of χ^2 is not significant indicates that the assumptions involved in finding the scale values of the 7 statements are tenable.

CALCULATION OF DISCRIMINAL DISPERSIONS

In some problems it may be desirable to have estimates of the discriminal dispersions of the various statements or stimuli being scaled. It may be recalled that in the procedure described earlier for finding the scale values of the stimuli, we assumed equality of the discriminal dispersions. Mosteller (1951a) has shown that if a single stimulus has an aberrant discriminal dispersion, all of the other stimuli

TABLE 3.4

Calculation of the standard deviations V for the columns of the Z matrix

STATEMENTS	1	2	3	4	5	6	7
1	.000	.499	.834	1.041	.834	1.372	1.522
2	− .499	.000	.108	.187	.412	.592	1.089
3	− .834	− .108	.000	.053	.327	.353	.440
4	−1.041	− .187	− .053	.000	.053	.440	.562
5	− .834	− .412	− .327	− .053	.000	.108	.215
6	−1.372	− .592	− .353	− .440	− .108	.000	.269
7	−1.522	−1.089	− .440	− .562	− .215	− .269	.000
(1) Σz_{ij}^2	6.923	2.002	1.135	1.634	1.033	2.635	4.130
(2) Σz_{ij}	−6.102	−1.889	− .231	.226	1.303	2.596	4.097
(3) $(\Sigma z_{ij})^2/n$	5.319	.510	.008	.007	.243	.963	2.398
(4) $\Sigma z_{ij}^2 - \dfrac{(\Sigma z_{ij})^2}{n}$	1.604	1.492	1.127	1.627	.790	1.672	1.732
(5) V^2	.229	.213	.161	.232	.113	.239	.247
(6) V	.479	.462	.401	.482	.336	.489	.497
(7) $1/V$	2.088	2.165	2.494	2.075	2.976	2.045	2.012

may still be properly spaced on the psychological continuum. It is only the position of the single stimulus with the atypical discriminal dispersion relative to the other stimuli that is displaced. If the scale value of the single aberrant stimulus is central with respect to the scale values of the other stimuli, that is, if it is at the mean of the remaining stimuli, then all of the stimuli, including the aberrant one, may be properly spaced.

In Thurstone's (1927a) original development of the law of comparative judgment, he called the solution of the scale values of the stimuli, without assuming equality of discriminal dispersions, his Case III model. Both Thurstone (1932) and, more recently, Burros (1951) have proposed solutions for the discriminal dispersions. If the discrepancies between the empirical p_{ij} and the theoretical p_{ij}' values seem unusually large and if the χ^2 test for goodness of fit indicates that the Case V model does not apply, we might desire to try to scale the stimuli using the Case III model. This can be done, once we have obtained estimates of the discriminal dispersions.

In Table 3.4 we repeat the z_{ij} values for the 7 statements of Table 2.6. We define the mean of the z values in the ith column as

$$\bar{z}_{i.} = \frac{\sum\limits_{j=1}^{n} z_{ij}}{n} \qquad (3.5)$$

Then the sum of squared deviations of the entries in the ith column about the mean of the column will be given by[2]

---

[2] This is a standard formula for the sum of squared deviations about the arithmetic mean. See Edwards (1954).

$$\sum_{j=1}^{n} (z_{ij} - \bar{z}_{i.})^2 = \sum_{j=1}^{n} z_{ij}^2 - \frac{\left(\sum_{j=1}^{n} z_{ij}\right)^2}{n}$$

(3.6)

We may denote the variance of the entries in the ith column by V_i^2 and this variance will be equal to the sum of squared deviations of formula (3.6) divided by n. Thus

$$V_i^2 = \frac{\sum_{j=1}^{n} (z_{ij} - \bar{z}_{i.})^2}{n}$$

(3.7)

Taking the square root of formula (3.7) we obtain the standard deviation of the entries in the ith column of the Z matrix. Thus

$$V_i = \sqrt{\frac{\sum_{j=1}^{n} (z_{ij} - \bar{z}_{i.})^2}{n}}$$

(3.8)

In the same way we could obtain the standard deviations V of the entries in the other columns of the Z matrix.

We then let a be a constant such that

$$a = \frac{2n}{\sum_{i=1}^{n} \left(\frac{1}{V_i}\right)}$$

(3.9)

where $\sum_{i=1}^{n} \left(\dfrac{1}{V_i}\right)$ is the sum of the reciprocals of the standard deviations of the columns of the Z matrix. Then, Thurstone

(1932) has shown that the discriminal dispersions of the stimuli can be estimated by

$$\sigma_1 = a\left(\frac{1}{V_1}\right) - 1$$

$$\sigma_2 = a\left(\frac{1}{V_2}\right) - 1$$

$$\sigma_3 = a\left(\frac{1}{V_3}\right) - 1$$

$$\sigma_i = a\left(\frac{1}{V_i}\right) - 1$$

$$\sigma_n = a\left(\frac{1}{V_n}\right) - 1 \qquad (3.10)$$

where a is given by formula (3.9) and $V_1, V_2, V_3, \ldots, V_i, \ldots, V_n$ are the standard deviations of the column entries of the Z matrix.

The calculations necessary for obtaining the discriminal dispersions of the 7 statements are shown at the bottom of Table 3.4. Row (1) gives the sum of the squared values in the columns or $\sum_{j=1}^{n} z_{ij}^2$. Row 2 gives the columns sums $\sum_{j=1}^{n} z_{ij}$. Squaring the sums in row (2) and dividing by n, we obtain the values of $\sum_{j=1}^{n}(z_{ij})^2 / n$ shown in row (3). Subtracting the values in row (3) from the corresponding values in row (1) we obtain the sums of squared deviations given by formula (3.6) and shown in row (4). Dividing the entries in row (4) by n, we obtain the V^2 values given in row (5). Taking the square root of the entries in row (5) we obtain the standard deviations V given in row (6), and row (7) gives the values of $1/V$.

The sum of the entries in row (7) of Table 3.4 gives us $\sum_{i=1}^{n} \left(\frac{1}{V_i} \right)$ and this sum is equal to 15.855. Substituting in formula (3.9), we obtain

$$a = \frac{(2)\,(7)}{15.855} = .883$$

and solving for the discriminal dispersions of formula (3.10) we get

$$\sigma_1 = (.883)\,(2.088) - 1 = .843$$
$$\sigma_2 = (.883)\,(2.165) - 1 = .911$$
$$\sigma_3 = (.883)\,(2.494) - 1 = 1.202$$
$$\sigma_4 = (.883)\,(2.075) - 1 = .832$$
$$\sigma_5 = (.883)\,(2.976) - 1 = 1.628$$
$$\sigma_6 = (.883)\,(2.045) - 1 = .806$$
$$\sigma_7 = (.883)\,(2.012) - 1 = .777$$

As a check we add the discriminal dispersions and we should find that $\sum_{i=1}^{n} \sigma_i = n$. Doing this for the 7 values obtained above we have

$$\sum_{i=1}^{n} \sigma_i = .843 + .911 + \ldots + .777 = 6.999$$

It may be observed that all of the discriminal dispersions are approximately of the same magnitude except σ_3 and σ_5. The scale value for Stimulus 3 is, however, very close to the mean of the scale values of the other stimuli, thus minimizing the possible displacement of this stimulus with respect to the other stimuli. To a somewhat lesser extent this is also true of Stimulus 5.[3]

---

[3] The scale value of Stimulus 3, expressed in terms of its deviation from the mean of the scale values is -.033, and that of Stimulus 5 is .186, as we found in the previous chapter.

DERIVATION OF FORMULAS USED IN CALCULATING DISCRIMINAL DISPERSIONS

Consider any three stimuli, i, j, and k, with i and j held constant and k varying. We shall assume independence of stimuli such that r_{ij}, r_{ik}, and r_{jk} are all zero. Then from formula (2.5) we have

$$\overline{S}_i - \overline{S}_k = z_{ik} \sqrt{\sigma_i^2 + \sigma_k^2} \tag{3.11}$$

$$\overline{S}_j - \overline{S}_k = z_{jk} \sqrt{\sigma_j^2 + \sigma_k^2} \tag{3.12}$$

Subtracting (3.12) from (3.11) we get

$$\overline{S}_i - \overline{S}_j = z_{ik} \sqrt{\sigma_i^2 + \sigma_k^2} - z_{jk} \sqrt{\sigma_j^2 + \sigma_k^2} \tag{3.13}$$

and solving for z_{ik}, we have

$$z_{ik} = \frac{\overline{S}_i - \overline{S}_i}{\sqrt{\sigma_i^2 + \sigma_k^2}} + z_{jk} \frac{\sqrt{\sigma_j^2 + \sigma_k^2}}{\sqrt{\sigma_i^2 + \sigma_k^2}} \tag{3.14}$$

As a first approximation, assume that the discriminal dispersions are all of the same order of magnitude. Then

$$\sqrt{\sigma_i^2 + \sigma_k^2} \doteq \sigma_i \sqrt{2} \doteq \frac{2\sigma_i\sqrt{2}}{2} \doteq \frac{(\sigma_i + \sigma_k)\sqrt{2}}{2} \tag{3.15}$$

and similarly

$$\sqrt{\sigma_j^2 + \sigma_k^2} \doteq \frac{(\sigma_j + \sigma_k)\sqrt{2}}{2} \tag{3.16}$$

Then, using (3.15) and (3.16), we can write (3.14) as

$$z_{ik} \doteq \frac{\overline{S}_i - \overline{S}_j}{\dfrac{(\sigma_i + \sigma_k)\sqrt{2}}{2}} + z_{jk} \frac{\dfrac{(\sigma_j + \sigma_k)\sqrt{2}}{2}}{\dfrac{(\sigma_i + \sigma_k)\sqrt{2}}{2}} \tag{3.17}$$

and multiplying both numerator and denominator of the right side of (3.17) by $\sqrt{2}$

$$z_{ik} \doteq \frac{\sqrt{2}\,(\overline{S}_i - \overline{S}_j)}{\sigma_i + \sigma_k} + z_{jk}\,\frac{\sigma_j + \sigma_k}{\sigma_i + \sigma_k}$$

$$(3.18)$$

We then let the sum of the discriminal dispersions be equal to n so that $\sum_{i=1}^{n} \sigma_i = n$, and then the mean of the discriminal dispersions will be equal to 1.00. Taking σ_k as equal to the mean discriminal dispersion (3.18) can be written

$$z_{ik} \doteq \frac{\sqrt{2}\,(\overline{S}_i - \overline{S}_j)}{\sigma_i + 1} + z_{jk}\,\frac{\sigma_j + 1}{\sigma_i + 1}$$

$$(3.19)$$

The only variables in the above expression are those involving the k subscript. If, as previously, we let V_i represent the standard deviation of the z_{ik} values in the ith column and V_j the standard deviation of the z_{jk} values in the jth column, then[4]

$$V_i \doteq V_j \left(\frac{\sigma_j + 1}{\sigma_i + 1} \right)$$

$$(3.20)$$

or

$$\frac{V_i}{V_j} \doteq \left(\frac{\sigma_j + 1}{\sigma_i + 1} \right)$$

$$(3.21)$$

---

[4] If we have an equation such that $X' = a + Xb$ where a and b are constants and X is a variable, then $\sigma_{x'} = \sigma_x b$. For a more complete discussion and proof, see Edwards (1954).

and a similar expression for the ratio of V_i to the standard deviation V of any other column of the Z matrix could also be written. For example, if we take V_1 the standard deviation of the first column, we would have

$$\frac{V_1}{V_1} \doteq \frac{\sigma_1 + 1}{\sigma_1 + 1}$$

$$\frac{V_1}{V_2} \doteq \frac{\sigma_2 + 1}{\sigma_1 + 1}$$

$$\frac{V_1}{V_3} \doteq \frac{\sigma_3 + 1}{\sigma_1 + 1}$$

and so on until the nth column for which we would have

$$\frac{V_1}{V_n} \doteq \frac{\sigma_n + 1}{\sigma_1 + 1}$$

Summing over the complete set, we obtain

$$V_1 \sum_{i=1}^{n} \left(\frac{1}{V_i} \right) \doteq \left(\frac{1}{\sigma_1 + 1} \right) \sum_{i=1}^{n} (\sigma_i + 1)$$

$$\doteq \left(\frac{1}{\sigma_i + 1} \right) \left(\sum_{i=1}^{n} \sigma_i + n \right) \quad (3.22)$$

and since we have taken $\sum_{i=1}^{n} \sigma_i$ as equal to n, we have

$$V_1 \sum_{i=1}^{n} \left(\frac{1}{V_i} \right) \doteq \frac{2n}{\sigma_i + 1}$$

or

$$\sigma_1 + 1 \doteq \frac{2n}{V_1 \sum_{i=1}^{n} \left(\frac{1}{V_i} \right)} \quad (3.23)$$

The expression $2n \, / \, \sum_{i=1}^{n} (1 \, / \, V_i)$ will be a constant for a given set of n stimuli and is defined as a by formula (3.9). Thus

$$\sigma_1 = a \left(\frac{1}{V_1} \right) - 1$$

as defined by formula (3.10).

SCALE VALUES USING THE CASE III MODEL

If we were so inclined, we might now compute new scale values for the 7 statements using the Case III model. The scale values would now be determined in terms of

$$\overline{S}_i - \overline{S}_j = z_{ij} \sqrt{\sigma_i^2 + \sigma_j^2} \tag{3.24}$$

According to formula (3.24), each entry in the z matrix must be multiplied by the square root of the sum of the two squared discriminal dispersions involved in the entry. The z_{13} entry, for example, would be multiplied by $\sqrt{\sigma_1^2 + \sigma_3^2}$. Multiplication of the z_{ij} values by the corresponding values of $\sqrt{\sigma_i^2 + \sigma_j^2}$ would give a new matrix, which we may designate by z_c to indicate that the entries have been corrected to take into account inequalities in the discriminal dispersions. The procedures described in the previous chapter for finding the scale values of the stimuli would now be followed using the entries in the z_c matrix.

CIRCULAR TRIADS AND THE COEFFICIENT OF CONSISTENCE

In making paired comparison judgments, a subject may sometimes be inconsistent. An inconsistency in judgments occurs whenever there is a *circular triad* present in the $n(n-1)/2$ judgments. As an illustration of what is meant by a circular triad, consider three statements, $i, j,$ and $k,$ included in a set of n statements judged on a psychological continuum from least to most favorable. If Statement i is judged more favorable than Statement $j,$ and Statement j is judged more favorable than Statement $k,$ then, to be consistent, the subject should also judge Statement i to be more favorable than Statement $k.$ If Statement $k,$ on the other hand, is judged more favorable than Statement $i,$ these three comparative judgments would constitute a circular triad. The greater the number of circular triads occurring in the set of $n(n-1)/2$ comparative judgments of a given subject, the more inconsistent the subject may be said to be.

Inconsistencies in comparative judgments may occur for a number of reasons. The subject may be disinterested in the task and therefore careless in his judgments. Some of the statements may fall so close together on the psychological continuum that the judgments are exceedingly difficult to make. Still another possibility is that the statements do not fall along the single dimension on which we are trying to scale them. If statements differ with respect to attributes or dimensions other than the one in which we are interested, these additional attributes may play a part in influencing the comparative judgments. It may also be true that inconsistencies in comparative judgments reflect a general personality or ability trait, that is, that there are some individuals who show a high degree of consistency, regardless of the nature of the comparative judgments they are asked to make, whereas others show a marked degree of inconsistency. Regardless of the conditions producing inconsistencies, it may often be desirable to obtain some measure of the degree of consistency a subject shows in making comparative judgments and this can be done in terms of Kendall's (1948) coefficient of consistence.

Kendall (1948) has shown that when the number of stimuli to be judged is odd, then the maximum number of circular triads that can occur is $(n^3 - n)/24$. When the number of stimuli is even, then the maximum number of circular triads is $(n^3 - 4n)/24$. If we let d be the observed number of circular triads for a given subject, then the coefficient of consistence, *zeta*, may be defined as

$$\zeta = 1 - \frac{24d}{n^3 - n} \quad \text{when } n \text{ is odd} \quad (3.25)$$

and

$$\zeta = 1 - \frac{24d}{n^3 - 4n} \quad \text{when } n \text{ is even} \quad (3.26)$$

For example, if we have $n = 10$ stimuli, then the maximum number of circular triads will be $[(10^3 - (4)(10)]/24 = 40$. If a subject makes the maximum number, that is, 40, then the coefficient of consistence would be

$$\zeta = 1 - \frac{(24)(40)}{10^3 - (4)(10)} = 0$$

If the subject does not have a single circular triad in his comparative judgments, then the coefficient of consistence will be 1.00. Zeta can thus range between 0, indicating the maximum number of circular triads, and 1.00 indicating the absence of any circular triads.

The number of circular triads made by a subject can be obtained from a table such as that shown in Table 3.5. When the column stimulus is judged more favorable than the row stimulus (the same arrangement we have used previously for showing comparative judgments) we have en-

TABLE 3.5

Comparative judgments for a judge with no circular triads

STATEMENTS	1	2	3	4	5	6	7
1	—	1	1	1	1	1	1
2	0	—	1	1	1	1	1
3	0	0	—	1	1	1	1
4	0	0	0	—	1	1	1
5	0	0	0	0	—	1	1
6	0	0	0	0	0	—	1
7	0	0	0	0	0	0	—
a	0	1	2	3	4	5	6
a^2	0	1	4	9	16	25	36

tered a 1 in the corresponding cell of the table. If the column stimulus is judged less favorable than the row stimulus, we have entered a 0 in the cell. If we let a equal the sum of the entries in a given column of Table 2.5, then the number of circular triads d will be given by

$$d = \left(\frac{1}{12}\right)(n)(n-1)(2n-1) - \frac{1}{2}\sum a^2 \tag{3.27}$$

For Table 3.5, it is obvious that the subject has been completely consistent in his comparative judgments and therefore d should be equal to 0. This is true, as substitution in formula (3.27) shows. Thus

$$d = \left(\frac{1}{12}\right)(7)(7-1)(14-1) - \frac{1}{2} \, 91$$

$$= 45.5 - 45.5$$

$$= 0$$

and ζ therefore equals 1.00.

Table 3.6 illustrates the case of a subject who made some

TABLE 3.6

Comparative judgments for a judge with 9 circular triads

Statements	1	2	3	4	5	6	7
1	—	1	0	1	1	1	1
2	0	—	1	1	0	1	1
3	1	0	—	0	1	0	1
4	0	0	1	—	0	1	1
5	0	1	0	1	—	1	0
6	0	0	1	0	0	—	1
7	0	0	0	0	1	0	—
a	1	2	3	3	3	4	5
a^2	1	4	9	9	9	16	25

inconsistent judgments. Substitution in formula (3.27) shows that the number of circular triads is equal to

$$d = 45.5 - \frac{1}{2} \, 73$$

$$d = 9$$

Using the value of d obtained above, we can substitute in formula (3.25) to find the coefficient of consistence. Thus

$$\zeta = 1 - \frac{(24)\,(9)}{7^3 - 7} = .357$$

SIGNIFICANCE TEST FOR THE COEFFICIENT OF CONSISTENCE

Often we are interested not only in knowing the degree of consistency or inconsistency in a set of comparative judgments for a given subject, but also in knowing the probability of obtaining a given value of ζ under the hypothesis that the subject's judgments were made at random. We might assume, for example, that a given subject is completely incompetent and that any degree of consistency shown in his comparative judgments is a matter of chance. Kendall (1948) gives tables showing the probability of obtaining a given value of ζ under the hypothesis that the comparative judgments were a matter of chance for stimuli varying in number from 2 to 7. Since it is unlikely that we would, in general, have fewer stimuli than 7, it is fortunate that when $n \geqq 7$, then ζ can also be tested for significance in terms of the χ^2 distribution.

We calculate χ^2 in terms of the following formula, given by Kendall (1948):

$$\chi^2 = \left(\frac{8}{n-4}\right)\left(\frac{1}{4} \; _nC_3 - d + \frac{1}{2}\right) + df \qquad (3.28)$$

where $n =$ the number of stimuli

$_nC_3 =$ the number of combinations of n things taken 3 at a time or $n!/3!(n-3)!$

$d =$ the observed number of circular triads

$df =$ the number of degrees of freedom associated with χ^2

The number of degrees of freedom for the χ^2 of formula (3.28) will be given by

$$df = \frac{n(n-1)(n-2)}{(n-4)^2} \qquad (3.29)$$

For the judgments of the subject shown in Table 3.6 we have already found d equal to 9. Since we have 7 stimuli, we have degrees of freedom, as given by formula (3.29),

$$df = \frac{7(7-1)(7-2)}{(7-4)^2} = \frac{210}{9} = 23.33$$

or 23 rounded to the nearest integer. Then substituting in

formula (3.28) with d, the number of circular triads equal to 9, $n = 7$, and $df = 23.33$, we obtain

$$\chi^2 = \left[\frac{8}{(7 - 4)} \right]\left[\frac{1}{4}\ 35 - 9 + \frac{1}{2} \right] + 23.33 = 24$$

To evaluate the obtained value of χ^2 equal to 24, we enter Table III in the appendix with df equal to 23. Since the distribution of χ^2 as given by formula (3.28) is from high to low values of d, the probability that d will be equaled or exceeded is the complement of the tabled probability for χ^2 For the data of Table 3.6 we have $\chi^2 = 24$, with $df = 23$. From the table of χ^2 in the appendix we find that the probability associated with χ^2 is approximately .41.[5] Then the probability of obtaining a value of d equal to or greater than the observed value of 9, is $1 - .41 = .59$.[6] Thus we may conclude that this subject did not make a significantly large number of circular triads, that is, he showed a certain degree of consistency in his judgments, despite a lack of perfection.

HILL'S STUDY USING THE COEFFICIENT OF CONSISTENCE

Hill (1953) has used the coefficient of consistence in a study of the relationship between inconsistent judgments and the spacing of statements on a psychological continuum. He also investigated individual differences in the ability of subjects to make comparative judgments. Hill states (p. 565):

If the rationale underlying the method of paired comparisons scale construction is valid, then the occurrence of inconsistent judgments

[5] The probability of .41 was obtained by approximate interpolation in the table of χ^2.

[6] Kendall's (1948) tables give .580 as the exact probability of $d \geq 9$, when $n = 7$.

of objects should increase as the difference between those objects on the underlying continuum decreases. In other words, the greater the difference between objects with respect to the attribute being judged, the less likely these objects are to be judged inconsistently.

A second problem to be discussed is that of individual differences in the ability to make the type of discriminations called for in paired comparisons. If there is some general ability concerned in the making of consistent discriminations, then individuals making inconsistent judgments in one situation would tend to make similar inconsistencies in a second situation.

Hill made use of two sets of attitude statements concerning the participation of the United States in the Korean conflict. These statements had previously been scaled by the method of equal-appearing intervals.[7] Set I consisted of 9 statements with scale values on a highly unfavorable to highly favorable continuum. Set II consisted of 7 statements selected so as to represent only the favorable portion of the psychological continuum. The range of scale values of the 9 statements in Set I was from .00 to 2.66, with the average scale separation for all possible pairs of statements being 1.12. For the 7 statements in Set II the range in scale values was from .00 to 1.71, with the average scale separation being .63. The statements in Set I might thus be considered as being more widely separated on the psychological continuum than those in Set II. Comparative judgments were obtained from 78 judges for the statements in Set I and from 94 judges for the statements in Set II. In addition, both groups of judges made comparative judgments of the prestige value of 9 occupations having professional status.

Coefficients of consistence were computed for each judge: one coefficient representing his comparative judgments of the particular set of attitude statements and the other, his judgments of the occupational titles. Hill found that signifi-

---

[7] A psychological scaling method to be discussed in Chapter 4.

cantly more of the judges who were given Set I of the attitude statements had lower coefficients of consistence than in the group given Set II, indicating that the more closely statements are spaced on the psychological continuum, the greater the tendency for inconsistencies to occur, in terms of the number of circular triads. For example, only 8 per cent of the subjects judging the statements in Set I had coefficients of consistence less than .85, whereas 26 per cent of those judging the statements in Set II had coefficients of consistence less than .85. That this relationship between inconsistencies in judgments and spacing of the stimuli being judged was not a function of any difference between the two groups of judges was indicated by the failure to find any difference in the values of the coefficients of consistence between the two groups for their comparative judgments of the occupational titles.

For the first set of 9 statements, $9!/3!6! = 84$ triads or groups of 3 statements are possible. Taking each of the 84 triads, Hill found the scale separation between the two ex-

TABLE 3.7

Frequency of occurrence of circularity and the scale distance between extreme members of a triad*

FREQUENCY OF OCCURRENCE	SCALE DISTANCE BETWEEN MEMBERS OF THE TRIAD			TOTAL
	.31 — 1.30	1.31 — 1.90	1.91 — 2.70	
2 or more	15	4	0	19
1	4	13	9	26
0	6	9	24	39
Total	25	26	33	84

*Reproduced from Hill (1953), Table 2, p. 566.

treme members. It was hypothesized that the frequency of occurrence of circular triads would be negatively related to to these scale separations. Table 3.7 indicates that this is the case.

Hill was also interested in determining whether there was any tendency for a subject who was inconsistent in his judgments of one set of stimuli to be inconsistent also in his judgments of a second set of stimuli. Since he had found that inconsistency of judgment was in part dependent upon the scale separations of the stimuli, he first determined whether the scale separations of the pairs of stimuli in each of the two sets were comparable. He found that the average scale separation between all possible pairs of the 9 occupational titles was .61 and for the set of 7 favorable attitude statements, the average scale separation was .63. He assumed, therefore, that approximately equal discriminal ability would be required for making comparative judgments for these two groups of stimuli.

The coefficient of consistence was then calculated for the

TABLE 3.8

Coefficients of consistence for the judges who judged Set II of the attitude statements and also the set of occupational titles*

VALUES FOR THE OCCUPATIONS	VALUES FOR THE ATTITUDE STATEMENTS			TOTAL
	1.000	.927 — .857	Less than .857	
1.000	21	12	4	37
.967 — .933	16	9	7	32
Less than .933	6	6	13	25
Total	43	27	24	94

*Reproduced from Hill (1953), Table 3, p. 566.

comparative judgments of each of the 94 subjects who judged the occupational titles. The coefficient of consistence was also calculated for each of the subjects based upon the comparative judgments of the attitude statements. Table 3.8 shows that there is some tendency for subjects who obtain a high coefficient of consistence for one set of judgments also to obtain a high coefficient for the second set of judgments. Subjects who have relatively low values for one set of judgments also tend to have low values for the second.

THE COEFFICIENT OF AGREEMENT

It should be clear that several subjects may each have a coefficient of consistence of 1.00 for their comparative judgments of a set of stimuli, and yet not agree in the judgments they have made. A statistic developed by Kendall (1948) which he designates as u, the coefficient of agreement, provides a means of determining the extent to which a group of judges agree in their comparative judgments.

Suppose that we have m judges each making $n(n-1)/2$ comparative judgments. If there is complete agreement among the judges, then using the recording system of Table 3.5, where we have entered a 1 if the column stimulus is judged more favorable than the row stimulus and a 0 if it is not, we would have $n(n-1)/2$ cells in which the frequency of judgments "i more favorable than j" was m and all of the other cells would be 0. Table 3.9 repeats the frequencies reported previously for 7 attitude statements judged by 94 judges. We wish to determine the extent of agreement among the 94 judges with respect to their comparative judgments of these 7 statements.

We consider only the entries *below the diagonal* of Table 3.9. Then we may define T as

$$T = (\Sigma f_{ij}^2 - m \Sigma f_{ij}) + ({}_mC_2)({}_nC_2) \qquad (3.30)$$

where $\Sigma_i f_{ij}{}^2 =$ the sum of the squared f_{ij} entries *below the diagonal*

$\quad m =$ the number of judges

$\quad \Sigma f_{ij} =$ the sum of the f_{ij} entries *below the diagonal*

$\quad {}_mC_2 =$ the number of combinations of the m judges taken 2 at a time or $m(m-1)/2$

$\quad {}_nC_2 =$ the number of combinations of the n stimuli taken 2 at a time or $n(n-1)/2$

The first row at the bottom of Table 3.9 gives the sum of the f_{ij} values in each column, remembering that the summation extends over the entries below the diagonal only. The last entry at the right of this row is the sum of the row entries below the diagonal and is equal to Σf_{ij} in formula (3.30). The second row at the bottom of the table gives the sum of squares of the f_{ij} values in each column, again remembering that the summation extends over the entries below the diagonal only. The last entry in the second row is the sum of all of the squared f_{ij} values below the diagonal and is equal to $\Sigma f_{ij}{}^2$ in formula (3.30).

Substituting with the values of $\Sigma f_{ij}{}^2 = 20{,}998$ and $\Sigma f_{ij} = 616$ in formula (3.30) we obtain

$$T = \left[\, 20{,}998 - (94)(616) \,\right] + \left[\, \frac{94(94-1)}{2} \,\right] \left[\, \frac{7(7-1)}{2} \,\right]$$

$$= -36{,}906 + 91{,}791$$

$$= 54{,}885$$

Kendall's coefficient of agreement is then defined as

$$u = \frac{2T}{({}_mC_2)({}_nC_2)} - 1 \qquad (3.31)$$

where T = the value obtained from formula (3.30)

$_mC_2$ = the number of combinations of the m judges taken 2 at a time

$_nC_2$ = the number of combinations of the n stimuli taken 2 at a time.

We have T equal to 54,885, and in calculating T we found $_mC_2 = 4,371$, and $_nC_2 = 21$. Substituting with these values in formula (3.31), we obtain

$$u = \frac{2(54,885)}{(4,371)\,(21)} - 1$$
$$= 1.196 - 1$$
$$= .196$$

The value of u can be 1.00 only if there is perfect agreement among the m judges. The greater the departure from complete agreement (as measured by agreement among pairs of judges), the smaller the value of u. If the number of judges is even, then the minimum value of u is $-1\,(m-1)$, and if m is odd, then the minimum value of u is $-1/m$. Thus, only if $m = 2$, can u be equal to -1.00. If u takes any positive value whatsoever, then there is a certain amount of agreement among the judges. To determine whether this agreement is greater than the agreement expected if the judgments of the m judges were made at random, we can make use of tables published by Kendall (1948).

χ^2 TEST FOR THE COEFFICIENT OF AGREEMENT

For m greater than 6 and for n greater than 4, and this will usually be true of data in which we are interested, then we can use Kendall's test of significance for u based upon the χ^2 distribution. We calculate

$$\chi^2 = \left[\frac{4}{m - 2} \right] \left[T - \frac{1}{2} \, (_nC_2) \, (_mC_2) \left(\frac{m - 3}{m - 2} \right) \right] \quad (3.32)$$

where $T =$ the value obtained from formula (3.30)

$m =$ the number of judges

$n =$ the number of stimuli

For the data of Table 3.9 we have already found

TABLE 3.9

Frequency with which the column statement was judged more favorable than the row statement by 94 judges

STATEMENTS	1	2	3	4	5	6	7
1	—	65	75	80	75	86	88
2	29	—	51	54	62	68	81
3	19	43	—	49	59	60	63
4	14	40	45	—	49	63	67
5	19	32	35	45	—	51	55
6	8	26	34	31	43	—	57
7	6	13	31	27	39	37	—
f_{ij}	95	154	145	103	82	37	$\Sigma f_{ij} = 616$
$f_{ij}{}^2$	1,859	5,318	5,367	3,715	3,370	1,369	$\Sigma f_{ij}{}^2 = 20,998$

$T = 54{,}885$, $_mC_2 = 4{,}371$, and $_nC_2 = 21$. Then substituting with these values in formula (3.32) we have

$$\chi^2 = \left[\frac{4}{94 - 2} \right] \left[54{,}885 - \frac{1}{2} \, (4{,}371) \, (21) \left(\frac{94 - 3}{94 - 2} \right) \right]$$

$$= \left(\frac{4}{92} \right) (9{,}494.35)$$

$$= 412.8$$

The degrees of freedom available for evaluating the χ^2 of formula (3.32) will be given by

$$df = \left({}_nC_2 \right) \frac{m\,(m\,-\,1)}{(m\,-\,2)^2} \qquad (3.33)$$

With $n = 7$, we have previously found ${}_nC_2 = 21$. Then, with $m = 94$ judges, we have

$$df = 21\,\frac{94\,(94\,-\,1)}{(94\,-\,2)^2} = 21.69$$

which rounded to the nearest whole number is 22.

Entering the table of χ^2 in the appendix with degrees of freedom equal to 22, we find a χ^2 of 412.8 is highly significant, and that the probability of a value of u as great as .196 is much less than .01 if the comparative judgments of all of the judges were made at random. We conclude, therefore, that the 94 judges do show significant agreement in their comparative judgments.

Such a finding, of course, does not imply that there are no inconsistencies in the comparative judgments, and this would be true even though u was equal to 1.00, indicating perfect agreement among the judges. If inconsistencies occur and u is equal to 1.00, this merely means that the judges are in agreement in their inconsistencies as well as their consistencies.

The table of χ^2 in the appendix gives values of χ^2 only for degrees of freedom equal to or less than 30. As n, the number of stimuli, increases, and m, the number of judges, decreases, the number of degrees of freedom given by formula (3.33 will tend to exceed 30. When this is the case, we can evaluate the significance of u by finding

$$z = \sqrt{2\chi^2} - \sqrt{2df - 1} \qquad (3.34)$$

The value of z obtained from formula (3.34) is approximately normally distributed with unit variance and can be evaluated in terms of Table I in the appendix.

QUESTIONS AND PROBLEMS

1. Find the discriminal dispersions for the 10 statements for which you obtained paired comparison judgments in Chapter 2.

2. Using the same data, test the significance of the difference between the observed and theoretical proportions.

3. For the same data, find the coefficient of agreement. Can you conclude that the agreement among the judges is greater than might be expected by chance?

4. Take the judgments obtained from five of the judges and find the coefficient of consistence for each judge. Test each of these coefficients for significance.

5. If paired comparison judgments are obtained for 10 statements, what is the maximum number of circular triads that could be present? What is the maximum number of circular triads that could be present for paired comparison judgments involving 7 statements?

6. Would you expect coefficients of consistence to be, in general, smaller for statements scaled close together on the psychological continuum than for statements fairly widely spaced on the psychological continuum? Why?

7. What are some of the psychological implications of Hill's research?

REFERENCES AND SUGGESTED READINGS

BLISS, C. I. The analysis of field experimental data expressed in percentages. *Plant Protection,* Leningrad, 1937, No. 12, 67-77.

*BURROS, R. H. The application of the method of paired comparisons to the study of reaction potential. *Psychol. Rev.*, 1951, 58, 60-66.

EDWARDS, A. L. *Statistical methods for the behavioral sciences*. New York: Rinehart, 1954.

FISHER, R. A. On the dominance ratio. *Proc. Roy. Soc.*, Edinburgh, 1922, 42, 321-341.

HILL, R. J. A note on inconsistency in paired comparison judgments. *Amer. soc. Rev.*, 1953, 18, 564-566.

KENDALL, M. G. *Rank correlation methods*. London: Griffin, 1948.

*MOSTELLER, F. Remarks on the method of paired comparisons: II. The effect of an aberrant standard deviation when equal standard deviations and equal correlations are assumed. *Psychometrika*, 1951a, 16, 203-206.

*——Remarks on the method of paired comparisons: III. A test of significance for paired comparisons when equal standard deviations and equal correlations are assumed. *Psychometrika*, 1951b, 16, 207-208.

SNEDECOR, G. W. *Statistical methods*. (5th Ed.) Ames, Iowa: Iowa State College Press, 1956.

THURSTONE, L. L. A law of comparative judgment. *Psychol. Rev.*, 1927, 34, 273-286.

*——Stimulus dispersions in the method of constant stimuli. *J. exp. Psychol.*, 1932, 15, 284-297.

4

The Method of
Equal-Appearing Intervals

The method of paired comparisons is useful in scaling statements when the number of statements to be scaled is not too large. We recall, however, that if comparative judgments are to be obtained for each pair of statements, then each subject will have to make $n(n - 1)/2$ comparative judgments. Twenty statements will thus require 190 comparative judgments, 30 statements will require 455 comparative judgments, and 40 will require 780 comparative judgments. If we have a fairly large number of statements to scale, we may not be able to obtain subjects who will give the necessary time required in making the comparative judgments. A solution to this problem is to use a scaling method that requires each subject to make only one comparative judgment for each statement. The *method of equal-appearing intervals* has been widely used in obtaining scale values for a large number of statements.

THE SORTING PROCEDURE

In the method of equal-appearing intervals, as originally described by Thurstone and Chave (1929), each statement concerning the psychological object of interest is printed on a separate card and subjects are then asked to sort the statements on the cards into a number of intervals.[1] Along with the cards containing the statements, each subject is given a set of 11 cards on which the letters *A* to *K* appear. These cards are arranged in order in front of the subjects with the *A* card to the extreme left and the *K* card to the extreme right. The *A* card is described as representing the card on which the statements that seem to express the most unfavorable feelings about the psychological object are to be placed. Statements that seem to express the most favorable feelings about the psychological object are to be placed on the *K* card. The middle or *F* card is described as the "neutral" card on which statements that express neither favorable nor unfavorable feelings about the psychological object are to be placed. Varying degrees of increasing favorableness expressed by the statements are represented by the cards lettered *G* to *K* and varying degrees of unfavorableness by the cards *D* to *A*. It may thus be observed that the psychological continuum from least to most favorable is regarded as continuous with the psychological continuum from least to most unfavorable and the *F* or "neutral" interval is, in essence, a zero point, as illustrated in Figure 4.1.

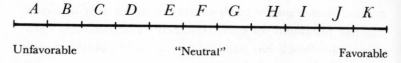

FIG. 4.1—The Thurstone equal-appearing interval continuum.

Each subject is asked to judge the degree of favorableness or unfavorableness of feeling expressed by each statement

---

[1] Variations in this procedure of obtaining equal-appearing interval judgments have been introduced by other research workers. We will describe some of these alternatives later.

in terms of the 11 intervals represented by the cards. It was found by Thurstone and Chave that subjects required about 45 minutes to judge the 130 statements that these investigators used in developing their scale to measure attitude toward the church. Comparative judgments of the kind described were obtained from 300 subjects.

Thurstone and Chave also believed that the sorting or judging of the statements would be done similarly by those judges who had favorable and those who had unfavorable attitudes toward the psychological object under consideration. A number of research studies bearing upon this contention will be discussed later.

Only the middle and the two extreme cards on which the statements were to be sorted were defined for the subjects. Thurstone and Chave believed it was essential that the other cards not be so defined in order that the intervals between successive cards would represent *equal-appearing intervals* or degrees of favorableness-unfavorableness for each subject. If the intervals are judged equal by the subjects, the successive integers from 1 to 11 can then be assigned to the lettered cards A to K, and, in essence, the subject has then rated each statement on an 11 point rating scale. The 11 point scale then becomes the psychological continuum on which the statements have been judged and all that is required is that some typical value be found for the distribution of judgments obtained for each statement. This typical or average value can then be taken as the scale value of the statement on the 11 point psychological continuum. As their measure of the average value of the distribution of judgments, Thurstone and Chave used the median of the distribution for a given statement. Before describing methods for finding the medians, however, another point should be considered.

As in the method of paired comparisons, some subjects in making equal-appearing interval judgments may undertake the task carelessly and with little interest. Still other subjects may misunderstand the directions and thus not be aware of the nature of the judgments desired. They may respond, for example, in terms of their *own agreement* or *disagreement* with the statements rather than in terms of the *judged degree of favorableness-unfavorableness*. A criterion used by Thurstone and Chave, for eliminating those subjects who apparently performed the judging task with carelessness or who otherwise failed to respond to the instructions for making the judgments, was to reject the judgments obtained from any subject who placed 30 or more statements on any one of the 11 cards.[2] They report that of 341 subjects making the judgments, 41 were eliminated by this criterion.

CALCULATION OF SCALE AND Q VALUES

The data obtained from a large number of judges can be arranged in the form shown in Table 4.1. Three rows are used for each statement. The first gives the frequency with which the statement was placed in each of the 11 categories. The second gives these frequencies as proportions. The proportions are obtained by dividing each frequency by N, the total number of judges or, more simply, by multiplying each of the frequencies by the reciprocal of N. The third row gives the cumulative proportions, that is, the proportion of judgments in a given category plus the sum of all of the proportions below that category.

If the median of the distribution of judgments for each

[2] Edwards and Kilpatrick (1948) report that they also examine the sortings for each subject and eliminate those subjects who show obvious reversals of the continuum. This can be quickly done by looking at the judgments made for two or three key statements believed to fall at each of the two extremes of the continuum.

TABLE 4.1

Summary table for judgments obtained by the method of equal-appearing intervals

STATEMENTS		SORTING CATEGORIES											SCALE VALUE	Q VALUE
		A	B	C	D	E	F	G	H	I	J	K		
		1	2	3	4	5	6	7	8	9	10	11		
1	f	2	2	6	2	6	62	64	26	18	8	4	6.8	1.7
	p	.01	.01	.03	.01	.03	.31	.32	.13	.09	.04	.02		
	cp	.01	.02	.05	.06	.09	.40	.72	.85	.94	.98	1.00		
2	f	0	0	0	10	40	28	50	26	28	14	4	6.9	2.8
	p	.00	.00	.00	.05	.20	.14	.25	.13	.14	.07	.02		
	cp	.00	.00	.00	.05	.25	.39	.64	.77	.91	.98	1.00		
3	f	0	0	0	2	8	6	26	44	56	44	14	8.7	2.0
	p	.00	.00	.00	.01	.04	.03	.13	.22	.28	.22	.07		
	cp	.00	.00	.00	.01	.05	.08	.21	.43	.71	.93	1.00		

statement is taken as the scale value of the statement, then the scale values can be found from the data arranged in the manner of Table 4.1 by means of the following formula

$$S = l + \left(\frac{.50 - \Sigma p_b}{p_w} \right) i \qquad (4.1)$$

where S = the median or scale value of the statement

l = the lower limit of the interval in which the median falls

Σp_b = the sum of the proportions below the interval in which the median falls

p_w = the proportion within the interval in which the median falls

i = the width of the interval and is assumed to be equal to 1.0

Substituting in the above formula to find the scale value for the first statement in Table 4.1, we have[3]

$$S = 6.5 + \left(\frac{.50 - .40}{.32} \right) 1.0 = 6.8$$

The other scale values shown in Table 4.1 are found in the same manner.

Thurstone and Chave used the interquartile range or Q as a measure of the variation of the distribution of judgments for a given statement. The interquartile range contains the middle 50 per cent of the judgments. To determine the value of Q, we need to find two other point measures, the 75th centile and the 25th centile. The 25th centile can be obtained from the following formula

$$C_{25} = l + \left(\frac{.25 - \Sigma p_b}{p_w} \right) i \qquad (4.2)$$

where C_{25} = the 25th centile

l = the lower limit of the interval in which the 25th centile falls

Σp_b = the sum of the proportions below the interval in which the 25th centile falls

p_w = the proportion within the interval in which the 25th centile falls

i = the width of the interval and is assumed to be equal to 1.0

The 75th centile will be given by

$$C_{75} = l + \left(\frac{.75 - \Sigma p_b}{p_w} \right) i \qquad (4.3)$$

[3] The interval represented by the number assigned to a given card or category is assumed to range from .5 of a unit below to .5 of a unit above the assigned number. Thus the lower limit of the interval represented by the card assigned the number 7 is 6.5 and the upper limit is 7.5

where $C_{75} =$ the 75th centile

$\Sigma p_b =$ the sum of the proportions below the interval in which the 75th centile falls

$p_w =$ the proportion within the interval in which the 75th centile falls

$i =$ the width of the interval and is assumed to be equal to 1.0

For the first statement in Table 4.1, we have

$$C_{25} = 5.5 + \left(\frac{.25 - .09}{.31} \right) 1.0 = 6.0$$

and

$$C_{75} = 7.5 + \left(\frac{.75 - .72}{.13} \right) 1.0 = 7.7$$

Then the interquartile range or Q will be given by taking the difference between C_{75} and C_{25}. Thus

$$Q = C_{75} - C_{25} \tag{4.4}$$

or for the first statement in Table 4.1, we have

$$Q = 7.7 - 6.0 = 1.7$$

The interquartile range is a measure of the spread of the middle 50 per cent of the judgments. When there is good agreement among the subjects in judging the degree of favorableness or unfavorableness of a statement, Q will be small compared with the value obtained when there is relatively little agreement among the subjects. A large Q value, indicating disagreement among the judges as to the degree of the attribute possessed by a statement, is therefore taken as an indication that there is something wrong with the statement. Thurstone and Chave regard large Q values primarily as an indication that a statement is ambiguous.

Large Q values may result from the fact that the statement is interpreted in more than one way by the subjects when making their judgments or from any of the other conditions producing large discriminal dispersions discussed in connec‑tion with the method of paired comparisons.

Scale and Q values for statements can also be found graphically. Figure 4.2 shows the cumulative proportion

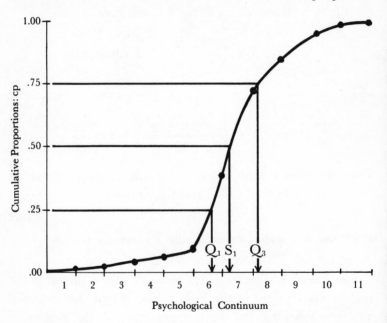

FIG. 4.2—Cumulative proportion graph for Statement 1 of Table 4.1.

graph for the first statement in Table 4.1 and Figure 4.3 shows the cumulative proportion graph for the second state‑ment. Dropping a perpendicular from the graph to the baseline at the value of cp equal to .50 will give the value of the median or the scale value of the statement. Dropping perpendiculars to the baseline at values of cp equal to .25

and .75 will give the values of C_{25} and C_{75} and the distance between these two on the baseline will give the value of Q.

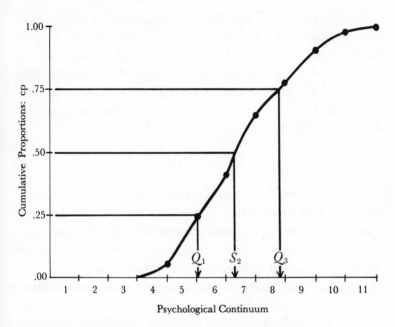

FIG. 4.3—Cumulative proportion graph for Statement 2 of Table 4.1.

Using graph paper ruled 10 to the inch, the scale and Q values of the statements can be found quite accurately by the graphic method.

A device used by Edwards and Kilpatrick (1948) facilitates the finding of scale and Q values by the graphic method. They prepared a master chart with the Y axis corresponding to the cumulative proportions and with the scale intervals on the X axis. This chart was taped to a ground-glass plate that fitted over the top of a small wooden box. Inside of the box was a 100 watt bulb. By placing tracing paper over the chart, the cumulative proportion graphs for the individual statements could be quickly drawn and the scale values and 75th and 25th centiles readily found.

Jurgensen (1943) has used a nomograph to obtain scale and Q values. He describes how the nomograph may be constructed and states it can be prepared in less than 10 minutes for any given number of judges. He estimates that scale and Q values for statements can be found using the nomograph in less than one-fourth the time required by direct calculation.

THE ATTITUDE SCALE

It may be observed that the scale values of the two statements whose cumulative proportion graphs are shown in Figures 4.2 and 4.3 are quite comparable. For the statement shown in Figure 4.2, for example, the scale value is 6.8 and for the one shown in Figure 4.3, the scale value is 6.9. The Q values for the two statements, however, differ considerably. For the first statement, the Q value is 1.7 and for the second it is 2.8. When there is a high degree of agreement among the judges, the cumulative proportion graph will, in general, have a steep slope and Q will be relatively small compared with the value obtained when the judgments are spread over the entire scale and the slope of the cumulative proportion graph is more gradual.

In general, what is desired in constructing an attitude scale by the method of equal-appearing intervals is approximately 20 to 22 statements such that the scale values of the statements on the psychological continuum are relatively equally spaced and such that the Q values are relatively small. Thus both S and Q are used as criteria for the selection of statements to be included in the attitude scale. If a choice is to be made among several statements with approximately the same S values, preference is given to the one with the lowest Q value, that is, to the one believed to be least ambiguous.

Assume that 22 statements have been selected from the much larger group for which we have scale and Q values. These statements can be arranged in random order and presented to subjects with instructions to indicate those that they are willing to accept or agree with and those that they reject or disagree with.[4] Taking only the statements with which the subject has agreed, an attitude score is obtained from the scale values of these statements that is regarded as an indication of the location of the subject on the psychological continuum on which the statements have been scaled. The attitude score is based upon the arithmetic mean or median of the scale values of the statements agreed with. If the subject has agreed with an odd number of statements, and if the median method of scoring is used, then the score is simply the scale value of the middle statement when they are arranged in rank order of their scale values. For example, if a subject has agreed with 5 statements with scale values of 3.2, 4.5, 5.6, 7.2, and 8.9, his score would be the scale value of the middle statement or 5.6. Using the arithmetic mean as the score would result in a value of 5.8 being assigned to the subject. If an even number of statements are agreed with and the median method of scoring is used, then the midpoint of the scale distance between the two middle statements is taken as the score. For example, if the subject has agreed with 4 statements with scale values of 4.5, 5.6, 7.2, and 8.9, his score would be $5.6 + (7.2 - 5.6)/2 = 6.4$.

[4] Research by Sigerfoos (1936) indicates that the arrangement of the statements in order of their scale values results in scores for subjects quite comparable to the scores obtained with a random arrangement of the statements. If this finding is, in general, true for equal-appearing interval scales, then the rank order arrangement would somewhat facilitate the scoring.

The arithmetic mean of these scale values would give a score of 6.6.

It has been customary among those working with the method of equal-appearing intervals to construct two comparable forms of the attitude scale. This is done by selecting from the initial group of statements for which scale and Q values have been obtained, in addition to the first set, a second set of 20 to 22 statements such that they also have scale values fairly equally spaced along the psychological continuum and with fairly low Q values. If both forms of the attitude scale are then given to the same group of subjects, the scores for the subjects on the two forms can be correlated and this correlation taken as a measure of the reliability of the scales. Reliability coefficients typically reported for the correlation between two forms of the same equal-appearing interval scale are above .85.

NUMBER OF JUDGES REQUIRED

Thurstone and Chave used 300 subjects in obtaining scale values for the 130 statements they used in constructing an attitude scale toward the church. Subsequent research by Nystrom (1933), Ferguson (1939), Rosander (1936), Uhrbrock (1934), and Edwards and Kenney (1946) indicates that reliable scale values can be obtained with much smaller groups of subjects.

Edwards and Kenney (1946), for example, report a correlation of .95 between the scale values for 129 statements obtained from a group of 72 judges with the scale values for the same statements based upon the judgments of 300 judges. Uhrbrock (1934) obtained judgments of 279 statements from two groups of 50 judges each. The correlation between the scale values obtained independently from the two groups of judges was .99. Correlations as high as .99 have been reported by Rosander (1936) for scale values obtained independently from two groups with as few as 15 judges in each group.

The evidence thus points to the conclusion that a relatively small number of judges can be used to obtain reliable scale values for statements using the method of equal-appearing intervals. It is obvious that reducing the number of judges from 300 to 50 will also reduce the amount of time and work involved in obtaining judgments and subsequent scale values for statements.

VARIATIONS IN THE METHOD OF OBTAINING JUDGMENTS

In order to obtain judgments from subjects following the procedure described by Thurstone and Chave, subjects must be provided with sufficient work space to spread out the 11 cards on which the statements are to be sorted. It would be convenient if it were possible to present the statements in some way so that large groups could do the judging at the same time. Ballin and Farnsworth (1941) have introduced a variation in the judging procedure through the use of a graphic-rating method that permits this. Instead of sorting statements into 11 categories, subjects give their judgments of the degree of favorableness or unfavorableness of the statements by making a check on an 11 inch line. It is possible, following Thurstone and Chave, to define one extreme of this line as favorable and the other as unfavorable with the midpoint being defined as "neutral." After subjects have made their judgments, the graphic-rating scale can be subdivided into 11, 10, 9 or any other number of equal intervals and the interval in which the rating or check-mark falls can be found. Scale and Q values can then be obtained in the usual manner. Ballin and Farnsworth (1941) report that scale values for 20 statements obtained by the graphic - rating method correlated .97 with those obtained using the sorting procedure of Thurstone and Chave, and .99 with a procedure suggested by Seashore and Hevner (1933).

In the Seashore and Hevner (1933) variation of the judging procedure, the statements are printed in booklets with the numbers from 1 to 11 printed at the left of the statements. Subjects then make their judgments by circling the number corresponding to the category in which they believe the statement falls. Edwards and Kenney (1946) used the Seashore and Hevner method to obtain judgments of 129 statements originally scaled by Thurstone and Chave. They found that the scale values of the statements correlated .95 with those originally reported by Thurstone and Chave. The fact that these scale values were obtained some 15 years later than the original values obtained by Thurstone and Chave speaks well for the stability of the ordering of the statements on the psychological continuum over a fairly long period of time.[5]

Edwards and Kilpatrick (1948) had subjects first sort statements relating to attitude toward science into three categories: those judged as favorable, those judged as unfavorable, and those judged as "neutral." The favorable statements were then further divided by the subjects into three categories: those judged to be most favorable, those judged to be least favorable, and a middle group. The unfavorable statements were also divided into three groups:

[5] See, however, the study by Farnsworth (1943). He reports changes as great as one scale interval for 2 out of 20 statements scaled twice with a 10-year interval separating the two sets of comparative judgments. The correlation between the scale values was, however, .97.

those judged most unfavorable, those judged to be least unfavorable, and a middle group. Finally, the "neutral" statements were divided into three piles, one pile representing statements with a slight degree of favorableness, another with a slight degree of unfavorableness, and a remaining "neutral" group. Edwards and Kilpatrick believed that this procedure enabled the subjects to gain a first impression of the complete set of statements and to form some judgment of the nature of the complete psychological continuum. After the statements had been sorted into the 9 categories, the subjects were then permitted to shift statements from one category to another until they were satisfied with the judgments they had made. No evidence is available as to the correlation of scale values obtained in this way with those obtained from the standard Thurstone and Chave procedure.

Webb (1951) had subjects judge statements relating to attitude toward science subjects. Judgments were obtained using standard IBM answer sheets with five categories of response in terms of which the subjects marked their judgments of each statement. The 1-column on the answer sheet was defined as very unfavorable and the 5-column as very favorable. Webb reports that the use of the IBM graphic-item counter in tabulating the judgments of the subjects reduced the labor involved in the scaling process considerably. Webb found that the scale values of 78 statements judged in terms of his categories correlated .99 with the scale values obtained by Remmers and Silance (1934), who used an 11 point scale and the Thurstone and Chave sorting procedure.

The evidence cited above would seem to point to the conclusion that of the various methods investigated, the particular one used in obtaining equal-appearing interval judgments is not an important variable related to the scale values of the statements. The relative ordering of the statements on the psychological continuum is much the same, regardless of which of the methods reported upon is used in obtaining the judgments.[6]

THE CRITERION OF IRRELEVANCE

Thurstone and Chave describe another criterion, in addition to Q, as a basis for rejecting statements in scales constructed by the method of equal-appearing intervals. This criterion, however, has not been used extensively in connection with the method of equal-appearing intervals. Nevertheless, we shall pay some attention to theory underlying the *criterion of irrelevance*, as it is called. The criterion of irrelevance is based, not upon the *judgments* of subjects of the degree of favorableness or unfavorableness of statements, but rather upon the *agreement* or *disagreement* of subjects with statements having known scale values. It requires, therefore, that the scale values of statements be known and that we also have available responses of agreement or disagreement with these same statements by another group.

Suppose, for example, that an equal-appearing interval scale has been given to a large group of subjects. For each subject we have a score that we take as an indication of his location on the same psychological continuum as that on which the statements have been scaled. Consider only a group of n subjects who are homogeneous with respect to

[6] Differences have been found, however, with respect to the Q values of statements. Edwards and Kenney (1946), using the Seashore and Hevner (1933) procedure, found that the Q values of their statements correlated only .18 with those originally reported by Thurstone and Chave (1929). Webb (1951), using the 5-point scale and IBM answer sheets, reports that his Q values correlated .42 with those originally reported by Remmers and Silance (1934). It is not known, however, whether these results are primarily due to differences in the methods of obtaining the judgments or due to the time intervals separating the judging situations.

their scores, that is, for example, a group of subjects all of whom have scale scores of 6.0. Let i be any statement with scale value S_i on the psychological continuum. Let n_i be the number of subjects in the group of n who endorse statement i. As S_i takes scale values closer and closer to 6.0, then we should expect n_i to increase and approach a maximum. As S_i becomes greater than 6.0 or less than 6.0, we should expect n_i to decrease also. Expressing n_i as a proportion of the n subjects with scale scores of 6.0, we may take this proportion, n_i/n, as the probability that a given statement will be endorsed by this particular group of n subjects. This probability should be a maximum for state-

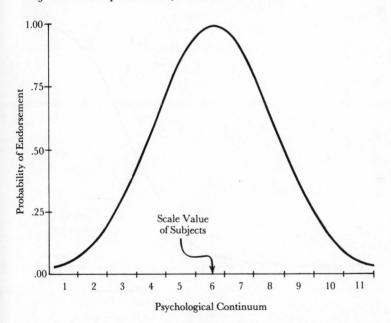

FIG. 4.4—Theoretical probability of endorsement of attitude statements with varying scale values on the psychological continuum by a group of subjects with attitude scale scores of 6.0 on the same continuum.

ments with the same scale value as the scale score of the subjects and should decrease systematically as S_i takes values larger than or smaller than 6.0. A theoretical distribution of these probabilities is shown in Figure 4.4.

Similarly, we might take a group of *n* subjects with scale scores of 11.0 and we should also expect the probability that they will *endorse* a given statement to be a function of the scale value of the statement. The closer a given statement is to the location of the subjects on the psychological continuum, the greater the probability that these subjects will endorse the statement, until we reach a maximum for

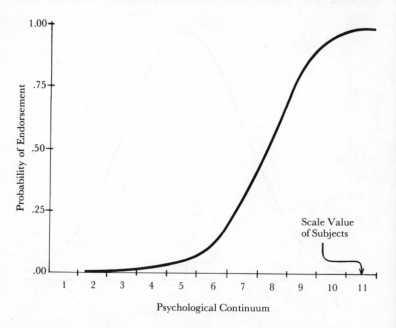

FIG. 4.5—Theoretical probability of endorsement of attitude statements with varying scale values on the psychological continuum by a group of subjects with attitude scale scores of 11.0 on the same continuum.

statements with scale values at 11.0. A theoretical distribution of these probabilities is shown in Figure 4.5.

ATTITUDE AS A LATENT VARIABLE

In the examples cited above, we have held *attitude*, represented by the scale score, constant, and varied the scale values of the statements. Suppose now that we *vary the attitude and hold the scale value of the statement constant*. We can think, for example, of an indefinitely large number of subjects as being distributed with respect to their attitudes over the psychological continuum at every point. For each point on the continuum we consider the *probability of endorsement* of a given statement by those individuals scaled at the point. If we now take a single statement with scale value S_i then we should expect a maximum probability of endorsement by those subjects whose scale locations are also at S_i and we should expect decreasing probabilities of endorsement by those subjects whose scale positions fall at points above or below S_i.

From a theoretical point of view, attitudes are sometimes regarded as latent variables. A *latent variable* is any variable that might be considered to underlie or produce certain behavior or responses. The behavior or response observed is then considered to be some function of the latent variable. The probability of endorsing a given statement relating to some psychological object, for example, might be regarded as a function of a latent attitude variable toward the object. The graph of this probability against the assumed or known values of the latent variable is called the *operating characteristic of the statement*.

Statements may be described as belonging to one of two major classes: those for which the operating characteristic is *monotonic* and those for which the operating characteristic is *nonmonotonic*. Monotonic statements, in turn, may be of two kinds. If the probability of endorsement of a given statement increases (or remains constant over a limited interval) but never decreases as the value of the latent variable increases, we may regard the probability of endorsement as an increasing monotonic function of the latent variable. If the probability of endorsement of a given statement decreases (or remains constant over a limited interval) but never increases as the latent variable increases, we may regard the probability of endorsement as a decreasing mono - tonic function of the latent variable. Various types of monotonic functions are shown in Figure 4.6.

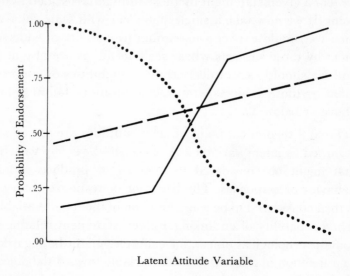

FIG. 4.6—Various types of monotonic operating characteristics for attitude statements.

If the probability of endorsement of a given statement shows an increase with an increase in the value of the latent variable, reaches some maximum value, and then shows a decrease, we may regard the probability of endorsement as a nonmonotonic function of the latent variable. Figure 4.7 shows some examples of nonmonotonic functions.

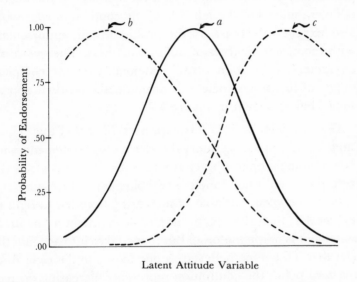

FIG. 4.7—Various types of nonmonotonic operating characteristics for attitude statements.

Attitude scales in which all of the statements are regarded as being increasing monotonic functions of the latent attitude variable have been referred to by Stouffer (1950) and Loevinger (1948) as *cumulative scales*. Attitude scales in which the statements are regarded as having nonmonotonic operating characteristics are referred to as *noncumulative scales*.

In equal-appearing interval scales, we have a theoretical zero point, the neutral interval, with increasing values of the latent variable as we move out from the zero point in both directions. To the right, for example, we have increasing degrees of favorableness and to the left increasing degrees of unfavorableness. For the right side of the continuum, we might expect a "neutral" statement to show a decreasing probability of endorsement with an increase in the degree of favorability. For the left side of the continuum we should also expect a decrease in the probability of endorsement with increasing degrees of unfavorableness. The operating characteristic for a "neutral" statement over the complete range of the psychological continuum should then appear somewhat as shown in Figure 4.7a.

Green (1954, p. 344) has expressed his belief that Thurstone equal-appearing interval scales require statements with nonmonotonic operating characteristics. If one neglects the zero point on Thurstone's psychological continuum, and regards the latent variable as increasing from left to right in Figure 4.7, then the operating characteristic of a "neutral" statement is nonmonotonic. But if one takes into account the fact that Thurstone believed as one moves to the right from the zero point, the continuum represents increasing degrees of favorableness and as one moves to the left the continuum represents increasing degrees of unfavorableness, the operating characteristic of the "neutral" statement shown in Figure 4.7a is essentially monotonic.

Thurstone's equal-appearing interval continuum is, in the sense described above, a joining together of *two continua,* the favorable and the unfavorable. Both Mosier (1941) and McNemar (1946) have raised the question as to whether these two continua can be assumed to represent a single continuum. Mosier (1941), for example, had subjects judge stimuli in terms of the method of equal-appearing intervals with the two extreme intervals defined as "favorable" and "unfavorable," in accordance with the usual Thurstone instructions. Mosier found that a number of stimuli had fairly large frequencies in the middle or "neutral" interval, but zero frequencies for all intervals on one or the other side of the "neutral" interval. On the basis of this finding, he raises the question as to whether the intervals from "favorable" to "neutral" might not represent one continuum and the intervals from "neutral" to "unfavorable" another continuum, with the second not necessarily collinear with the first. Mosier suggests that perhaps if his judges had been instructed to judge the stimuli in terms of "degree of favorableness" rather than in terms of "favorableness-unfavorableness," the piling up or end-effect in the "neutral" interval might not have occurred. This possibility has been tested by Carlson (1956) with 130 statements used by Thurstone and Chave (1929) in establishing their attitude scale toward the church.

Carlson (1956) had three groups of subjects judge the 130 statements under differing sets of instructions. For one group, the two extreme intervals were defined as "most unfavorable" and "most favorable," in accordance with the usual Thurstone instructions. The second group judged the same statements with the two extreme intervals defined as "least unfavorable" and "most unfavorable." The third group judged the same statements with the two extreme intervals defined as "least favorable" and "most favorable." Scale values of the 130 statements were found independently for each of the three groups of judges. The plots of each set of scale values against every other set were all linear with only a small degree of scatter, and Carlson estimates that the intercorrelations among the three sets of scale values are all above .90. The relative ordering of the statements as to the degree of affect expressed by each, in other words, was much the same, regardless of which of the three sets of instructions was given to the judges, that is, how the two extreme intervals were defined. These results would seem to indicate that only a single continuum is involved and that "degree of favorableness" is, in fact, collinear with "degree of unfavorableness."

From data reported by Thurstone and Chave (1929, pp. 49-54), it is apparent that, although one might expect to obtain nonmonotonic operating characteristics for statements with scale values that deviate from the zero point on the psychological continuum, expectation is not in accord with fact. As Green (1954, p. 365) has pointed out, "In practice, Thurstone items with scale values near the extremes tend to have monotonic operating characteristics."

In Figure 4.7a we have shown the *theoretical* operating characteristic of a "neutral" statement in an equal-appearing interval scale. As Edwards (1946) has suggested, it is also doubtful whether in practice the operating characteristics of "neutral" statements are in accord with theoretical expectations. The examples he cites suggest that the operating characteristics of "neutral" statements may be straight lines with zero slope. This would mean, for "neutral" statements, that the probability of endorsement remains relatively constant as the latent attitude variable goes from highly unfavorable through the "neutral" point to highly favorable. Regardless of the value of the latent variable, the probability of endorsement of the "neutral" statement does not change. Such "neutral" statements, in other words, are just as likely to be endorsed by those with favorable and unfavorable attitudes as by those with "neutral" attitudes on the equal-appearing interval continuum.

THE INFLUENCE OF ATTITUDE ON SCALE VALUES

A basic assumption of the method of equal-appearing

intervals is that the scale values of the statements are independent of the attitudes of the judges who do the sorting. If the scale values of statements are not independent of the attitudes of the judges doing the sorting, this would, of course, result in difficulties in the interpretation of attitude scores based upon the scale values.

Since the publication of the Thurstone and Chave monograph, much research has been done concerning the relationship between the scale values of statements and the attitudes of the judges doing the sorting. In one of the early studies, Hinckley (1932) used three groups of judges who he had some reason to believe differed in their attitudes toward the Negro. One was a group of southern white subjects who might be likely to have unfavorable attitudes toward the Negro. Another group consisted of white northerners who were favorable in their attitudes toward the Negro and the third group consisted of Negroes. Each group of subjects sorted 114 statements about the Negro into 11 categories following the procedure of the method of equal-appearing intervals. Scale values for the statements were then obtained separately from the judgments of each group. Hinckley found that the scale values obtained from the judgments of the two white groups correlated .98. The correlation between the scale values based upon the judgments of the unfavorable whites and the judgments of the Negro group was .93. Since essentially the same ordering of the statements on the psychological continuum was obtained from groups with differing attitudes, Hinckley concluded that the scale values of the statements were independent of the attitudes of the judging group.

In another study, Beyle (1932) reports the same results as Hinckley. Beyle used statements relating to a particular candidate for political office. These statements were scaled by supporters of the candidate and also by nonsupporters.

Beyle found that the scale values obtained from the two groups with opposed attitudes correlated .99.

Ferguson (1935) used scores on an equal-appearing interval attitude scale, designed to measure attitude toward war, to divide subjects into three groups with differing attitudes. One group he describes as strongly opposed to war, another as moderately opposed, and a third group as "neutral." He then used the method of paired comparisons to obtain comparative judgments for the 20 statements in the scale from the three groups of subjects. He reports that the correlations between the scale values based upon the judgments of these three groups of subjects were all above .98.

Pintner and Forlano (1937) used a procedure similar to Ferguson's. They gave their subjects an equal-appearing interval attitude scale designed to measure "patriotism." Immediately after they had taken the scale, the subjects were told how the scale was constructed and were asked to make comparative judgments of the degree of favorableness-unfavorableness of the statements. On the basis of their scores on the scale, the subjects were divided into three groups, the 27 per cent with the most favorable scores, the 27 per cent with the most unfavorable scores, and the middle 46 per cent. The rank ordering of the statements from the most unfavorable to the most favorable was determined separately for each of these three groups and the rank orders correlated. All of the correlations were above .98.

More recently, Eysenck and Crown (1949) gave subjects a scale designed to measure anti-Semitism. On the basis of scores on the scale, they selected the 40 most anti-Semitic and the 40 least anti-Semitic subjects. Each group of subjects then judged 150 statements relating to anti-Semitism. Scale values were obtained for the statements based upon the judgments of each group. The correlation between the two sets of scale values was .98.

The various studies cited above would seem to give support to McNemar's (1946) contention that all attempts to disprove the Thurstone and Chave assumption that the scale values of statements are independent of the attitudes of sorters have failed. However, Edwards and Kenney (1946) indicate that they are not satisfied with the evidence on this point. They state (p. 82):

Would similar results obtain from judgments derived from those with sympathetic attitudes toward fascism and those violently opposed to fascism in the construction of a scale measuring attitude toward fascism? And in the case of communist sympathizers and non-communists, in the construction of a scale measuring attitude toward communism? When social approval or disapproval attaches to a favorable or unfavorable attitude toward an issue, different scale values might result from groups with differing attitudes. An individual with a highly generalized unfavorable attitude toward fascism, for example, might scale an item such as: "Superior races are justified in dominating inferior races by force" as very favorable toward fascism. But would "native fascists" tend to scale it toward the same end of the continuum? The research so far, it seems to us, also neglects the related problem of ego-involved attitudes and the bearing they might have upon scale values of items.

Hovland and Sherif (1952) have also expressed their concern over the evidence presented relating to the independence of scale values and attitudes of the judging group. These writers believe insufficient evidence has been presented that the judging groups, supposedly differing in attitude, do, in fact, include individuals at opposite extremes of the psychological continuum. In the Hinckley study, previously cited, for example, Hovland and Sherif believe that perhaps the application of Thurstone's criterion for removing careless judges may, at the same time, have restricted the range by eliminating those judges who had the most extreme attitudes toward the Negro. Thurstone's criterion, it may be recalled, is to regard as careless those judges who place 30 or more statements in a single category.

On the basis of various studies of the influence of values

on perception and judgment, Hovland and Sherif (p. 824) advance the hypothesis that judges with extremely favorable or extremely unfavorable attitudes should, in fact, "show a tendency to concentrate their placement of items into a small number of categories." A second hypothesis they raise is that judges with extreme attitudes should be highly discriminating in the statements they place toward their own end of the scale and should show a corresponding tendency to lump together statements at the opposite end of the scale. Still a third hypothesis they formulate is that the displacement in the scale positions of statements should be greater for those statements in the "neutral" section of the psychological continuum and less for those at the two extremes.

Using much the same procedure as Hinckley had used and working with Hinckley's original statements, Hovland and Sherif obtained equal-appearing interval judgments from a group of Negro subjects, a group of white subjects with favorable attitudes toward the Negro, and a group of white subjects with unfavorable attitudes toward the Negro. They found that if the criterion of eliminating judges with 30 or more statements in a single category were applied to their data, over three-fourths of the Negro judges and two-thirds of the white judges with favorable attitudes toward Negroes would be eliminated.

Taking 11 statements that seemed to be equally appropriate for the Negro and white groups and that were fairly evenly spaced over the 11 point continuum, the scale values obtained for these 11 statements are shown in Figure 4.8. Figure 4.8 shows that the scale values originally obtained by Hinckley for the 11 statements and those obtained by Hovland and Sherif, using the Thurstone criterion for the elimination of careless judges are much the same. The scale values obtained from white subjects with favorable attitudes toward the Negro and from Negro subjects are also much the same. For the latter two groups, however, there is considerable displacement of statements judged as "neutral" and moderately favorable by the first two groups toward the unfavorable end of the continuum. A similar displacement of moderately unfavorable and "neutral" statements toward the favorable end of the continuum, though not as great, occurs for the anti-Negro white subjects.[7]

By introducing various checks made in the process of obtaining the judgments, Hovland and Sherif reached the conclusion that the subjects who placed a large number of statements in a single category were not being careless. They point out, however, that the "data do not indicate whether the distortions and displacements are caused by the fact that individuals with extreme positions lack the ability to discriminate between adjacent items at the opposite extreme,

[7] A study by Prothro (1955) bears upon this point. Prothro gave 40 statements to two groups of Arab students at the American University of Beirut to sort in terms of the method of equal-appearing intervals. There were 60 students in each group. For the experimental group all of the statements referred to the Jews. For the control group the reference to the Jews in each statement was deleted. Instead the members of the control group were told that the statements could refer to "any group," such as a "group of students in a class." Scale values were found independently for the experimental and control groups. Assuming that the Arab students in the experimental group had strongly unfavorable attitudes toward Jews, one might expect statements with central scale values for the control group to show a displacement effect for the experimental group. Prothro reports that this is not the case: displacement of the central statements was no greater than it was for those scaled at the two extremes. Only one of the 40 statements scaled by the two groups had a scale difference greater than two intervals on the psychological continuum. Furthermore, the scale values obtained from the control group and those obtained previously from a group of college students in the United States correlated highly and positively.

While the members of Prothro's experimental group may be assumed to have strongly unfavorable attitudes toward the Jews, it is extremely unlikely that they had any kind of personal identification with the Jews. On the other hand, the Negro subjects in the Hovland and Sherif study were judging statements relating to Negroes as a group with which they could identify themselves. Prothro suggests that the factor of identification or non-identification may account for the difference between his findings and those of Hovland and Sherif.

and hence place them in the same category or whether they reflect variations in the judge's interpretation of the total scale and the magnitude of the category intervals" (p. 830).[8]

It is possible, as Hovland and Sherif note, that the second

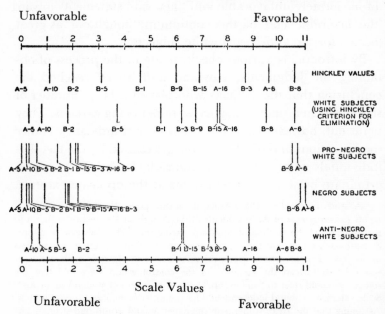

FIG. 4.8—Scale values of 11 selected statements obtained from 5 different groups of judges. Reproduced from Hovland and Sherif (1952), Fig. 2, p. 829.

[8] Research by Granneberg (1955) indicates that there may be other possible explanations for the "displacement phenomenon." He had 448 judges make equal-appearing interval judgments with respect to 130 statements relating to attitude toward religion. Granneberg found that scale values for these statements obtained from a religious group and a non-religious group differed significantly, although the correlation between the two sets of scale values was quite high. Differences were also observed in the scale values obtained from a group of mentally superior and a group of low intelligence. Further investigation indicated that attitudes of the judges toward religion and their intelligence levels interacted in a complex fashion to influence scale values. Granneberg believes that his findings indicate that the displacement phenomenon is a product of this interaction rather than the simple result of attitudinal involvement.

alternative would account for the results they obtained, since the rank ordering of the scale values of the 11 statements, as can be seen in Figure 4.8, is much the same, regardless of the particular group involved. The method of equal-appearing intervals is an absolute scaling method that does not require or force the judges to make fine discriminations. It is possible, for example, for a judge to place statements with differing scale values within the same category, since there is nothing in the instructions of the method of equal-appearing intervals to require him to make discriminations within an interval. This is not true of the method of paired comparisons where two statements may be close together on the psychological continuum, yet the judge is asked to judge one or the other as being more favorable or more unfavorable, as the case may be. If it could be shown, for example, that displacements of the kind shown in Figure 4.8 did not occur for groups with varying attitudes when judgments were obtained by the method of paired comparisons, this would indicate that the particular results observed by Hovland and Sherif are peculiar to the scaling method of equal-appearing intervals.

A subsequent study by Kelley, Hovland, Schwartz, and Abelson (1955) was done in which 20 of the Hinckley statements were judged by the method of paired comparisons. These statements were so selected that they were distributed over the psychological continuum in terms of their scale values as previously determined by the judgments of an "average" white group. These 20 statements were also known to show the displacement effect found in the Hovland and Sherif study. A group of Negro and a group of white subjects, comparable to those used in the Hovland and Sherif study, made comparative judgments of the $n(n-1)/2 = 190$ pairs of statements.

Before comparing the relationship between the paired-

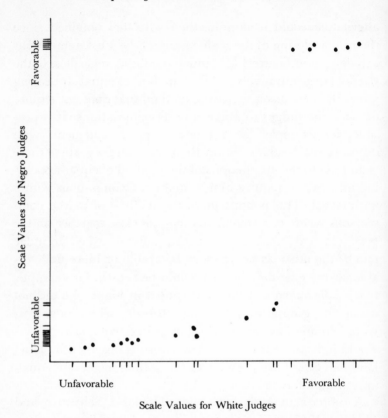

FIG. 4.9—Scatter diagram of equal-appearing interval scale values of 20 attitude statements obtained from a group of 103 Negro judges and a group of 175 white judges. Reproduced from Kelley, Hovland, Schwartz, and Abelson (1955), Fig. 1, p. 153.

comparison scale values for these 20 statements as obtained from the Negro and white groups, we should examine the equal-appearing interval scale values for these same statements. Figure 4.9 shows the plot of equal-appearing-interval scale values as obtained from 103 Negro subjects against the corresponding values obtained from 175 white subjects. It may be observed that for the white subjects the 20 statements are fairly uniformly distributed over the psychological continuum. For the Negro subjects, however, the statements are bunched at the two ends of the continuum, revealing the kind of displacement effect described by Hovland and Sherif.

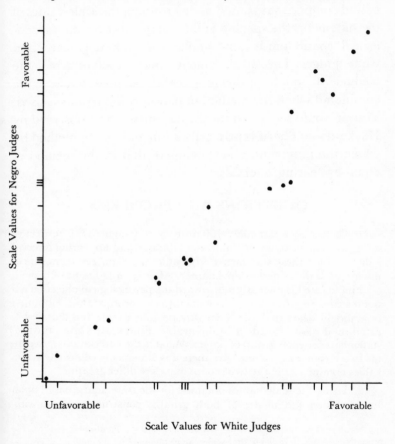

FIG 4.10—Scatter diagram of paired-comparison scale values of 20 attitude statements obtained from a group of 71 Negro judges and from a group of 78 white judges. Reproduced from Kelley, Hovland, Schwartz, and Abelson (1955), Fig. 2, p. 154.

Figure 4.10 shows the plot of the paired-comparison scale values for the same 20 statements as obtained from a group of 71 Negro subjects against the corresponding paired-comparison scale values for the statements obtained from a group of 78 white subjects. It is clear that when the method of paired comparisons is used in determining the scale values of the statements the spacing of the statements over the psychological continuum is quite similar for both the Negro and white judges. The displacement effect observed when the method of equal-appearing intervals is used tends to be eliminated when the method of paired comparisons is used. Thus it would seem as if the displacement effect observed by Hovland and Sherif is primarily a function of the method by which the judgments were obtained, that is, the method of equal-appearing intervals.[9]

QUESTIONS AND PROBLEMS

1. Collect approximately 100 attitude statements with respect to some psychological object of interest. Obtain equal-appearing interval judgments for these statements from at least 100 judges using one of the methods described in the chapter. After each judge has finished, ask him to rate his own attitude toward the psychological object on a 9 point scale. Separate the judgments into two groups: those obtained from judges who rated their own attitude as favorable and those who rated their own attitude as unfavorable. Find scale values for the statements for each group of judges. What is the correlation between the two sets of scale values? Are there any statements where the scale values obtained from the two groups of judges differ greatly?

2. Using the scale values obtained for the statements, based upon the combined judgments of both groups, construct a scale with

[9] See, however, the research by Granneberg (1955) mentioned earlier. He presents evidence to indicate that scale values obtained by the method of equal-appearing intervals are influenced by the thoroughness of the instructions given to the judges, the serial position of the statement, and various other factors. In addition, the research by Fehrer (1952) is important in indicating the extent to which the scale value of a statement may possibly be influenced by the context of other statements in the set being scaled.

approximately 20 to 22 statements fairly evenly spaced over the psychological continuum and with small Q values.

3. What is meant by a latent variable? What is meant by the operating characteristic of an attitude statement?

4. Sketch the theoretical operating characteristic of a favorable statement, an unfavorable statement, and a "neutral" statement.

5. Could two sets of scale values, obtained from two groups of judges, correlate highly, and yet differ? Why?

6. If it is true that the "displacement phenomenon" discovered by Hovland and Sherif disappears when statements are scaled by the method of paired comparisons, what would account for this result?

7. What factors, in addition to those suggested by Granneberg and Fehrer, might influence scale values of statements scaled by the method of equal-appearing intervals? Describe a research project that would provide evidence concerning the importance of these factors.

REFERENCES AND SUGGESTED READINGS

BALLIN, M., and FARNSWORTH, P. R. A graphic rating method for determining the scale values of statements in measuring social attitudes. *J. soc. Psychol.*, 1941, 13, 323-327.

BEYLE, H. C. A scale for the measurement of attitude toward candidates for elective governmental office. *Amer. polit. Sci. Rev.*, 1932, 26, 527-544.

CARLSON, G. A study of polarity in attitude scaling. Unpublished master's thesis. Univ. of Washington, 1956.

EDWARDS, A. L. A critique of "neutral items" in attitude scales constructed by the method of equal-appearing intervals. *Psychol. Rev.*, 1946, 53, 159-169.

——— and KENNEY, KATHERINE C. A comparison of the Thurstone and Likert techniques of attitude scale construction. *J. appl. Psychol.*, 1946, 30, 72-83.

——— and KILPATRICK, F. P. A technique for the construction of attitude scales. *J. appl. Psychol.*, 1948, 32, 374-384.

EYSENCK, H. J., and CROWN, S. An experimental study in opinion-attitude methodology. *Int. J. Opin. Attitude Res.*, 1949, 3, 47-86.

FARNSWORTH, P. R. Shifts in the values of opinion items. *J. Psychol.*, 1943, 16, 125-128.

——— Further data on the obtaining of Thurstone scale values. *J. Psychol.*, 1954a, 19, 69-73.

────── Attitude scale construction and the method of equal-appearing intervals. *J. Psychol.*, 1954*b*, 20, 245-248.

*FEHRER, ELIZABETH. Shifts in scale values of attitude statements as a function of the composition of the scale. *J. exp. Psychol.*, 1952, 44, 179-188.

FERGUSON, L. W. The influence of individual attitudes on construction of an attitude scale. *J. soc. Psychol.*, 1935, 6, 115-117.

────── The requirements of an adequate attitude scale. *Psychol. Bull.*, 1939, 36, 665-673.

GRANNEBERG, R. T. The influence of individual attitude and attitude-intelligence upon scale values of attitude items. *Amer. Psychol.*, 1955, 10, 330-331. (Abstract.)

GREEN, B. F. Attitude measurement. In G. Lindzey (Ed.), *Handbook of social psychology*. Cambridge, Mass.: Addison-Wesley, 1954. pp. 335-369.

*HINCKLEY, E. D. The influence of individual opinion on construction of an attitude scale. *J. soc. Psychol.*, 1932, 3, 283-296.

*HOVLAND, C. I., and SHERIF, M. Judgmental phenomena and scales of attitude measurement: Item displacement in Thurstone scales. *J. abnorm. soc. Psychol.*, 1952, 47, 822-832.

JURGENSEN, C. E. A nomograph for rapid determination of medians. *Psychometrika*, 1943, 8, 265-269.

*KELLEY, H. H., HOVLAND, C. I., SCHWARTZ, M., and ABELSON, R. P. The influence of judges' attitudes in three methods of attitude scaling. *J. soc. Psychol.*, 1955, 42, 147-158.

LOEVINGER, JANE. The technic of homogeneous tests compared with some aspects of "scale analysis" and factor analysis. *Psychol. Bull.*, 1948, 45, 507-529.

McNEMAR, Q. Opinion-attitude methodology. *Psychol. Bull.*, 1946, 43, 289-374.

MOSIER, C. I. A psychometric study of meaning. *J. soc. Psychol.*, 1941, 13, 123-140.

NYSTROM, G. H. The measurement of Filipino attitudes toward America by the use of the Thurstone technique. *J. soc. Psychol.*, 1933, 4, 249-252.

PINTNER, R., and FORLANO, G. The influence of attitude upon scaling of attitude items. *J. soc. Psychol.*, 1937, 8, 39-45.

PROTHRO, E. T. The effect of strong negative attitudes on the placement of items in a Thurstone scale. *J. soc. Psychol.*, 1955, 41, 11-18.

REMMERS, H. H., and SILANCE, ELLA BELLE. Generalized attitude scales. *J. soc. Psychol.*, 1934, 5, 298-311.

ROSANDER, A. C. The Spearman-Brown formula in attitude scale construction. *J. exp. Psychol.*, 1936, 19, 486-495.

SEASHORE, R. H., and HEVNER, KATE. A time-saving device for the construction of attitude scales. *J. soc. Psychol.*, 1933, 4, 366-372.

*SHERIF, M. and HOVLAND, C. I. Judgmental phenomena and scales of attitude measurement: Placement of items with individual choice of number of categories. *J. abnorm. soc. Psychol.*, 1953, 48, 135-141.

SIGERFOOS, C. C. The validation and application of a scale of attitude toward vocations. In H. H. Remmers (Ed.), *Further studies in attitudes, Series II, Studies in Higher Education, Bulletin of Purdue University*. Lafayette, Indiana: Purdue Univ., 1936, pp. 177-191.

STOUFFER, S. A. An overview of the contributions to scaling and scale theory. In S. A. Stouffer *et al.*, *Measurement and prediction*. Princeton, N. J.: Princeton Univ. Press, 1950. pp. 3-45.

*THURSTONE, L. L., and CHAVE, E. J. *The measurement of attitude*. Chicago: Univ. Chicago Press, 1929.

UHRBROCK, R. S. Attitudes of 4430 employees. *J. soc. Psychol.*, 1934, 5, 365-377.

WEBB, S. C. A generalized scale for measuring interest in science subjects. *Educ. psychol. Measmt.*, 1951, 11, 456-469.

5

The Method of Successive Intervals

The fundamental assumption involved in scaling by the method of equal-appearing intervals is, as the name of the method indicates, that the intervals into which the statements are sorted or rated are, in fact, equal. There is nothing contained within the procedure of equal-interval scaling to provide a check on this assumption. An empirical study by Hevner (1930) does indicate, however, that when the same stimuli are scaled both by the method of paired comparisons and the method of equal-appearing intervals, the relationship between the two sets of scale values is approximately linear except at the two extremes of the equal-appearing interval continuum.

Hevner's results indicate that if a statement has an extreme value on the psychological continuum established by the method of paired comparisons, then its scale value on the equal-appearing interval continuum will be less extreme, that is, closer toward the center of the equal-appearing interval continuum. Attneave (1949, p. 334) has pointed out that:

The source of this distortion is fairly evident on *a priori* grounds. The ratings of a given item by a number of judges will, when unrestricted, tend to distribute themselves normally about the hypothetically "true" rating; but when the "true" rating falls at an extreme, variability is possible in only one direction. The distribution obtained in the latter case will therefore be skewed away from the end of the scale, yielding a mean (or median) too close to the center.

We note that it is also true that equal-appearing interval scaling does not require the judges to discriminate between statements placed within the same category. If a judge encounters a statement that he regards as extremely unfavorable early in the judging process, he will undoubtedly place that statement in the extreme category. Later he may encounter another statement that is more extreme than the first. Since he does not have a category falling beyond the one previously used, he sorts the second statement in the same category as the first. He is not forced, in other words, to discriminate between the two statements, as would be the case in the method of paired comparisons. He could, of course, later move the first statement into a less extreme category, but it is unlikely that many judges will make the effort to consider and to make these finer adjustments of their sortings.

We might thus expect that if many statements fall close together in terms of their scale values, at one or the other extreme of the equal-appearing interval continuum, the scale values of these same statements would show a much greater spread when determined by a method of scaling which forces a discrimination between them. That this is, in fact, the case is indicated by data reported by Hevner (1930) and also by Kelley, Hovland, Schwartz, and Abelson (1955).

Figure 5.1 shows the theoretical relationship between the equal-appearing interval scale values and those obtained by the method of paired comparisons. It may be observed that the theoretical equal-appearing interval scale values for stimuli falling at the two extremes of the continuum show relatively little spread compared with the scale values for the same stimuli as determined by the method of paired comparisons. Other than at the two extremes, the theoretical expectation is that the scale values obtained by the two methods are approximately linearly related.

It would be desirable to have a scaling method that retains

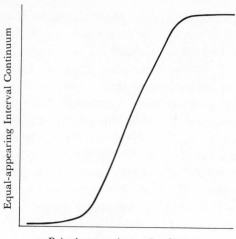

FIG. 5.1—Theoretical relationship between scale values obtained by the method of equal-appearing intervals and the method of paired comparisons for the same set of statements.

the simplicity of the method of equal-appearing intervals, that is, one that requires only one judgment from each subject for each statement, but one that, at the same time, yields scale values that are linearly related to those obtained by the method of paired comparisons over the complete range. But to obtain a linear relationship over the complete range would require that we manage, in some way, to stretch or pull out the two extremes of the equal-appearing interval scale of Figure 5.1. If we do this, however, it would mean that we are no longer dealing with equal intervals, but rather with unequal intervals.

Various procedures have been suggested for taking into account possible inequalities in the widths of the intervals on the psychological continuum. Saffir (1937), for example, describes a previously unpublished technique, developed by Thurstone, called the *method of successive intervals*. Guilford

(1938) calls his procedure the *method of absolute scaling,* while Attneave (1949), using a similar technique, calls it the *method of graded dichotomies,* and Garner and Hake (1951) use the term *equal discriminability scale.* The term *method of successive intervals* seems to describe all of these procedures and, following Edwards and Thurstone (1952), it will be used in that way in this chapter.

The method of successive intervals, like the method of equal-appearing intervals, requires but a single judgment from each subject for each statement to be scaled. It is, therefore, a convenient method to use when the number of statements to be scaled is large. The instructions given to the subjects who are to judge the statements are similar to those used in the method of equal-appearing intervals. Any of the judging methods previously described in connection with the method of equal-appearing intervals may be used to obtain successive-interval judgments.

In obtaining judgments by the method of equal-appearing intervals, one of the extreme intervals was described as "highly unfavorable" and the other as "highly favorable." The middle category was described as "neutral." We may use a similar anchoring of the extreme categories and the middle category when obtaining successive-interval judgments. If it seems desirable, additional descriptive phrases may be used to anchor other successive intervals.

If the various statements are now sorted or rated into the successive intervals by a group of judges according to the degree of favorableness-unfavorableness that each statement is assumed to express, our basic data will be in the same form as when we obtain equal-appearing interval judgments. For each statement we will have a frequency distribution showing the number of times that the statement has been placed in each of the successive intervals. These frequencies may be cumulated, from left to right, and the cumulative frequencies

TABLE 5.1

Arrangement of successive interval data showing the frequencies, cumulative frequencies, and cumulative proportions for each statement

STATEMENTS		SUCCESSIVE INTERVALS								
		Unfavorable			*Neutral*				*Favorable*	
		1	2	3	4	5	6	7	8	9
1	f	2	4	12	12	26	52	60	26	6
	cf	2	6	18	30	56	108	168	194	200
	cp	.010	.030	.090	.150	.280	.540	.840	.970	1.000
2	f	0	0	0	2	4	20	88	74	12
	cf	0	0	0	2	6	26	114	188	200
	cp	.000	.000	.000	.010	.030	.130	.570	.940	1.000
3	f	0	0	0	2	8	46	64	80	10
	cf	0	0	0	2	10	56	110	190	200
	cp	.000	.000	.000	.010	.050	.230	.550	.950	1.000

may be expressed as cumulative proportions by multiplying each one by the reciprocal of the number of judges.

The basic data may be entered in a single table as shown in Table 5.1. For each statement we have three rows. The first row gives the frequency with which the statement was placed in a given interval, the second gives the cumulative frequencies, and the third gives the cumulative proportions.

ESTIMATING INTERVAL WIDTHS

The scaling problem in the method of successive intervals is to determine estimates of the widths of the intervals making up the psychological continuum from the cumulative proportion distributions for a given set of statements. We make the assumption that these cumulative proportion distributions are normal for each statement when they are projected on the unknown psychological continuum. The scale values of the statements are then defined as the medians or means of the cumulative proportion distributions as projected on the psychological continuum.

For purposes of illustrating the calculations involved in the method of successive intervals, we give the cumulative proportion distributions for a group of 14 statements in Table 5.2. We may designate the general element or cell entry of Table 5.2 as p_{ij}, with the subscript i referring to the state-

TABLE 5.2

Cumulative proportions p_{ij} for 14 statements judged in terms of the method of successive intervals ($N = 200$)

STATE-MENTS	SUCCESSIVE INTERVALS								
	1	2	3	4	5	6	7	8	9
1	.010	.030	.090	.150	.280	.540	.840	.970	1.000
2				.010	.030	.130	.570	.940	1.000
3	.010	.070	.230	.370	.550	.810	.930	.980	1.000
4	.040	.130	.290	.460	.710	.850	.950	.970	1.000
5	.020	.140	.320	.510	.580	.740	.860	.960	1.000
6			.010	.030	.100	.300	.670	.850	1.000
7		.030	.090	.200	.350	.550	.830	.970	1.000
8		.020	.070	.150	.360	.610	.850	.970	1.000
9	.010	.060	.180	.380	.630	.860	.950	.980	1.000
10	.010	.070	.270	.490	.660	.850	.950	.990	1.000
11	.010	.020	.100	.190	.390	.550	.860	.990	1.000
12		.010	.040	.100	.220	.400	.690	.950	1.000
13			.010	.020	.070	.320	.670	.940	1.000
14				.010	.050	.230	.550	.950	1.000

ment and subscript j to the upper limit or boundary of the jth category. Thus p_{ij} means the proportion of judges who placed Statement i below the upper limit or boundary of category j and $1 - p_{ij}$ means the proportion of judges who placed Statement i above the upper limit or boundary of category j. In Table 5.2, for example, we see that p_{25} is equal to .030. Thus we know that .030 of the judgments for this statement fall below the upper limit or boundary of the 5th category and that $1 - .030 = .970$ of the judgments fall above this point.

From the assumptions we have previously made, we know that if the value of p_{ij} is exactly .50, then the scale value of Statement i would fall precisely at the upper limit of the jth interval (or the lower limit of the jth + 1 interval) on the psychological continuum. The corresponding normal deviate for this boundary would be 0.0. If the value of p_{ij} is greater than .50, say .75, then we know that the upper limit or boundary of the jth interval (or the lower limit of the jth + 1 interval) deviates *positively* from the scale value of Statement i. The normal deviate corresponding to $p_{ij} = .75$ is found from Table I in the appendix to be equal to .674. Similarly, if p_{ij} is less than .50, say .20, then we know that the boundary of the upper limit of the jth interval (or lower limit of the jth + 1 interval) deviates *negatively* from the scale value of Statement i. From the table of the normal curve in the appendix we find that the normal deviate corresponding to $p_{ij} = .20$ is $- .842$.

Entering the table of the normal curve with the cumulative proportions of Table 5.2, we can find the normal deviates corresponding to the boundaries of the successive intervals for each statement. These normal deviates are shown in Table 5.3.[1] We designate the cell entries of Table 5.3 as z_{ij} values with the subscript i referring to a particular statement and j to the upper limit or boundary of the jth interval. Thus z_{25} means that we have expressed the upper limit of category 5 as a normal deviate in terms of Statement 2.

If we now consider the entries in a single row of Table 5.3,

[1] In obtaining the z_{ij} values of Table 5.3, we ignore any values of p_{ij} less than .02 or greater than .98 as we did previously in connection with the method of paired comparisons.

TABLE 5.3

Normal deviates z_{ij} corresponding to the upper limits of the successive intervals for the data of Table 5.2

STATEMENTS	SUCCESSIVE INTERVALS							
	1	2	3	4	5	6	7	8
1		−1.881	−1.341	−1.036	− .583	.100	.994	1.881
2					−1.881	−1.126	.176	1.555
3		−1.476	− .739	− .332	.126	.878	1.476	2.054
4	−1.751	−1.126	− .553	− .100	.553	1.036	1.645	1.881
5	−2.054	−1.080	− .468	.025	.202	.643	1.080	1.751
6					−1.881	−1.282	− .524	.440	1.036
7		−1.881	−1.341	− .842	− .385	.126	.954	1.881
8		−2.054	−1.476	−1.036	− .358	.279	1.036	1.881
9		−1.555	− .915	− .305	.332	1.080	1.645	2.054
10		−1.476	− .613	− .025	.412	1.036	1.645	
11		−2.054	−1.282	− .878	− .279	.126	1.080	
12			−1.751	−1.282	− .772	− .253	.496	1.645
13				−2.054	−1.476	− .468	.440	1.555
14					−1.645	− .739	.126	1.645

we can obtain an estimate of the width of a given interval on the psychological continuum in terms of the difference between the entries z_{ij} and $z_i(j-1)$. Thus we may define

$$w_{ij} = z_{ij} - z_i(j-1) \tag{5.1}$$

where w_{ij} is an estimate of the width of the jth interval provided by Statement i. By taking the differences between the successive entries in each of the rows of Table 5.3, we obtain additional estimates of the various interval widths. These differences are shown in Table 5.4. All of the entries in a given column of Table 5.4 are estimates of the width of the same interval. We assume that the best estimates of the widths of the various successive intervals are the arithmetic means of the column entries of Table 5.4.[2]

---

[2] If the Z matrix is complete, that is, if we have no p_{ij} values greater than .98 or less than .02, then the interval widths or $\bar{w}_{.j}$ values would simply be the differences between the means of the entries in the successive columns of the Z matrix.

TABLE 5.4

Estimates of interval widths w_{ij} obtained from the differences between the upper limits of the intervals as shown in Table 5.3

STATEMENTS	SUCCESSIVE INTERVALS						
	2 - 1	3 - 2	4 - 3	5 - 4	6 - 5	7 - 6	8 - 7
1		.540	.305	.453	.683	.894	.887
2					.755	1.302	1.379
3		.737	.407	.458	.752	.598	.578
4	.625	.573	.453	.653	.483	.609	.236
5	.974	.612	.493	.177	.441	.437	.671
6				.599	.758	.964	.596
7		.540	.499	.457	.511	.828	.927
8		.578	.440	.678	.637	.757	.845
9		.640	.610	.637	.748	.565	.409
10		.863	.588	.437	.624	.609	
11		.772	.404	.599	.405	.954	
12			.469	.510	.519	.749	1.149
13				.578	1.008	.908	1.115
14					.906	.865	1.519
(1) Sum	1.599	5.855	4.668	6.236	9.230	11.039	10.311
(2) n	2	9	10	12	14	14	12
(3) $\bar{w}._j$	.800	.651	.467	.520	.659	.788	.859
(4) Cum. $\bar{w}._j$	.800	1.451	1.918	2.438	3.097	3.885	4.744

In the first row at the bottom of Table 5.4 we give the column sums. The second row gives the number of entries in each column and the third row gives the arithmetic means $\bar{w}._j$ of the column entries. These means are our estimates of the widths of the various intervals on the psychological continuum. We may take as our arbitrary origin the upper limit of the first interval (or the lower limit of the second interval). Our psychological continuum is then obtained by cumulating the widths of the various intervals, as shown in row (4) at the bottom of Table 5.4. This is the common psychological continuum upon which all of the statements are now to be scaled.

SCALE VALUES OF THE STATEMENTS

When there is knowledge of the psychological continuum it is a simple matter to find the scale values of the various statements. We project each of the cumulative distributions of Table 5.2 on the psychological continuum shown at the bottom of Table 5.4. The scale values of the statements may then be taken as the medians of the corresponding cumulative proportion distributions on this continuum. The medians may be computed by formula, interpolating within a given interval to find the point below which and above which 50 per cent of the judgments fall. Thus

$$S_i = l + \left(\frac{50 - \Sigma p_b}{p_w} \right) \overline{w}._j \qquad (5.2)$$

where S_i = the scale value of the ith stimulus

l = the lower limit of the interval on the psychological continuum in which the median falls

Σp_b = the sum of the proportions below the interval in which the median falls

p_w = the proportion within the interval in which the median falls

$\overline{w}._j$ = the width of the interval on the psychological continuum

Substituting in the above formula to find the scale value of the first statement, we have

$$S_1 = 2.438 + \left(\frac{.50 - .28}{.54 - .28} \right) .659 = 2.996$$

The scale values of the other statements are found in the same way and are given at the right of Table 5.5.

TABLE 5.5

Computation of scale values for the 14 statements in terms of the psychological continuum given at the bottom of Table 5.4

STATEMENTS	l	+	$[(.50 - \Sigma p_b)/p_w]$	$(\bar{w}_{.j})$	=	SCALE VALUE
1	2.438	+	$[(.50 - .28)/.26]$	(.659)	=	2.996
2	3.097	+	$[(.50 - .13)/.44]$	(.788)	=	3.760
3	1.918	+	$[(.50 - .37)/.18]$	(.520)	=	2.293
4	1.918	+	$[(.50 - .46)/.25]$	(.520)	=	2.001
5	1.451	+	$[(.50 - .32)/.19]$	(.467)	=	1.893
6	3.097	+	$[(.50 - .30)/.37]$	(.788)	=	3.523
7	2.438	+	$[(.50 - .35)/.20]$	(.659)	=	2.932
8	2.438	+	$[(.50 - .36)/.25]$	(.659)	=	2.807
9	1.918	+	$[(.50 - .38)/.25]$	(.520)	=	2.168
10	1.918	+	$[(.50 - .49)/.17]$	(.520)	=	1.949
11	2.438	+	$[(.50 - .39)/.16]$	(.659)	=	2.891
12	3.097	+	$[(.50 - .40)/.29]$	(.788)	=	3.369
13	3.097	+	$[(.50 - .32)/.35]$	(.788)	=	3.502
14	3.097	+	$[(.50 - .23)/.32]$	(.788)	=	3.762

From the description of the method of successive intervals given above it is clear that if we have k successive intervals and if the judgments for a statement are distributed over all intervals, then these judgments will provide us with estimates of the widths of the middle $k - 2$ categories. A statement for which the judgments are distributed into categories 1, 2, 3, 4, and 5 will provide estimates of the widths of categories 2, 3, and 4. The procedure described, therefore, does not permit us to obtain an estimate of the width of either of the two extreme intervals. That is because no estimate can be obtained for the lower limit of the first interval or for the upper limit of the last interval. The widths of these two intervals are indeterminate.

In general, the successive intervals used in obtaining judgments should be sufficient in number to offset the possibility that the scale value of any statement will fall in either of the two extreme categories, that is, so that no more than 50 per cent of the judgments for any given statement will fall in either extreme interval. If more than 50 per cent of the judgments do fall in either of the two extreme intervals for a given statement, then the psychological scale value for this statement cannot be determined by the method described.

Statements with Scale Values in the First Interval

Since it is not always possible to anticipate correctly that we have a sufficient number of successive intervals, we shall describe a procedure that can be used to obtain estimates of the scale values of statements when we do find more than 50 per cent of the judgments in one or the other extreme category.

Suppose, for example, that upon examination of the cumulative proportion distributions, we find that over 50 per cent of the judgments fall in the first interval for one or more statements. We wish to obtain scale values for these statements. We consider every statement that has an entry of at least .04 in the first interval. If the proportion of judgments in the first interval is less than .04, we shall ignore it.[3] We shall assume that if we take 1/2 the proportion in the first interval, this will provide us with an estimate of the midpoint of the interval.[4] Using the table of the normal curve, we can find normal deviates or z values corresponding to these values of $p/2$. Then each of the differences between these z values and those corresponding to the upper limits of the first interval will provide us with an estimate of the dis-

---

[3] We are here following the same rule previously stated with respect to ignoring extreme proportions.

[4] Analytical methods, described by Attneave (1949) and Green (1954), avoid this assumption. They define the scale values in terms of means rather than medians and their procedure for finding the scale values is not influenced by proportions greater than .50 in either extreme category.

tance from the midpoint to the upper limit of the interval. The average of these differences will be our best estimate of the distance from the midpoint of the first interval to the upper limit of the first interval on the psychological continuum. We have, in essence, simply extended the psychological continuum to the left and shifted our point of origin from the upper limit of the first interval to the midpoint of the first interval. Using the midpoint as our origin, it is now possible to find the scale value of any statement for which we have more than 50 per cent of the judgments falling within the first interval.

TABLE 5.6

Proportions falling below the midpoint and upper limit of the first interval and normal deviates corresponding to the proportions for 7 statements

STATEMENTS	PROPORTION FALLING BELOW		NORMAL DEVIATE		DIFFERENCE
	Midpoint	Upper Limit	Midpoint	Upper Limit	
	(1)	(2)	(3)	(4)	(4)−(3)
1	.100	.200	−1.282	− .842	.440
2	.150	.300	−1.036	− .524	.512
3		.020			
4	.280	.560	− .583	.151	.734
5	.020	.040	−2.054	−1.751	.303
6	.075	.150	−1.440	−1.036	.404
7	.040	.080	−1.751	−1.405	.346
				Sum	2.739

In Table 5.6 we illustrate the procedure described above. Column (2) of the table gives the proportion of judgments falling below the upper limit of the first interval for 7 statements. Statement 4 has more than .50 of the judgments in the first interval and we want to find the scale value of this statement. It is necessary, therefore, that we shift our origin on the psychological continuum from the upper limit of the first interval to the midpoint of the first interval. In column (1) of the table we give the values of ½ the proportions shown in column (2). These are the estimated proportions falling below the midpoint of the first interval for the various statements. We have ignored the value of .02 for Statement 3, since it is less than our minimum of .04. Column (3) gives the z values corresponding to the proportions falling below the midpoints, that is, for the proportions shown in column (1). Column (4) gives the z values corresponding to the proportions falling below the upper limit of the first interval, that is, for the proportions shown in column (2). In the last column of the table we give the differences between the z values of columns (3) and (4), that is, the entry in column (4) minus the corresponding entry in column (3). The sum of these differences is 2.739 and the mean is $2.739/6 = .456$. The value .456 is the estimated distance from the midpoint of the first interval to the upper limit of the first interval on the psychological continuum.

If we take as our origin the midpoint of the first interval, then for Statement 4 we have .28 of the judgments falling below the origin and .28 between the origin and the upper limit of the first interval, a distance which is equal to .456 on the psychological continuum. Interpolating within this distance by means of formula (5.2) we obtain

$$S_4 = \left(\frac{.50 - .28}{.28} \right) .456 = .358$$

as the scale value for Statement 4.

Statements with Scale Values in the Last Interval

If we have statements for which we have more than 50 per cent of the judgments falling in the last interval and if we wish to find scale values for these statements, we shall have to extend the psychological continuum beyond the upper limit of the next to last interval (or the lower limit of the last interval). We do this by finding the estimated distance between the lower limit of the last interval and the midpoint of the interval. The necessary calculations are shown in Table 5.7.

The first column of Table 5.7 gives the cumulative proportion falling below the lower limit of the last interval. We

TABLE 5.7

Proportions falling below the lower limit and midpoint of the last interval and normal deviates corresponding to the proportions for 7 statements

	PROPORTIONS			NORMAL DEVIATES		
	Below	*Within*	*Below*			*Diff.*
STATEMENTS	*Lower Limit*	*Interval*	*Midpoint*	*Lower Limit*	*Mid-point*	
	(1)	(2)	(3)	(4)	(5)	(5) − (4)
1	.900	.100	.950	1.282	1.645	.363
2	.800	.200	.900	.842	1.282	.440
3	.400	.600	.700	− .253	.524	.777
4	.950	.050	.975	1.645	1.960	.315
5	.980	.020				
6	.700	.300	.850	.524	1.036	.512
7	.850	.150	.925	1.036	1.440	.404
					Sum	2.811

know that the cumulative proportion entries for the last interval will all be 1.00. Therefore, if we subtract the cumulative proportion entry in column (1) from 1.00, we shall have the proportion of judgments falling within the last interval. These values are shown in column (2). In estimating the distance from the lower limit of the last interval to the midpoint of the interval, we again use only those statements for which the proportion of judgments falling in the last interval is at least .04. We thus eliminate Statement 5 from consideration. If we now take 1/2 the proportion falling within the last interval for each statement and add these values to the corresponding entries in column (1), we will have the cumulative proportions up to the midpoint of the last interval. These are shown in column (3). We now find the normal deviates or z values for the cumulative proportions in column (1) and these are given in column (4). Column (5) gives the normal deviates corresponding to the cumulative proportions of column (3). The differences between the z values of columns (5) and (4) will give us the desired estimates of the distance between the lower limit of the last interval and the midpoint of the interval. These differences are shown in the last column of the table. The sum of the differences is 2.811 and the arithmetic mean is $2.811/6 = .468$.

Knowing the distance of the lower limit of the last interval from the point of origin on the psychological continuum, it is now possible to find the scale value of any statement that has more than 50 per cent of the judgments falling in the last interval. Assume, for example, that the distance from the origin to the lower limit of the last interval is 3.580. Then the scale value for Statement 3 in Table 5.7 would be

$$S_3 = 3.580 + \left(\frac{.50 - .40}{.30} \right) .468 = 3.736$$

AN INTERNAL CONSISTENCY TEST

Having determined the scale values of a given set of statements by the method of successive intervals, we can then apply a test of internal consistency similar to that used with the method of paired comparisons. In the method of paired comparisons, we used the n scale values of the statements to obtain a set of $n(n-1)/2$ theoretical proportions. The discrepancies between our observed and theoretical proportions were then obtained. When these discrepancies are small, we have reason to believe that our scale values are consistent with the empirical data. In addition, we are able to reproduce, within the observed margin of error, the complete set of $n(n-1)/2$ independent empirical proportions by means of a limited number of parameters, the n scale values.

For the internal consistency test applied to successive interval scaling, we have available the n scale values and also the $k-2$ interval widths on the psychological continuum, where k is the number of successive intervals used in scaling the statements. For the data of Table 5.2, for example, we have 14 scale values and $9-2 = 7$ interval widths, a total of 21 parameters. Using these parameters, we can obtain a theoretical cumulative distribution for each of the 14 statements we have scaled.

For the empirical data of Table 5.2 we have only $n(k-1)$ proportions potentially free to vary, since the entry in the kth or last successive interval must of necessity be equal to 1.00 for all n stimuli. Thus for a single statement we have only $k-1$ entries that can vary and for n statements we have a total of $n(k-1)$ proportions free to vary. We shall thus use 21 parameters in an attempt to reproduce the $14(9-1)$ $= 112$ proportions of Table 5.2.[5]

At the left of Table 5.8 we give the scale values of the 14 statements on the psychological continuum. At the top of

[5] If the 14 statements had been scaled by the method of paired comparisons we would have used only the 14 scale values in the internal consistency test. Thus we would have used fewer parameters, but we would also have had fewer independent proportions to reproduce, that is, $14(14-1)/2 = 91$.

the table we give the cumulative interval widths on the psychological continuum. If we now subtract the scale value of each statement from the cumulative interval widths, we can obtain a matrix of theoretical normal deviates z_{ij}'. These z_{ij}' values will be the boundaries of the successive intervals as expressed in terms of normal deviates from the scale values of the statements on the psychological continuum. They are shown in the body of Table 5.8.

We now refer to the table of the normal curve, Table I in the appendix, to obtain the theoretical cumulative proportions p_{ij}' corresponding to the theoretical normal deviates

TABLE 5.8

Theoretical normal deviates z_{ij}' corresponding to the upper limits of the successive intervals as obtained from the scale values and interval widths on the psychological continuum

SCALE VALUES OF STATEMENTS	CUMULATIVE INTERVAL WIDTHS							
	.000	.800	1.451	1.918	2.438	3.097	3.885	4.744
(2.996) 1	−2.996	−2.196	−1.545	−1.078	− .558	.101	.889	1.748
(3.760) 2	−3.760	−2.960	−2.309	−1.842	−1.322	− .663	.125	.984
(2.293) 3	−2.293	−1.493	− .842	− .375	.145	.804	1.592	2.451
(2.001) 4	−2.001	−1.201	− .550	− .083	.437	1.096	1.884	2.743
(1.893) 5	−1.893	−1.093	− .442	.025	.545	1.204	1.992	2.851
(3.523) 6	−3.523	−2.723	−2.072	−1.605	−1.085	− .426	.362	1.221
(2.932) 7	−2.932	−2.132	−1.481	−1.014	− .494	.165	.953	1.812
(2.807) 8	−2.807	−2.007	−1.356	− .889	− .369	.290	1.078	1.937
(2.168) 9	−2.168	−1.368	− .717	− .250	.270	.929	1.717	2.576
(1.949) 10	−1.949	−1.149	− .498	− .031	.489	1.148	1.936	2.795
(2.891) 11	−2.891	−2.091	−1.440	− .973	− .453	.206	.994	1.853
(3.369) 12	−3.369	−2.569	−1.918	−1.451	− .931	− .272	.516	1.375
(3.502) 13	−3.502	−2.702	−2.051	−1.584	−1.064	− .405	.383	1.242
(3.762) 14	−3.762	−2.962	−2.311	−1.844	−1.324	− .665	.123	.982

z_{ij}' of Table 5.8. These theoretical proportions are shown in Table 5.9. The entries in each row of Table 5.9 are theoretical distributions obtained by using only our knowledge of the interval widths on the psychological continuum and the scale values of the various statements. If the assumptions we have made in scaling the statements are tenable, we should expect the theoretical values of Table 5.8 to reproduce the empirical values of Table 5.2.

If we now subtract the entries in Table 5.9 from the corresponding entries of Table 5.2, we can obtain the dis-

TABLE 5.9

Theoretical cumulative distributions obtained from the theoretical normal deviates of Table 5.8

STATEMENTS	SUCCESSIVE INTERVALS							
	1	2	3	4	5	6	7	8
1	.001	.014	.061	.141	.288	.540	.813	.960
2	.000	.002	.010	.033	.093	.254	.550	.837
3	.011	.068	.200	.354	.558	.789	.944	.993
4	.023	.115	.291	.467	.669	.863	.970	.997
5	.029	.137	.329	.510	.707	.886	.977	.998
6	.000	.003	.019	.054	.139	.335	.641	.889
7	.002	.016	.069	.155	.311	.565	.830	.965
8	.003	.022	.088	.187	.356	.614	.860	.974
9	.015	.086	.237	.401	.606	.824	.957	.995
10	.026	.125	.309	.488	.688	.875	.974	.997
11	.002	.018	.075	.165	.325	.582	.840	.968
12	.000	.005	.028	.073	.176	.393	.697	.915
13	.000	.003	.020	.057	.144	.343	.649	.893
14	.000	.002	.010	.033	.093	.253	.549	.837

tribution of values of $p_{ij} - p_{ij}'$. Summing the absolute values of these discrepancies over all entries, and dividing by 112, the total number of discrepancies summed, we have as our absolute average deviation, $2.702/112 = .024$. This is fairly typical of the values reported for the average error obtained when the method of successive intervals is used to scale stimuli. Edwards and Thurstone (1952), for example, report an average error of .025 for 10 stimuli scaled by the method of successive intervals into 9 categories and Edwards (1952) reports a value of .021 for 17 stimuli scaled into 10 categories.

INFLUENCE OF ATTITUDE ON SCALE VALUES

When Saffir (1937) scaled 25 stimuli both by the method of paired comparisons and by the method of successive intervals, he found that the relationship between the two sets of scale values was linear. Saffir also used Hevner's (1930) data to obtain successive-interval scale values for 20 stimuli for which Hevner had found equal-appearing interval scale values and paired-comparison scale values. Although the

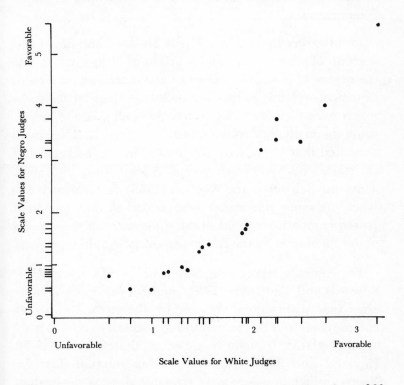

FIG. 5.2—Scatter diagram of successive-interval scale values of 20 attitude statements obtained from a group of 103 Negro judges and from a group of 175 white judges. Modified from Kelley, Hovland, Schwartz, and Abelson (1955), Fig. 3, p. 156.

equal-appearing interval scale values were not linearly related to the paired-comparison values, as pointed out earlier in the chapter, when the same data were scaled by the method of successive intervals, the relationship between the successive-interval scale values and the paired-comparison scale values was linear. Attneave (1949), Edwards and Thurstone (1952), and Edwards (1952) also report finding linear relationships between scale values obtained by the method of successive intervals and the method of paired comparisons.

In an earlier chapter, a study by Hovland and Sherif had a group of white judges and a group of Negro judges rate the degree of favorableness and unfavorableness of a set of statements relating to the Negro. Scale values for the statements were then found separately for each group of judges, using the method of equal-appearing intervals. The results indicated that there were differences in the placement of the statements by the two groups. A later study by Kelley, Hovland, Schwartz, and Abelson (1955) demonstrated that when the same statements were scaled by the method of paired comparisons, most of the differences in the spacing of the statements by the two groups of judges disappeared.

The evidence reported by Saffir (1937), Attneave (1949), Edwards and Thurstone (1952), and Edwards (1952) indicates that scale values obtained by the method of paired comparisons and by the method of successive intervals are linearly related. It might be expected, therefore, that if the Hovland and Sherif equal-appearing interval data for Negro and white judges were reanalyzed using the method of successive intervals, this method would also result in similar spacings of the statements on the psychological continuum. This reanalysis of the Hovland and Sherif data was done by Kelley, Hovland, Schwartz, and Abelson (1955) with the results shown in Figure 5.2.

Figure 5.2 shows the plot of the successive-interval scale values for 20 statements obtained from the Negro judges against the corresponding values obtained from the white judges. Again, it is apparent that the method of successive intervals tends to make for a more comparable spacing of the statements along the psychological continuum for the two groups, although with not quite the success with which this was accomplished by the method of paired comparisons. [6]

DISCRIMINAL DISPERSIONS

Rimoldi and Hormaeche (1955) and Burros (1955) have independently reported solutions for the discriminal dispersions of stimuli scaled by the method of successive intervals. [7] Suppose we have statements or stimuli a to n with corresponding scale values $S_a, S_b, S_c, \ldots, S_n$, and discriminal dispersions $\sigma_a, \sigma_b, \sigma_c, \ldots, \sigma_n$. We designate the upper limit of the jth interval as L_j. Then expressing the upper limit of the jth interval as a normal deviate in terms of Stimulus a, we have

$$z_{aj} = \frac{L_j - S_a}{\sigma_a} \tag{5.3}$$

or

$$\sigma_a z_{aj} + S_a = L_j \tag{5.4}$$

We can also express the upper limit of the jth interval as

[6] See Figure 4.10 for the plot of the two sets of paired comparison scale values.

[7] See also the procedures used by Saffir (1937) and Mosier (1940).

a normal deviate in terms of Stimulus b so that we also have

$$z_{bj} = \frac{L_j - S_b}{\sigma_b} \qquad (5.5)$$

or

$$\sigma_b z_{bj} + S_b = L_j \qquad (5.6)$$

Substituting from (5.6) into (5.4) we get

$$\sigma_a z_{aj} + S_a = \sigma_b z_{bj} + S_b \qquad (5.7)$$

or

$$z_{aj} = \frac{S_b - S_a}{\sigma_a} + \frac{\sigma_b}{\sigma_a} z_{bj} \qquad (5.8)$$

We thus see that the z_{aj} values are a linear function of the z_{bj} values. The z_{aj} values are, of course, the entries in the first row of the normal deviate table, such as Table 5.3, used in successive interval scaling, and the z_{bj} values are the entries in the second row of the same table. We designate the standard deviation of the z_{aj} entries in the first row as V_a and the standard deviation of the z_{bj} entries in the second row as V_b. Then from (5.8) above, we have

$$V_a = \frac{\sigma_b}{\sigma_a} V_b \qquad (5.9)$$

or

$$\frac{V_a}{V_b} = \frac{\sigma_b}{\sigma_a} \qquad (5.10)$$

Writing the complete set of equations for Stimulus a with

each of the other n stimuli, in the form of (5.10) we would have

$$\frac{V_a}{V_a} = \frac{\sigma_a}{\sigma_a}$$

$$\frac{V_a}{V_b} = \frac{\sigma_b}{\sigma_a}$$

$$\frac{V_a}{V_c} = \frac{\sigma_c}{\sigma_a}$$

$$\cdot \qquad \cdot$$
$$\cdot \qquad \cdot$$
$$\cdot \qquad \cdot$$

$$\frac{V_a}{V_n} = \frac{\sigma_n}{\sigma_a}$$

and summing the above equations we get

$$V_a \sum_1^n \left(\frac{1}{V}\right) = \frac{1}{\sigma_a} \sum_1^n \sigma \tag{5.11}$$

If, as we did previously in the method of paired comparisons, we let the sum of all the discriminal dispersions be equal to n, then we can write (5.11) as

$$V_a \sum_1^n \left(\frac{1}{V}\right) = \frac{n}{\sigma_a} \tag{5.12}$$

and solving for σ_a, we get

$$\sigma_a = \frac{1}{V_a} \left[\frac{n}{\sum_1^n \left(\frac{1}{V}\right)} \right] \tag{5.13}$$

The term in the brackets in (5.13) will be a constant and is equal to n, the number of stimuli, divided by the sum of the reciprocals of the standard deviations of the rows of the z_{ij} table used in successive interval scaling, that is, the standard deviations of the rows of Table 5.3. If we designate this constant term by k, then we have

$$\sigma_a = \left(\frac{1}{V_a} \right) k \qquad (5.14)$$

or, in general, for the ith stimulus

$$\sigma_i = \left(\frac{1}{V_i} \right) k \qquad (5.15)$$

ATTITUDE SCALES

When statements have been scaled by the method of successive intervals, we develop our attitude scale for measuring the attitudes of individuals in much the same way that we did when we scaled statements by the method of equal-appearing intervals. Once having discovered the psychological continuum on which the statements have been scaled, we can then graph the cumulative proportion distributions for each statement on this continuum. Scale and Q values can then easily be determined from these graphs.

As in the case of equal-appearing interval scales, we can select 20 to 22 statements such that their scale values are fairly evenly spaced over the psychological continuum. We can also use either the Q value or the discriminal dispersion associated with each statement as a basis for eliminating those statements considered to be relatively ambiguous.

If the 20- to 22-item scale is then given to a group of

subjects with instructions to check those statements with which they agree, we determine scores for each subject by finding the median of the scale values of the statements checked. Because the interpretation we place on these scores is essentially the same as that described previously in the case of scores on equal-appearing interval scales, the discussion will not be repeated here. [8]

THE DISTRIBUTION OF JUDGMENTS ON THE PSYCHOLOGICAL CONTINUUM

One of the assumptions we made in developing the method of successive interval scaling was that the projection of the cumulative proportion distributions for the various statements would be normal on the psychological continuum. There is evidence, reported by Mosier (1941), Edwards and Thurstone (1952), Edwards (1952), and Jones and Thurstone (1955), to indicate that this, in general, is the case.

Whether the assumption of normality of distribution on the psychological continuum holds true for any particular statement can be determined by plotting the cumulative proportion distribution for the statement on normal probability paper with the psychological continuum along the base line. If the cumulative proportion distribution is normal on the psychological continuum, the graph should be a straight line.

Figure 5.3 shows the cumulative proportion distribution for Statement 3 of Table 5.2 plotted on normal probability paper. It is apparent that this graph is approximately linear. If the distributions for the other statements of Table 5.2 were plotted in Figure 5.3, we would see that they also are

[8] It may be pointed out, however, that the procedure used by Edwards, described earlier in Chapter 2 in connection with paired comparison scales, can also be used with statements scaled by either the method of equal-appearing intervals or by the method of successive intervals.

approximately linear. It is evident also that we could find the scale value for Statement 3 from Figure 5.3. The scale value would be given by dropping a perpendicular from the point at which the line crosses the 50th centile to the base line. Scale values for the other statements could also be found graphically by plotting their cumulative proportion distributions on normal probability paper. The scale values would

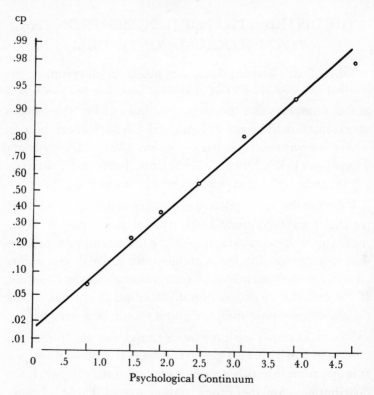

FIG. 5.3—Cumulative distribution of the judgments for Statement 1 plotted on normal probability paper. The abscissa represents the psychological continuum obtained by the method of successive interval scaling for the data of Table 5.2. The boundaries of the successive intervals are also marked on the abscissa.

be given by the points on the base line at which the linear plots intersect the 50th centile.

QUESTIONS AND PROBLEMS

1. Mosier has suggested that the psychological continuum involved in successive interval scaling could be obtained by a sampling of the statements, rather than through the use of the entire set. Using the equal-appearing interval data obtained in Chapter 5, divide the statements at random into four sets. Find the psychological continuum for each set of statements, using the method of successive intervals. Are approximately the same interval widths obtained from each set of statements?

2. Using only the distributions of judgments for the statements contained in the 20- to 22-statement equal-appearing interval scale constructed previously, find the successive-interval scale values for these statements. Plot the equal-appearing interval scale values against the successive interval scale values for these statements. Is the plot linear?

3. Plot the cumulative proportion distributions for the 20 to 22 statements on normal probability paper, marking off the abscissa in terms of the successive intervals on the psychological continuum. Are these plots linear?

4. Select every other statement, in terms of scale values, from the 20 to 22 statements so that you have a set of 10 or 11 statements, and obtain paired comparison judgments for these statements. Find the paired comparison scale values and determine whether the successive interval-scale values are linearly related to those obtained by the method of paired comparisons. Find the discriminal dispersions for these statements in terms of both successive intervals and paired comparisons. Are the discriminal dispersions obtained by the two methods related?

5. Using the above set of 10 or 11 statements, find the successive interval scale values using the procedure described by Attneave (1949) or Green (1954). Are these values comparable to those obtained using the method described in the text?

REFERENCES AND SUGGESTED READINGS

*ATTNEAVE, F. A method of graded dichotomies for the scaling of judgments. *Psychol. Rev.*, 1949, 56, 334-340.

*BURROS, R. H. The estimation of the discriminal dispersion in the method of successive intervals. *Psychometrika*, 1955, 20, 299-306.

EDWARDS, A. L. The scaling of stimuli by the method of successive intervals. *J. appl. Psychol.*, 1952, 36, 118-122.

—— A technique for increasing the reproducibility of cumulative attitude scales. *J. appl. Psychol.*, 1956, 40, 263-265.

*—— and THURSTONE, L. L. An internal consistency check for scale values determined by the method of successive intervals. *Psychometrika*, 1952, 17, 169-180.

GARNER, W. R., and HAKE, H. W. The amount of information in absolute judgments. *Psychol. Rev.*, 1951, 58, 446-459.

GREEN, B. F. Attitude measurement. In G. Lindzey (Ed.), *Handbook of social psychology*. Cambridge, Mass.: Addison-Wesley, 1954. Pp. 335-469.

GUILFORD, J. P. The computation of psychological values from judgments in absolute categories. *J. exp. Psychol.*, 1938, 22, 32-42.

GULLIKSEN, H. A least squares solution for successive intervals assuming unequal standard deviations. *Psychometrika*, 1954, 19, 117-140.

HEVNER, KATE. An empirical study of three psychophysical methods. *J. gen. Psychol.*, 1930, 4, 191-212.

HOVLAND, C. I., and SHERIF, M. Judgmental phenomena and scales of attitude measurement: Item displacement in Thurstone scales. *J. abnorm. soc. Psychol.*, 1952, 47, 822-832.

JONES, L. V., and THURSTONE, L. L. The psychophysics of semantics: An experimental investigation. *J. appl. Psychol.*, 1955, 39, 31-36.

KELLEY, H. H., HOVLAND, C. I., SCHWARTZ, M., and ABELSON, R. P. The influence of judges' attitudes in three methods of scaling. *J. soc. Psychol.*, 1955, 42, 147-158.

*MOSIER, C. I. A modification of the method of successive intervals. *Psychometrika*, 1940, 5, 101-107.

MOSIER, C. I. A psychometric study of meaning. *J. soc. Psychol.*, 1941, 13, 123-140.

*RIMOLDI, H. J. A., and HORMAECHE, M. The law of comparative judgment in successive intervals and graphic rating scale methods. *Psychometrika*, 1955, 20, 307-318.

*SAFFIR, M. A. A comparative study of scales constructed by three psychophysical methods. *Psychometrika*, 1937, 2, 179-198.

6

The Method of Summated Ratings

Suppose that we have a large number of statements for which the scale values on the psychological continuum are unknown. We assume, however, that we can obtain agreement in classifying the statements into two classes, favorable and unfavorable, with approximately the same number of statements in each class. These statements are then given to a group of subjects who are asked to respond to each one in terms of their own agreement or disagreement with the statements. In obtaining responses from subjects we permit them to use any one of five categories: strongly agree, agree, undecided, disagree, or strongly disagree. For any given statement we have available the proportion of subjects giving each of the five categories of response. We want to weight these categories of response in such a way that the response made by individuals with the most favorable attitudes will always have the highest positive weight. For the favorable statements, we assume that this is the "strongly agree" category, and for the unfavorable statements, we assume that it is the "strongly disagree" category.

NORMAL DEVIATE WEIGHTING OF
RESPONSE CATEGORIES

In row (1) of Table 6.1 we show the proportion of subjects falling in each response category for a favorable

TABLE 6.1

The proportion of subjects ($N = 200$) falling in each of five response categories for a favorable statement and the normal deviate weights for these response categories based upon the proportions

	STRONGLY DISAGREE	DISAGREE	UNCERTAIN	AGREE	STRONGLY AGREE
(1) p	.130	.430	.210	.130	.100
(2) cp	.130	.560	.770	.900	1.000
(3) Midpoint cp	.065	.345	.665	.835	.950
(4) z	-1.514	$-.399$	.426	.974	1.645
(5) $z + 1.514$	.000	1.115	1.940	2.488	3.159
(6) z rounded	0	1	2	2	3

statement. In row (2) of the table we give the cumulative proportions, and in row (3) the proportions below a given category plus 1/2 the proportion within the category. For example, the second entry in row (3) is obtained by

$$.130 + \frac{1}{2} (.430) = .345$$

From the table of the normal curve we find the normal deviates corresponding to the proportions of row (3). The normal deviates are shown in row (4) and they are one set of weights we might use for the response categories. We can make the weights all positive by adding the absolute value of the largest negative value, -1.514, to all of the other entries in row (4) thus obtaining the values shown in row (5). But it may be observed that if we round the entries in row (5) to the nearest integer, we obtain the weights 0, 1, 2, 2, 3 and these are close to the values 0, 1, 2, 3, 4. Table 6.2 illustrates that much the same thing happens when we deal with the responses to an unfavorable statement, although here we have reversed the weightings for the response categories so that the strongly disagree category has the highest positive weight.

In the development of the method of attitude scale construction described in this chapter, Likert (1932)[1] found that scores based upon the relatively simple assignment of integral weights correlated .99 with the more complicated normal deviate system of weights. He therefore used the simpler system. We shall do the same. For favorable statements, the strongly agree response will be given a weight of 4, the agree response a weight of 3, the undecided response a weight of 2, the disagree response a weight of 1, and the strongly disagree response a weight of 0. For unfavorable statements, the scoring system is reversed, with the strongly disagree response being given the 4 weight and the strongly agree response the 0 weight.

For each subject we obtain a total score by summating his

TABLE 6.2

The proportion of subjects ($N = 200$) falling in each of five response categories for an unfavorable statement and the normal deviate weights for these response categories based upon the proportions

	STRONGLY AGREE	AGREE	UNCERTAIN	DISAGREE	STRONGLY DISAGREE
(1) p	.180	.200	.320	.220	.080
(2) cp	.180	.380	.700	.920	1.000
(3) Midpoint cp	.090	.280	.540	.810	.960
(4) z	-1.341	$-.583$	.100	.878	1.751
(5) $z + 1.341$	.000	.758	1.441	2.219	3.092
(6) z rounded	0	1	1	2	3

[1] Likert's (1932) monograph reporting his research was subsequently reprinted (with a few changes) in a volume by Murphy and Likert (1937). The latter publication also contains a more detailed report of applications of scales constructed by the Likert technique.

scores for the individual items. Because each response to a statement may be considered a rating and because these are summated over all statements, Bird (1940, p. 159) called the Likert method of scale construction the *method of summated ratings* and this term has come into rather general use.

SELECTION OF ITEMS

In the method of equal-appearing intervals we had a basis for the rejection of statements in terms of Q and the criterion of irrelevance. As basis for rejecting statements in the method of summated-ratings, use is made of some form of item analysis. We consider the frequency distribution of scores based upon the responses to all statements. We may then take the 25 (or some other) per cent of the subjects with the highest total scores and also the 25 per cent of the subjects with the lowest total scores. We assume that these two groups provide criterion groups in terms of which to evaluate the individual statements. In evaluating the responses of the high and low groups to the individual statements we might find the ratio

$$t = \frac{\bar{X}_H - \bar{X}_L}{\sqrt{\dfrac{s_H{}^2}{n_H} + \dfrac{s_L{}^2}{n_L}}} \tag{6.1}$$

where $\bar{X}_H$ = the mean score on a given statement for the high group

$\bar{X}_L$ = the mean score on the same statement for the low group

$s_H{}^2$ = the variance of the distribution of responses of the high group to the statement

s_L^2 = the variance of the distribution of responses of the low group to the statement

n_H = the number of subjects in the high group

n_L = the number of subjects in the low group

If $n_H = n_L = n$, as will be the case if we select the same percentage of the total number of subjects for the high and low groups, then formula (6.1) can be written

$$t = \frac{\bar{X}_H - \bar{X}_L}{\sqrt{\dfrac{\Sigma (X_H - \bar{X}_H)^2 + \Sigma (X_L - \bar{X}_L)^2}{n(n-1)}}} \qquad (6.2)$$

where $\Sigma (X_H - \bar{X}_H)^2 = \Sigma X_H^2 - \dfrac{(\Sigma X_H)^2}{n}$

and $\Sigma (X_L - \bar{X}_L)^2 = \Sigma X_L^2 - \dfrac{(\Sigma X_L)^2}{n}$

The calculation of t in terms of formula (6.2) is illustrated in Table 6.3.

The value of t is a measure of the extent to which a given statement differentiates between the high and low groups. As a crude and approximate rule of thumb, we may regard any t value equal to or greater than 1.75 as indicating that the average response of the high and low groups to a statement differs significantly, provided we have 25 or more subjects in the high group and also in the low group. [2]

In the method of summated-ratings, what is desired is a set of 20 to 25 statements that will differentiate between the high

---

[2] More exact interpretations of the t test can be found in elementary statistical books. See, for example, Edwards (1954).

TABLE 6.3

The calculation of t for evaluating the difference in the mean response to an attitude statement by a high group and a low group

RESPONSE CATEGORIES	LOW GROUP				HIGH GROUP			
	X	f	fX	fX^2	X	f	fX	fX^2
Strongly agree	4	2	8	32	4	15	60	240
Agree	3	3	9	27	3	20	60	180
Uncertain	2	20	40	80	2	10	20	40
Disagree	1	15	15	15	1	4	4	4
Strongly disagree	0	10	0	0	0	1	0	0
Sums		50	72	154		50	144	464
		n_L	ΣX_L	$\Sigma X_L{}^2$		n_H	ΣX_H	$\Sigma X_H{}^2$

$$\bar{X}_L = \frac{72}{50} = 1.44 \qquad\qquad \bar{X}_H = \frac{144}{50} = 2.88$$

$$\Sigma (X_L - \bar{X}_L)^2 = 154 - \frac{(72)^2}{50} \qquad\qquad \Sigma (X_H - \bar{X}_H)^2 = 464 - \frac{(144)^2}{50}$$

$$= 50.32 \qquad\qquad\qquad\qquad = 49.28$$

$$t = \frac{2.88 - 1.44}{\sqrt{\dfrac{50.32 + 49.28}{50(50 - 1)}}} \qquad = 7.13$$

and low groups. These statements can be selected by finding the t value for each statement and then arranging the statements in rank order according to their t values. We then select the 20 to 25 statements with the largest *t* values for our attitude scale.

Other methods of item analysis, such as correlational methods, may be used in evaluating the individual statements instead of the *t* test described above. It is doubtful, however, whether any of the methods of item analysis in current use would result in an ordering of the statements that is essentially different from the ordering we obtain in terms of *t* values. Indeed, often a simpler procedure than the *t* test will prove to be sufficient.

Murphy and Likert found, for example, that the rank ordering of 15 statements upon the basis of the magnitude of the difference between the means of a high and low group agreed very well with the ordering of the same statements in terms of the magnitude of the correlation between the item response and total score. As a simple and convenient procedure, therefore, we might use the difference between the means of the high and low groups on the individual statements as a basis for selecting the 20 to 25 items desired for the scale.

Approximately half of the selected statements should be favorable so that the strongly agree response carries the 4 weight and the strongly disagree response the 0 weight. The other half should consist of unfavorable statements so that the scoring system is reversed. The advantage of having both kinds of statements represented in the final scale is to minimize possible response sets of subjects that might be generated if only favorable or unfavorable statements were included in the scale.

If the set of selected statements is given to a new group of subjects, an attitude score for each subject can be obtained by summing the weights that have been assigned to the responses made to the statements. The reliability of the scores on the scale can be obtained by correlating scores on the odd-numbered statements with those on the even-numbered statements. The reliability coefficients typically reported for scales constructed by the method of summated-ratings are above .85, even when fewer than 20 items make up the scale.

INTERPRETATION OF SCORES

In equal-appearing interval scales, the attitude score obtained by a single subject has an absolute interpretation in terms of the psychological continuum of scale values of the statements making up the scale. That is because the attitude score is taken as the median of the scale values of the statements with which the subject agrees. Each attitude score is thus itself a scale value on the psychological continuum on which the statements have been scaled. In scaling the statements, one end of this continuum has been defined as unfavorable and the other as favorable, with the middle category being defined as "neutral." If an attitude score thus falls in the middle section of the psychological continuum, it, in turn, can be described as "neutral." If it falls toward the favorable end of the continuum, it can be described as favorable, and if it falls toward the unfavorable end, it can be described as unfavorable. This interpretation of an attitude score on an equal-appearing interval scale can be made independently of the distribution of scores for a particular group of subjects.

In general, the interpretation of an attitude score on a summated-rating scale cannot be made independently of the distribution of scores of some defined group. If a subject obtains a score of 0 on a 25-item summated-rating scale, we could interpret this score as indicating an unfavorable attitude, since, in order to obtain this score, the subject would have had to have given a strongly agree response to every unfavorable statement and a strongly disagree response to every favorable statement in the scale. Similarly, we could interpret a score of 100 as indicating a favorable attitude, since this score could be obtained only if the subject gave a strongly agree response to every favorable statement and a strongly disagree response to every unfavorable statement. The interpretation of scores falling between the maximum and minimum possible scores is more difficult, if our interest is in describing an individual as having either a favorable or an unfavorable attitude toward the object under consideration. That is because the summated-rating score corresponding to the zero or "neutral" point on a favorable-unfavorable continuum is not known as it is assumed to be known in the case of equal-appearing interval scores. Nor is there any evidence to indicate that the "neutral" point on a summated-rating scale necessarily corresponds to the mid-point of the possible range of scores, that is, to the score of 50 on a 25-item scale.

The absence of knowledge of such a point is a handicap only if our major interest is in being able to assign, on the basis of an attitude score, a single subject to the class of those favorable or unfavorable in attitude toward the psychological object under consideration.

If, in terms of research, our interest is in comparing the mean change in attitude scores as a result of introducing some experimental variable, such as a motion picture film, then the lack of knowledge of a zero point should cause no concern. Similarly, if our interest is in comparing the mean attitude scores of two or more groups, this can be done with summated-rating scales as well as with equal-appearing interval scales. Or if we wish to correlate scores on an attitude scale with scores on other scales or with other measures of interest, this can also be done without any reference to the zero point on the favorable-unfavorable continuum. [3]

[3] One of the most promising approaches to the location of a zero point is the intensity analysis of Guttman and Suchman (1947). See also Suchman (1950) and Katz (1944).

EXPRESSING ATTITUDE SCORES AS *T* SCORES

If our interest is in the attitude of the single subject relative to the attitudes of other subjects, then scores on summated-rating scales can be interpreted in this relative sense—as can also scores on equal-appearing interval scales. A relative interpretation of attitude scores is made in the same manner in which relative interpretations of scores on other psychological tests are made, that is, in terms of the distribution of scores obtained from a particular group.

We can define the mean attitude test score for a particular group of subjects as

$$\bar{X} = \frac{\Sigma X}{n} \tag{6.3}$$

where $\bar{X}$ = the arithmetic mean

ΣX = the sum of scores of all subjects on the attitude scale

n = the number of subjects in the group under consideration

If we use the mean of the group as our point of origin, then each of the individual attitude scores can be expressed as a deviation from this origin. We assume that the mean represents the typical or average attitude of the group. Then scores that are higher than the mean can be interpreted as scores that are more favorable than the average for the group and scores that are lower than the mean can be interpreted as scores that are less favorable than the average.

As a convenient frame of reference, the distribution of attitude scores for a given group can be translated into *T* scores in terms of the following formula.

$$T = 50 + 10 \left(\frac{X - \bar{X}}{s} \right) \tag{5.4}$$

where T = a T score

X = the score of a given subject

$\bar{X}$ = the arithmetic mean of the distribution

s = the standard deviation of the distribution of scores

Expressing the attitude scores as T scores yields a new distribution of scores that will have a mean of 50 and a standard deviation of 10. Scores on psychological tests are frequently translated into T scores in order to provide a standard interpretation of scores free from differences in means and standard deviations of the various tests.

RELIABILITY OF ATTITUDE SCORES [4]

Some confusion has centered around the subject of the comparative reliabilities of scales constructed by the method of summated ratings and by the method of equal-appearing intervals, largely as a result of Likert's study of the reliability of a Thurstone-type scale which was scored by both methods.[5] Two forms of the scale were given to a group of subjects with instructions to check the statements in accordance with the usual Thurstone instructions. The same scales were then given to the subjects with instructions to check for each item one of the five alternatives (strongly agree, agree, undecided, disagree, strongly disagree) in accordance with the usual Likert instructions. Four of the statements on the Thurstone scales were not adaptable to Likert-type responses and were omitted when the subjects were asked to check their

[4] The material in this and following sections is reproduced with minor changes from an article by Edwards and Kenney (1946) by permission of the American Psychological Association.

[5] See also the studies by Likert, Roslow, and Murphy (1934) and Eysenck and Crown (1949).

reactions according to the method of summated ratings scoring system.

The reliability coefficient between the two forms of the scale (22 versus 22 items), when scored by the equal-appearing interval method, was .88, corrected by the Spearman-Brown formula. The reliability coefficient for the two forms (18 versus 18 items), as scored by the method of summated ratings was .94, corrected by the Spearman-Brown formula. What this demonstrates, of course, is that it is possible to take a scale constructed by the method of equal-appearing intervals and apply to most of the statements the scoring system of the method of summated ratings. When this is done, a somewhat higher reliability coefficient will, in general, be obtained.

Ferguson (1941), however, in criticizing the method of summated ratings, seems to believe that Likert, because he found a higher reliability coefficient with his method of scoring rather than with the equal-appearing interval method of scoring, erroneously concluded that "his technique is the better one" (p. 52). The higher reliability coefficient obtained by the Likert method of scoring, Ferguson notes, may be due to the fact that "increasing the number of steps on a psychological scale increases reliability" (p. 52). As a matter of record, this is precisely the same explanation offered originally by Murphy and Likert (1937, p. 47 and p. 55) for the higher reliability coefficient obtained by the Likert method of scoring. The entire discussion, pro and con, on this point has little bearing upon the question of whether the *method* of summated ratings or the *method* of equal-appearing intervals will yield scales of higher reliability. The real problem concerns the reliabilities of scales constructed by the two methods, not the reliability of a particular scoring scheme isolated from the technique of scale construction of which it is a part.

Ferguson (1939) has quoted Thurstone as reporting the reliabilities of scales constructed by the method of equal-appearing intervals, under his direction, as being "all over .8, most of them being over .9" (p. 670). Ferguson adds that in his own studies he has found reliabilities for equal-appearing interval scales ranging from ".52 to .80 for the 20-item forms and from .68 to .89 for the 40-item forms" (p. 670). If we take these coefficients as representative, how do they compare with those reported for scales constructed by the method of summated-ratings?

Murphy and Likert (1937, p. 48) found reliability co-efficients for their Internationalism Scale of 24 items ranging from .81 to .90. Their Imperialism Scale of 12 statements gave coefficients ranging from .80 to .92; the Negro Scale of 14 statements yielded coefficients ranging from .79 to .91. Rundquist and Sletto (1936, p. 110) report coefficients ranging from .78 to .88 for various summated-rating scales of 22 statements each. [6]

That Likert-type scales with even fewer statements will give high reliability coefficients is indicated by Hall (1934, p. 19). Reliability coefficients for his scale of 10 statements measuring attitude toward religion ranged from .91 to .93; for his scale of 7 statements measuring attitude toward em-ployers the coefficients ranged from .77 to .87; and his morale scale of 5 statements gave coefficients from .69 to .84.

All of these coefficients compare favorably with those obtained from scales constructed by the method of equal-

---

[6] The reliability coefficients of the summated-rating scales are based upon split-half correlations, and all of those reported here have been "corrected" to indicate the reliability of the scale taken as a whole. For purposes of comparison, it does not seem proper to raise the coefficients for the equal-appearing interval scales which are based upon equivalent forms of 20 to 22 items each. To do so would indicate the reliability to be expected from a Thurstone scale of 40 to 44 statements, while in practice the scale generally used contains only half as many statements.

appearing intervals. According to the evidence at hand, there is no reason to doubt that scales constructed by the method of summated-ratings will yield reliability coefficients as high as or higher than those obtained with scales constructed by the method of equal-appearing intervals.

THURSTONE SCALE VALUES OF STATEMENTS IN LIKERT SCALES

From the description of the method of summated-ratings, it is clear that no consideration is given to the problem of the scale values of the individual statements. It is sufficient if the statements relating to a given psychological object can be classified as favorable or unfavorable. This classification determines the direction of the weighting system to be assigned to the response categories. In the scaling methods such as the method of equal-appearing intervals, however, a judging group is required in order to determine first the scale values of the statements on the favorable-unfavorable continuum.

The confusion which followed Likert's rescoring of the statements in an equal-appearing interval scale by the weighted response method, unfortunately, was not confined to the subject of reliability; it spread to involve the question of whether or not there is a need for a judging group in the construction of attitude scales. Ferguson (1941) for example, seems to believe that Likert implied, as a result of obtaining a higher reliability coefficient with his method of scoring than with the customary Thurstone method of scoring, that he had demonstrated that the method of summated-ratings does away entirely with the need for a judging group. Ferguson argues against this and bases his criticism on the following grounds (p. 52):

Since the statements (used by Likert in the above study) had been sifted through the sorting procedure (Thurstone's), it would seem unjustifiable to conclude that Likert's method did away with the need for a judging group. To test this point adequately one should compare scales constructed (independently of the Thurstone method) by the Likert technique with those constructed by the equal-appearing interval method.

We are in complete agreement with this argument of Ferguson's. It is therefore somewhat difficult to understand why he proceeded to do precisely what he criticized Likert for doing. Ferguson proposes, for example (p. 52), that:

> A more adequate test (of the two methods?) can be provided by rescaling items using Thurstone's method in scales constructed by Likert's technique. If Likert's technique does away with the need for a judging group, the two methods of treating the statements should give the same result.

But this particular experimental design will not give a test of the two *methods* of scale construction; it is an investigation of where Likert-selected statements will fall along the continuum posited by Thurstone or, stated somewhat differently, what Thurstone scale values will be attached to the particular statements included in a particular Likert-type scale.

What Ferguson found by following this line of investigation was that Likert-selected statements, when scaled according to the method of equal-appearing intervals, failed to spread evenly over the scale continuum of Thurstone; the statements failed to represent all degrees of attitude but fell largely at the favorable and unfavorable ends of the scale with the middle categories neglected. [7] This is illustrated in Figure 6.1. Only one of the Likert-type scales which Ferguson attempted to scale by the Thurstone technique, the economic conservatism scale, gave a fairly even spread of statements (see Figure 6.1),

[7] Edwards (1946) presents evidence to indicate that statements falling in the central sections of the equal-appearing interval continuum tend to be statements that fail to differentiate between "high" and "low" groups in the method of summated ratings. Thus statements selected in terms of the item analysis procedures used in the method of summated ratings would, in general, not include these "neutral" statements on the Thurstone continuum.

and the correlation between the Thurstone and Likert methods of scoring this scale was .70. [8] Because of these findings, that is, the failure of the Likert-selected statements to spread evenly over the Thurstone continuum and the "low" correlation between the Thurstone and Likert methods of

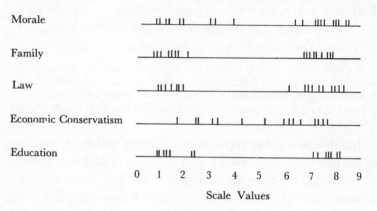

FIG. 6.1—The Thurstone equal-appearing interval scale values of attitude statements contained in five scales constructed by the method of summated ratings. Reproduced from Ferguson (1941), Fig. 1, p. 56.

scoring the one that did, Ferguson (1941) concluded that he had successfully demonstrated "that Likert's technique for the construction of attitude scales does not obviate the need for a judging group (p. 57).

In essence, however, what Ferguson demonstrated was that Likert-selected statements do not necessarily fall at equally-spaced intervals along the theoretical continuum. That they do not may be of theoretical interest, but this finding has little bearing upon the problem of whether or not there is need for

[8] Assuming that the reliability coefficient of this scale when scored by the Thurstone method is approximately that obtained when the scale is scored by the Likert method, which is reported by Rundquist and Sletto (1936) as .85, and correcting for attenuation, the correlation would be .82.

a judging group. Attitude scales are constructed primarily for the purpose of obtaining attitude scores for individuals and thus being able to order individuals with respect to the degree of favorableness or unfavorableness they associate with a psychological object. If this ordering is essentially the same as determined by scales independently constructed by each of the two methods, then it would be difficult to argue that a judging group is necessary for the construction of an attitude scale. But, it may be noted, this is not the problem investigated by either Likert or Ferguson.

It might seem that the correlation of .70 (.82 corrected for attenuation), reported by Ferguson, between the Thurstone and Likert methods of scoring the economic conservatism scale would bear upon the problem. But this correlation is biased in that Ferguson failed to give the Thurstone method a fair trial, that is, he limited the Thurstone scale to the statements already selected by Likert's technique. Nor can we accept the correlations of .75 and .81 (corrected for attenuation) which Murphy and Likert report for their Internationalism Scale and scores on the Thurstone-Droba War Scale. These correlations also fail to do justice to the question of whether comparable results can be obtained with independently constructed Thurstone and Likert scales, since it is possible that the attitudes under consideration are not the same.

THE EDWARDS AND KENNEY STUDY

A valid comparison of the method of equal-appearing intervals and the method of summated ratings, should start with an original set of statements, not with statements already sifted by the Thurstone procedure and then scored by Likert's method, and not with statements sifted by the Likert procedure and then scaled by the Thurstone technique. The same group of subjects should then be used in the construction of the two scales, but the steps for each method should be carried through independently. To carry out this comparison, Edwards and Kenney (1946) used the original statements of Thurstone and Chave in their study of attitudes toward the church.

Subjects used in the construction of the scale were 72 members of an introductory psychology class at the University of Maryland. Half the class, selected at random, was asked to judge the degree of favorableness or unfavorableness expressed by the statements in accordance with the Thurstone method, while the other half of the class was requested to give Likert-type responses to the same statements. Two days later the procedure was reversed; the first half of the class gave Likert-type responses to the statements, while the other half gave Thurstone-type judgments. The Seashore and Hevner (1933) method of rating items was used instead of the Thurstone and Chave procedure of sorting the items into categories.

Statements were selected for two "equivalent" forms of an equal-appearing interval scale, each form containing 20 statements. Selection of statements was made on the basis of Thurstone's informal standards, Q values, and scale values. Insofar as possible, the final scales contained statements with low Q values and with scale values which were spread along the entire scale at relatively equally-spaced distances. Since only a few statements, however, were found to have scale values near the center of the continuum and, at the same time, low Q values, this was not entirely possible.

In constructing the Likert scale, 25 statements were selected all with a mean difference between the statement responses of the high group and the low group of 1.8 or greater. In approximately half of these statements the strongly agree response was assigned the maximum weight and in the other half the strongly agree response was assigned the minimum weight. Of the 25 statements selected for the Likert scale, three were also used in Form *A* of the equal-appearing interval scale and two were used in common with Form *B*.

To obtain data on the reliabilities of the scales and to find out the relationship existing between scores on the independently constructed Likert and Thurstone scales, members of another introductory psychology class and an applied psychology class were tested. One group of subjects was presented with the Thurstone scales followed by the Likert scale; for the second group of subjects the order of presentation was reversed. There were 80 subjects altogether, each group containing approximately half this number.

The reliability coefficient for the Likert scale of 25 items was .94. This coefficient compares favorably with those usually reported for scales constructed by the method of summated-ratings. The reliability coefficient for the two forms of the equal-appearing interval scales of 20 items each was .88. This is comparable to reliability coefficients of .85 and .89 which Thurstone and Chave (1929, p. 66) originally reported for scores on their Forms *A* and *B* for two different groups of subjects.

The correlation coefficient between scores on the Likert scale and Form *A* of the Thurstone scale was .72, which, when corrected for attenuation becomes .79. The correlation between the Likert scale and Form *B* of the Thurstone scale was .92. When corrected for attenuation, this coefficient indicates a perfect relationship between scores on the two scales. Unfortunately, we have no way of knowing which of these two coefficients is more representative of the "true" relationship existing between scores on independently constructed Thurstone and Likert scales in general. It might be suggested, however, that if Edwards and Kenney had constructed only one form of the equal-appearing interval scale so that greater care could have been exercised in terms of the scale and Q values of the 20 statements to be included in the scale, the correlation between scores on this scale and the Likert scale would have been closer to the observed value of .92 than to the observed value of .72. In other words, choosing the best 20 from the 40 statements that they used in the two forms would perhaps have resulted in a more adequate equal-appearing interval scale than either of the two forms they constructed. Under these circumstances, we might predict that the relative ordering of subjects on either an equal-appearing interval scale or a summated-rating scale would be, for all practical purposes, essentially the same.

EASE OF CONSTRUCTION OF SUMMATED-RATING AND EQUAL-APPEARING INTERVAL SCALES

It has been claimed by Likert (1932) that the method of summated ratings is simpler and easier to apply in the development of an attitude scale than is the method of equal-appearing intervals. Some support to this claim has been given by others who have used the method of summated ratings. Hall (1934), for example, states that he used the method of summated ratings in his survey of attitudes of employed and unemployed men because of its relative simplicity. Rundquist and Sletto (1936) used the method of summated ratings in developing the attitude scales contained in the Minnesota Survey of Opinions and they also express their belief that the method "is less laborious than that developed by Thurstone" (p. 5).

Edwards and Kenney (1946), in their comparative study of the method of equal-appearing intervals and the method of summated ratings, estimate that the time required to construct an equal-appearing interval scale is approximately twice that required by the method of summated ratings. However, we now know that it is not necessary to use an excessively large group of judges in order to obtain reliable scale values. It is also true that judgments can be obtained quickly and conveniently in terms of the methods used by Seashore and Hevner (1933) or Ballin and Farnsworth (1941). Once judgments have been obtained, scale and Q values can be rapidly determined through the use of a nomograph, as described by Jurgensen (1943) or a device such as that used by Edwards and Kilpatrick (1948). It therefore seems likely that in terms of these developments the method of summated ratings and the method of equal-appearing intervals would be fairly comparable with respect to the time and labor required.

QUESTIONS AND PROBLEMS

1. Examine the statements with "neutral" scale values obtained when the statements were scaled by the method of equal-appearing intervals in an earlier exercise. Could these statements, in general, be scored in terms of the method of summated ratings? If not, why not?

2. Give the statements previously scaled by the method of equal-appearing intervals to a new group of approximately 100 subjects with Likert directions. Select a few of the statements and find the proportion in each of the response categories. Find normal deviate weights for the response categories. Are these weights approximately the same as the weights 0, 1, 2, 3, and 4 used by Likert?

3. Using the data obtained above, construct a summated-rating scale of approximately 20 to 22 statements and give the scale to a new group of 100 subjects.

4. Since equal-appearing interval scale values are known for the above statements, it is possible to find scores on the Thurstone continuum using the median method of scoring for those statements that a subject agrees with. Correlate these scores with those obtained by scoring the statements in terms of the method of summated ratings. Do your results agree with those reported by Likert? Which method of scoring would you predict to result in a higher reliability coefficient? Why?

5. What reasons might be offered to support the notion that not many Thurstone "neutral" statements would be expected to be included in a scale constructed by the method of summated ratings?

6. How would one interpret scores on a summated-rating scale? On an equal-appearing interval scale?

7. Read the article by Edwards (1946). What are some of the characteristics of "neutral" statements that he found?

REFERENCES AND SUGGESTED READINGS

BALLIN, M., and FARNSWORTH, P. R. A graphic rating method for determining the scale values of statements in measuring social attitudes. *J. soc. Psychol.*, 1941, 13, 323-327.

BIRD, C. *Social psychology*. New York: Appleton-Century-Crofts, Inc., 1940.

*EDWARDS, A. L. A critique of "neutral items" in attitude scales constructed by the method of equal-appearing intervals. *Psychol. Rev.*, 1946, 53, 159-169.

——— *Statistical methods for the behavioral sciences*. New York: Rinehart, 1954.

* ——— and KENNEY, KATHERINE C. A comparison of the Thurstone and Likert techniques of attitude scale construction. *J. appl. Psychol.*, 1946, 30, 72-83.

——— and KILPATRICK, F. P. A technique for the construction of attitude scales. *J. appl. Psychol.*, 1948, 32, 374-384.

EYSENCK, H. J. and CROWN, S. An experimental study in opinion-attitude methodology. *Int. J. Opin. Attitude Res.*, 1949, 3, 47-86.

*FERGUSON, L. W. The requirements of an adequate attitude scale. *Psychol. Bull.*, 1939, 36, 665-673.

* ——— A study of the Likert technique of attitude scale construction. *J. soc. Psychol.*, 1941, 13, 51-57.

GUTTMAN, L., and SUCHMAN, E. A. Intensity and a zero point for attitude analysis. *Amer. sociol. Rev.*, 1947, 12, 57-67.

HALL, O. M. Attitudes and unemployment. *Arch. Psychol.*, 1934, No. 165.

*KATZ, D. The measurement of intensity. In H. Cantril *et al.*, *Gauging public opinion*. Princeton, N. J.: Princeton Univ. Press, 1944. Pp. 51-65.

JURGENSEN, C. E. A nomograph for rapid determination of medians. *Psychometrika*, 1943, 8, 265-269.

*LIKERT, R. A technique for the measurement of attitudes. *Arch. Psychol.*, 1932, No. 140.

——— ROSLOW, S., and MURPHY, G. A simple and reliable method of scoring the Thurstone attitude scales. *J. soc. Psychol.*, 1934, 5, 228-238.

*MURPHY, G., and LIKERT, R. *Public opinion and the individual*. New York: Harper, 1937.

RUNDQUIST, E. A., and SLETTO, R. F. *Personality in the depression*. Minneapolis: Univ. Minnesota Press, 1936.

SEASHORE, R. H., and HEVNER, KATE. A time-saving device for the construction of attitude scales. *J. soc. Psychol.*, 1933, 4, 366-372.

SUCHMAN, E. A. The intensity component in attitude and opinion research. In S. A. Stouffer *et al.*, *Measurement and prediction*. Princeton, N. J.: Princeton Univ. Press, 1950. Pp. 213-276.

7

Scalogram Analysis

Scalogram analysis differs considerably from the methods of constructing attitude scales that we have previously described. In one sense, scalogram analysis is not a method for constructing or developing an attitude scale, although it has been referred to as such by other writers. In practice, scalogram analysis can perhaps be most accurately described as a procedure for evaluating sets of statements or existing scales to determine whether or not they meet the requirements of a particular kind of scale, set forth in some detail by Guttman (1944, 1945, 1947a, 1947b). We shall refer to this particular kind of scale as a *Guttman scale* or a *cumulative scale*.

If a set of statements with a common content is to constitute a Guttman scale, then an individual with a higher rank (or score) than another individual on the same set of statements must also rank just as high or higher on every statement in the set as the other individual (Guttman, 1950b, p. 62). In the case of attitude statements, we might say that this means that a person with a more favorable attitude score than another person must also be just as favorable or more favorable in his response to every statement in the set than the other person. When responses to a set of attitude statements meet this requirement, the set of statements is said to constitute a *unidimensional scale*.

172

UNIDIMENSIONAL SCALES

Let us examine an important property of a unidimensional scale. Suppose that we have five rods arranged in order of magnitude with respect to length. We pay no attention to the actual measured differences in lengths of the rods, but only to their ordering with respect to length. Any set of *n* objects arranged in order of magnitude of some variable or attribute is said to be *ranked*. The object with the highest value of the variable can be assigned rank 1, the next highest rank 2, and so on, with the object having the least value being assigned rank *n*. We should note that the ranks of the objects tell us nothing about the magnitude of the differences between the objects. In the case of our five rods, for example, that with rank 1 may have a measured length of 80 inches, that with rank 2 a measured length of 70 inches, and that with rank 3 a measured length of 40 inches. Clearly, the ranks themselves do not tell us that the difference in measured length between rank 1 and rank 2 is only 1/3 the difference in measured length between rank 2 and rank 3.

Assuming errors of measurement are nonexistent, anyone who knows how to use a ruler or yardstick could rank the five rods under consideration with respect to length and these ranks, we would expect, would be the same for anyone who performed the necessary operations. As long as we confine our observations to the dimension of length, the ranking of the rods is invariant. Of course, they might differ with respect to weight, hardness, overall size, and various other attributes. And the ordering of the rods with respect to these other attributes would not necessarily be the same as the ordering we obtain in terms of length. The length continuum, however, is a single continuum or, as we might say, length is a unidimensional continuum or scale that permits only an invariant ordering of objects on this dimension.

When objects can be ordered along a single dimension or continuum, interesting relations exist among the objects. For example, we know that the rod with rank 1 is longer than any of the other remaining $n - 1$ rods. We also know that the rod with rank 2 is longer than any of the other remaining $n - 2$ rods with larger ranks, and that the only rod that is longer is the one that has rank 1.

Suppose now we have a group of sticks of varying but unknown lengths. We have no measurement of length available, but only our five rods with their known ranks on the length continuum. Can we use these rods and their known ranks to obtain an ordering of the sticks with respect to length also? Let us assume that we take each stick in turn and we compare it with each of the five rods. If the stick is longer than a given rod, we assign it a weight of 1 and if it is shorter, we assign it a weight of 0 for the comparison. We do this for each of the sticks and for each

TABLE 7.1

Possible outcomes in comparing a set of sticks with each of 5 rods of known rank with respect to length. A weight of 1 has been assigned to the stick if it is longer than the rod and a weight of 0 if it is shorter

STICKS	RANKS OF RODS					SCORES OF STICKS	RANKS OF STICKS
	1	2	3	4	5		
a	1	1	1	1	1	5	1
b	0	1	1	1	1	4	2
c	0	0	1	1	1	3	3
d	0	0	0	1	1	2	4
e	0	0	0	0	1	1	5
f	0	0	0	0	0	0	6

stick we obtain a score consisting of the sum of numbers (0, 1) that it has been assigned in the comparisons with the rods of known ranks. Table 7.1 shows the *only* possible outcomes of our comparisons.

We may note, in Table 7.1, that any stick with a higher score than another also has a score that is just as high or higher on every one of the possible comparisons than the other. The scores assigned to the sticks thus meet Guttman's requirements for a scale and we may say that these scores fall along a unidimensional continuum. Knowing the nature of the continuum on which the rods were ranked and also the nature of the comparisons we have made, we would have no doubts at all as to the rank order of the sticks on the length continuum. The interesting point is that if we have a set of objects of known ranks or order on a unidimensional continuum, then we can, by comparisons of the kind described, obtain information relative to the rank order of a new set of objects on the same continuum.

At this point let us shift our discussion from five rods as ranked in terms of a length continuum to five attitude statements with respect to some psychological object. We shall assume that these statements fall along a single continuum from least to most favorable. The most favorable statement on this continuum is assigned rank 1, the next most favorable rank 2, and so on, with the least favorable statement being assigned the rank of n. We now have a group of individuals and we assume that they possess unknown but varying degrees of favorable attitudes toward the psychological object under consideration. We compare each individual with each statement. If he agrees with the statement we assign him a weight of 1 and if he disagrees we assign him a weight of 0. For each individual we obtain a score based upon the sum of weights of his responses to the statements. If we are correct in our assumption that the attitude statements fall along a single dimension and if the responses of the subjects to the statements are determined only by their position on this same dimension, then the only possible outcomes of the comparisons are the same as those shown in Table 7.1.

In general, of course, we do not know in advance that a given set of attitude statements necessarily falls along a single continuum from least to most favorable. It is the purpose of scalogram analysis to determine whether, if we start with this as a hypothesis, the responses of the subjects to the statements are in accord with the hypothesis of a single dimension. If, for example, in a set of five attitude statements, we find that all individuals who agree with four statements do so with respect to the same four; that those who agree with three do so with respect to the same three, and that furthermore these three are among the four agreed with by those who agree with four; that those who agree with two do so with respect to the same two, and furthermore that these two are among the three agreed with by those who agree with three, and so on, then these results would offer strong evidence that the statements do fall along a single dimension. Thus, if the responses of subjects to the statements were in accord with our theoretical model of a unidimensional scale of statements, we would have confidence in interpreting scores of subjects based upon the statements as also falling along the same unidimensional continuum.

UNIVERSE OF CONTENT

An area of content may be quite general such as "attitude toward the United Nations." General areas of content may also be broken down into more specific areas. such as "attitude toward the United Nations as a means of settling international disputes," "attitude toward the United Nations World Health Program," and so on. It has been found that the chances of obtaining a scalable set of statements, in Guttman's sense, are better if the universe of content is made specific rather than general.

When an area of content has been defined, a number of statements relating to this universe are then selected. In particular, Guttman and his associates have worked with a selected set of four to six statements, with a maximum of perhaps ten to twelve statements. Just how these statements are selected remains something of a mystery. As we know, in the various scaling methods previously described, we started with a relatively large number of statements relating to some psychological object. Then, by means of item analysis techniques or various other statistical procedures, we selected various statements for inclusion in our scales and rejected others. Thus we ended with a relatively small number of statements selected on the basis of objective criteria.

Guttman (1945) has expressed his belief that the selection of a small number of statements from the large number of possible statements representing a universe of content should be done upon the basis of intuition and experience. He has also said that the statements selected should be those that seem to have the most "homogeneous content" (Guttman, 1947a).[1] Perhaps as Festinger (1947, p. 159) has indicated, one should look for statements "all of which are, to a large extent, rephrasings of the same thing." We shall return to

---

[1] Loevinger (1948) has stressed the essential similarity between what she calls a cumulative homogeneous test and a Guttman scale. She also develops a coefficient, H_{ij}, to measure the degree of homogeneity of two statements and a coefficient H_t for a given set of statements.

this problem of statement selection later. For the time being, we shall merely say that contrary to Guttman's early advice, it may be desirable to subject the statements relating to a given area of content to item analysis procedures prior to testing for scalability. There is some reason to believe, for example, that statements that have been found to meet an internal consistency test are more apt to meet the requirements of a cumulative scale than unselected statements (Edwards and Kilpatrick, 1948). We agree with Guttman (1945), however, that item analysis procedures are not a *necessary* part of scale analysis.

As in the case of all attitude statements to be included in a scale, an important test for each statement is whether or not one can expect subjects with varying attitudes toward the psychological object to respond differentially to the statements. If it can be inferred that an "agree" (or disagree) response will be given by subjects with more favorable attitudes and a "disagree" (or agree) response by subjects with less favorable attitudes, then a statement may be judged satisfactory.

THE CORNELL TECHNIQUE

For the time being we shall assume that each statement is to have only two response categories, such as agree-disagree. For each statement we assign weights of 0 and 1 to the two response categories. These weights are so assigned that the 1 is always given to the response category that indicates more of whatever it is that is being measured. In the case of attitude statements, for example, the 1 weight may be assigned to the response category that indicates a more favorable attitude toward the psychological object and the 0 weight to the response category that indicates a less favorable attitude.

The statements are then given to a sample of at least 100

persons. If more subjects have been tested, it is often sufficient to select a sample of 100 from the larger number. Subjects are asked to respond to each statement in terms of their agreement or disagreement with it. A score is obtained for each subject by summing the weights assigned to the response categories he has selected. The test papers are then arranged in rank order of the scores, from high to low.

From this point on there are several procedures that may be used to evaluate the scalability of the set of statements. [2] Since all "are virtually equivalent in the results they yield" (Guttman 1947*a*, p. 458), we shall describe first a method which Guttman (1947*b*) calls the "Cornell technique," and then a variation of this technique which seems to have certain advantages in terms of objectivity of the routine.

Using the Cornell technique, a table is constructed with one column for each response category for each statement and one row for each subject.[3] For 10 statements with two possible responses to each statement and 100 subjects, this would mean a table with 20 columns and 100 rows.

Starting with the person having the highest score, the responses of each subject to each statement are recorded by placing a check mark in the appropriate cell of the table. When completed the table provides a record of all the available data. If the statements are to be considered a Guttman scale, then certain conditions must be met with respect to the pattern of check marks recorded in the table, the most important of which is that "from a person's rank

---

[2] Suchman (1950) provides a good description of the *scalogram board,* a device used by members of the Research Branch, Information and Education Division, Army Service Forces, in doing scalogram analyses.

Kahn and Bodine (1951), and Ford (1950) describe procedures involving IBM equipment.

[3] In Table 7.2 we have an example of this table for four statements and 20 subjects.

alone we can reproduce his response to each of the items in a simple fashion" (Guttman, 1947*b*, p. 249). The other conditions which must be met will be discussed later.

What would this mean in the case of *perfect reproducibility*? Let us suppose that for the first statement we have 80 individuals giving the response weighted 1 and 20 individuals giving the response weighted 0. Now, if the 1 response has been judged more favorable than the 0 response, then the 80 subjects who give the 1 response should all have higher

TABLE 7.2

An illustration of a perfect scale of 4 statements responded to by 20 subjects. A response of 1 to a given statement is judged to be more favorable than a response of 0

| | STATEMENTS | | | | | | | | |
| SUBJECTS | 1 | | 2 | | 3 | | 4 | | SCORES |
	1	0	1	0	1	0	1	0	
1	x		x		x		x		4
2	x		x		x		x		4
3	x		x		x		x		4
4	x		x		x		x		4
5	x		x		x		x		4
6	x		x			x	x		3
7	x		x			x	x		3
8	x		x			x	x		3
9		x	x			x	x		2
10	x		x			x	x		2
11	x		x			x		x	1
12	x		x			x		x	1
13	x		x			x		x	1
14	x		x			x		x	1
15	x			x		x		x	0
16	x			x		x		x	0
17	x			x		x		x	0
18	x			x		x		x	0
19	x			x		x		x	0
20	x			x		x		x	0

total scores than the 20 subjects who give the 0 response. A similar statement could be made for each of the other statements, assuming the set constitutes a perfect scale. Thus, it would be possible to reproduce the responses of the individuals to the various statements in terms of their total scores alone.

In Table 7.2 we have an example, using only four statements and 20 subjects, that illustrates the point that in the case of a perfect scale it is possible to reproduce the responses to the individual statements from knowledge of total scores. An examination of this table indicates that all of the information provided by the individual responses is contained in the total score. Thus five scores, 4, 3, 2, 1, and 0 permit us to reproduce a total of 20 x 4 = 80 responses without any error whatsoever.

But since perfect reproducibility is not to be expected in practice, it becomes a matter of some importance to measure the degree of reproducibility present for any given set of responses to attitude statements. This is accomplished by setting *cutting points* for the response categories of each statement. A cutting point marks that place in the rank order of subjects where the most common response shifts from one category to the other. With overlapping between responses in different categories, some choice as to the location of the cutting point is possible.[4] Guttman (1947*b*) offers two rules to be used in locating cutting points. The first is that the cutting point should be located so as to minimize error (p. 258). The second is that "no category should have more error in it than non-error" (p. 261).

If a set of statements had perfect reproducibility, then all

---

[4] Some of the difficulties involved in locating cutting points are described in a study by Clark and Kriedt (1948).

responses above a given cutting point for a statement would fall in the same category and all those below would fall in the other category. This can be seen in Table 7.2 where we have recorded the pattern of responses for a set of statements constituting a perfect scale. Thus, responses falling outside the column or category in which they theoretically belong may be counted as errors.

In Table 7.3, for purposes of illustration, we give the responses of 20 subjects to a set of four statements and show the possible cutting points for the various statements following Guttman's two rules. The cutting points are indicated by the horizontal lines in the body of the table. It may be observed in this table that no category has *more* error than non-error and that the cutting points have been located so as to *minimize* errors. The errors for each category are counted and are recorded at the bottom of the table. We see, for example, that for the 1 category of the first statement, one response falls below the cutting point and it should theoretically fall above the cutting point. It thus constitutes an error and the number 1 has been recorded in the error row "*e*" at the bottom of the table. For the second category of Statement 1, we also have one response falling above the cutting point and it also constitutes an error. The number 1 has thus been recorded at the bottom of the table under the 0 category for Statement 1. Errors for the other statements are counted in the same manner and recorded at the bottom of the table.

We now sum the errors for each category for each statement over all statements. This gives a total of 12 errors. We express the total number of errors as a proportion of the total number of responses and subtract this value from unity. For the data of Table 7.3 we have 12 errors and a total of $(20) (4) = 80$ responses. The proportion of errors is there-

TABLE 7.3

The Cornell technique applied to a 4 statement scale responded to by 20 subjects. The horizontal lines in the body of the table are possible cutting points for the statements

	STATEMENTS								SCORES
SUBJECTS	1		2		3		4		
	1	0	1	0	1	0	1	0	
1	x		x		x		x		4
2	x			x	x		x		3
3	x		x			x	x		3
4	x		x			x	x		3
5	x			x	x		x		3
6	x			x	x		x		3
7	x			x	x		x		3
8	x			x	x		x		3
9	x			x		x	x		2
10		x	x			x	x		2
11	x			x		x	x		2
12	x			x		x	x		2
13		x	x			x	x		2
14		x		x	x		x		2
15		x	x			x		x	1
16		x		x		x	x		1
17	x			x		x		x	1
18		x		x	x			x	1
19		x		x		x	x		1
20		x		x		x		x	0
f	12	8	6	14	8	12	16	4	
p and *q*	.6	.4	.3	.7	.4	.6	.8	.2	
e	1	1	3	1	2	2	2	0	$\Sigma e = 12$

fore $12/80 = .15$. Subtracting this value from unity gives us $1 - .15 = .85$. This value, which Guttman calls the *coefficient of reproducibility*, is supposed to indicate the per cent accuracy with which responses to the various statements can be reproduced from the total scores.

But further examination of the data of Table 7.3 demonstrates that it would be impossible to reproduce the individual responses to the statements with this degree of accuracy. The value of .85 represents a spurious degree of accuracy because we have followed Guttman's rule for "minimizing error" in locating cutting points.

With perfect reproducibility, of course, there is no problem in locating the cutting points. The cutting points would be the dividing points in the total scores where the response shifts from the more to the less favorable category. All subjects with scores above a cutting point for a given statement would respond by checking the more favorable alternative and all those below by checking the less favorable, as in Table 7.2. There would thus be an exact correspondence between cutting points and scores, with no overlap whatsoever in the responses of subjects below and above the cutting point of a given statement. But, as we have noted before, perfect scales exist only as ideal models and in practice it is necessary to determine the extent to which the data or observed patterns of response fit the model of a perfect scale.

ANOTHER METHOD OF SCALOGRAM ANALYSIS

We turn now to another method of scalogram analysis suggested by Goodenough (1944). This method, as Edwards (1948) has shown, enables us to determine the coefficient of reproducibility in such a way that the coefficient does accurately represent the degree of accuracy with which we can reproduce the responses to statements from total scores alone.

A score matrix is prepared with rows corresponding to subjects and columns to statements. This matrix will be of order n x c where n is the number of subjects, usually 100, and c is the number of statements in the scale. The responses of a subject to the various statements are recorded in the row of the matrix in terms of the 0 and 1 weights. The response patterns are recorded with the subject with the highest score assigned to the first row. The second row will correspond to the subject with the next highest score, and so on. In Table 7.4 we give this score matrix based upon the data presented in Table 7.3.

TABLE 7.4

A score method for recording the data of Table 7.3

SUBJECTS	STATEMENTS				SCORES	e
	1	2	3	4		
1	1	1	1	1	4	0
2	1	0	1	1	3	0
3	1	1	0	1	3	2
4	1	1	0	1	3	2
5	1	0	1	1	3	0
6	1	0	1	1	3	0
7	1	0	1	1	3	0
8	1	0	1	1	3	0
9	1	0	0	1	2	0
10	0	1	0	1	2	2
11	1	0	0	1	2	0
12	1	0	0	1	2	0
13	0	1	0	1	2	2
14	0	0	1	1	2	2
15	0	1	0	0	1	2
16	0	0	0	1	1	0
17	1	0	0	0	1	2
18	0	0	1	0	1	2
19	0	0	0	1	1	0
20	0	0	0	0	0	0
f	12	6	8	16	42	16
p	.6	.3	.4	.8		
q	.4	.7	.6	.2		

Summing across the rows of the score matrix will give the scores for the various subjects and these are recorded at the right of the last statement column, as in Table 7.4. Summing down the columns will give the frequencies with which the 1 response has been made to each of the various statements. The sum of the column sums will equal the sum of scores for all subjects, as shown at the bottom of Table 7.4.

The sums for each column of the score matrix are divided by the total number of subjects to obtain the proportions p

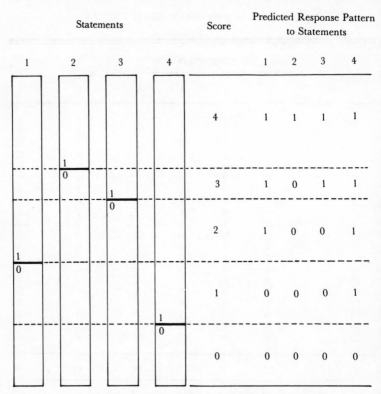

FIG. 7.1—Bar charts used in determining the predicted response patterns corresponding to the scores of Table 7.4.

giving the 1 response to each of the statements. The proportions giving the 0 response will be $1 - p = q$. The values of p and q for the illustrative data of Table 7.4 are shown at the bottom of the table.

A bar chart can now be drawn for each statement in the manner of Figure 7.1. In drawing the bar chart, it is convenient to use graph paper ruled 20 to the inch. The top part of the bar chart indicates the proportion giving the 1 response to a statement and the lower part represents the proportion giving the 0 response. The points of division are indicated by the solid lines. Each point of division is extended through the other bar charts in terms of the dotted lines shown in Figure 7.1.

For the four-statement scale the possible range of scores is from 0 to 4. On the hypothesis that the statements constitute a perfect scale, as discussed earlier, the predicted patterns of response to the statements corresponding to each score can be determined. These predicted patterns of response are obtained directly from the bar charts as shown in Figure 7.1.

The predicted patterns of response for each score can now be compared with the observed patterns which have been recorded in the original score matrix. Each deviation of an observed response from the predicted response is counted as an error. The errors for each subject are summed and recorded at the right of the column of scores, as shown in Table 7.4. There we see, for example, that the observed pattern of response for Subject 10, who has a score of 2, is 0 1 0 1. The predicted response pattern for a score of 2, as shown in Figure 7.1, is 1 0 0 1. We thus have two errors, and this value is recorded in the error column in the row corresponding to Subject 10.

If we now sum the entries in the error column of Table 7.4, we obtain the total number of errors. This is equal to 16. The proportion of errors is therefore $16/80 = .20$, and the coefficient of reproducibility is $1 - .20 = .80$.

The coefficient of reproducibility, computed in the manner described, *is* a measure of the degree of accuracy with which the statement responses can be reproduced from knowledge of the total scores alone. [5]

MORE THAN TWO CATEGORIES OF RESPONSE

The discussion above has assumed dichotomous scoring for each of the statements, that is, only two categories of response for each statement. If three categories of response are permitted, such as agree, undecided, disagree, then weights of 2, 1, and 0 may be assigned to the categories, with the largest weight always being assigned to the most favorable response and the 0 weight to the least favorable response. Under these circumstances, the score matrix will now have entries of 2, 1, and 0, but will otherwise be the same as that described for two categories of response. Summing the weights across rows will give the scores for the subjects.

With more than two categories of response, however, it will be necessary to count separately the number of 2, 1, and 0 entries in each column of the score matrix. These frequencies, when divided by the total number of subjects,

[5] By way of comparison, we may note that using the Cornell technique, the number of errors for the same data was 12. Our total of 16 errors represents an increase of approximately 33 per cent. The coefficient of reproducibility is not changed too greatly, from .85 to .80, for the illustrative data, though this will not necessarily be the case in actual practice.

will yield the proportions making each of the responses. Each bar chart will thus have two solid lines, showing the proportion giving each of the possible responses to the statement, unless one of the response categories has zero frequency, in which case the bar chart will again have only a single solid line.

In Table 7.5 we give the proportion of subjects falling in each response category for three statements with more than

TABLE 7.5

The proportion of subjects falling in each response category for three statements with more than two categories of response

RESPONSE CATEGORIES	WEIGHTS	STATEMENTS		
		1	2	3
		p	p	p
Agree	2	.30	.25	.80
Uncertain	1	.40	.25	.20
Disagree	0	.30	.50	.00

two categories of response permitted. Figure 7.2 illustrates the bar charts for these three statements. It may be observed that for Statement 2, no one gave the 0 response, and the bar chart for this statement has only a single solid line showing the proportion giving the 2 and the proportion giving the 1 response. From these bar charts, the predicted pattern of response for each score is determined and is shown at the right of Figure 7.2. These predicted patterns of response, assuming a perfect scale, may then be compared with the patterns actually observed in the score matrix. The errors of prediction are recorded for each subject and the coefficient of reproducibility is obtained in the manner described earlier. This procedure may be generalized to any number of response categories.

If a relatively large number of response categories are used, say five, then one will usually find that the discrepancies between the predicted patterns of response and those actually observed are so great that the number of errors is quite large, resulting in a value of less than .85 for the coefficient of reproducibility. When this is the case, Guttman suggests that a second score matrix be constructed. Where the recorded weights in a given column of the original score matrix appear to overlap considerably, then the categories of response assigned these weights may be combined. The combined categories are then reweighted. Assume, for example, that initially we have five categories of response, weighted 4, 3, 2, 1, and 0. If we have combined categories with weights of 4 and 3, and categories with weights of 2 and 1, then a response of 4 or 3 to the original statement would be given a weight of 2, and a response of 2 or 1 to the same statement would now be given a weight of 1. The original weight of 0 would still be given to all responses in that category.

New scores, based upon the new weights, would now be computed for each of the subjects and a new rank ordering obtained based upon the new scores. A new score matrix would then be constructed using the new weights. Following the same procedures described before, new predicted patterns of response would be obtained and compared with the observed patterns and a new coefficient of reproducibility obtained. If the coefficient of reproducibility is still not satisfactory, successive combinations of response categories can be continued until the response categories for all statements have been dichotomized.

Let us assume that a coefficient of reproducibility of .90

or greater is not obtained with any of the successive score matrices. Guttman (1945, p. 4) then suggests that if it seems that one or more subsets of the statements may scale separately, this in turn may mean that the original universe of content can be broken up into subuniverses which will scale.

To test the hypothesis that a scalable subset is part of a scalable subuniverse, it is necessary to show that the content of this subuniverse is ascertained by *inspection*, and is distinguished by inspection from that of the rest of the universe. The practical procedure to test this hypothesis is as follows: construct new items of two types of content, one type which should belong in the original universe but should not belong to the scalable subuniverse. If the new items designed for the apparently scalable subuniverse do scale, and scale together with the old subset; and if the new items designed not to be in this subuniverse do not scale with the subscale; then the hypothesis is sustained that a subuniverse has been defined and has been found scalable.

MODAL CATEGORIES AND MINIMAL MARGINAL REPRODUCIBILITY [6]

If a coefficient of reproducibility of .90 or greater is obtained with any of the successive score matrices, this constitutes evidence for the scalability of the set of statements. But this is not a *sufficient* condition, for the simple reason that the reproducibility of any single statement can never be less than the frequency present in the modal category. For example, if we had a statement with only two categories of response and found that .9 of the 100 subjects fell in one of the categories, this statement would have as its minimum reproducibility 90 per cent. Thus, it might be possible to have a set of 10 statements, each with just two categories of response, and each with a very high modal frequency, and

[6] The following paragraphs are reprinted, with minor changes in wording, from an article by Edwards and Kilpatrick (1948).

these statements would yield—would have to yield — a very high coefficient of reproducibility. This fact should always be taken into consideration when categories are combined by the method of successive approximations. It may happen that the reduction in error is simply the result of obtaining a larger modal frequency for the various statements.

Obviously, in the case of statements with only two categories of response (agree, disagree), statements for which the response frequencies divide .5 and .5 are valuable in keeping the coefficient of reproducibility from being spuriously high. Similar arguments apply to statements with more than two categories of response: the more evenly distributed the frequencies are in the various categories, the less the possibility of obtaining a spuriously high coefficient of reproducibility. But it should be noted that statements with non-uniform frequencies are also needed in order to obtain a range of scores. With a perfect scale and all statements dividing .5 and .5, only two scores would be possible. This fact will be grasped easily if one thinks of the bar charts for such a set of statements. Although Guttman (1945) recognizes the desirability of including in the original set of statements those which will yield a wide range of marginal frequencies, he fails to suggest how this is to be accomplished. As will be pointed out later, techniques of item analysis and other procedures seem to be called for here.

The minimum coefficient of reproducibility which it is possible to obtain with a given set of statements having known frequencies in each of the categories of response can easily be determined. Simply find the proportion of responses in the modal category for each statement. If these values are then summed and divided by the number of statements, the resulting value indicates the *minimal marginal reproducibility* present for the set of statements.

For the data of Table 7.4, for example, the proportions corresponding to the modal categories are .6, .7, .6, and .8, and the sum of these values is 2.7. Dividing by 4, the number of statements, we have $2.7/4 = .675$ as the value of the minimal marginal reproducibility. The response weights corresponding to the modal categories are 1 0 0 1. If we were now to predict this response pattern for *every* individual in Table 7.4, regardless of total scores, we would have a total of 26 errors and the coefficient of reproducibility would be equal to .675.[7]

The minimal marginal reproducibility of .675 may be compared with the coefficient of reproducibility of .80 that we obtained from the same data to note the improvement in our predictions from knowledge of the total scores. [8]

SCALE AND NON-SCALE TYPES

Even when a coefficient of reproducibility of .90 is obtained with a set of statements and when the minimal marginal reproducibility is not excessively high, these findings alone are not sufficient evidence to conclude that the statements constitute a scale in the sense in which Guttman (1945, 1947*a*) uses the term. If the coefficient of reproducibility is .90, then the remaining 10 per cent error may be the result of (*a*) random errors and/or (*b*) the presence of a second variable other than the one originally defined. The presence or absence of a second variable is determined by examination of the patterns of response of the subjects to find out whether "non-scale types" exist (Guttman, 1945).

The total number of possible types (patterns of response)

[7] This can be verified by reference to Table 7.4.

[8] The limitations and implications of the minimal marginal coefficient are discussed in greater detail by Guttman (1947*a*).

is a function of the number of statements under consideration and the number of response categories for each statement. For 10 statements, each with only two categories of response, the number of types (scale and non-scale) is 1024. This can easily be determined from the fact that either one of two responses to the first statement may be followed by either one of two responses to the second statement, and this in turn may be followed by either one of two responses to the third statement, and so on. We thus have 2^{10} or 1024 possible response patterns, generating scores ranging from 0 to 10. In general, the number of possible types is simply the product of the number of categories of the various statements. By the familiar rules of permutations and combinations, we know that there is only one pattern of response that will result in a score of 10, while there are 10 different ways in which a score of 9 may be obtained, 45 different patterns of response which will yield a score of 8, and so on. But, by Guttman's definition of a scale, there should be one and only one pattern of response for each possible score. Thus with 10 statements, each with only two categories of response, we would have only 11 possible scale types. In general, the number of possible scale types, for any set of statements, may be determined by summing the number of response categories for each of the statements, subtracting the number of statements, and adding unity. Not all possible types, scale or non-scale, will necessarily appear in the sample of individuals under observation.

We may illustrate these procedures with a hypothetical example which, in the interests of simplicity, we shall assume consists of three statements all of which have three categories of response. The number of possible types is $3 \times 3 \times 3 = 27$; the number of scale types would be equal to $3 + 3 + 3 - 3 + 1 = 7$. Let us suppose that the response categories for the statements are "agree," "uncertain," and "disagree." The weights assigned to these categories and the observed proportions in our sample making each of the various responses are the same as those shown in Table 7.5.

Figure 7.2 shows the bar charts corresponding to the data of Table 7.5. The response patterns shown in Figure 7.2 indi-

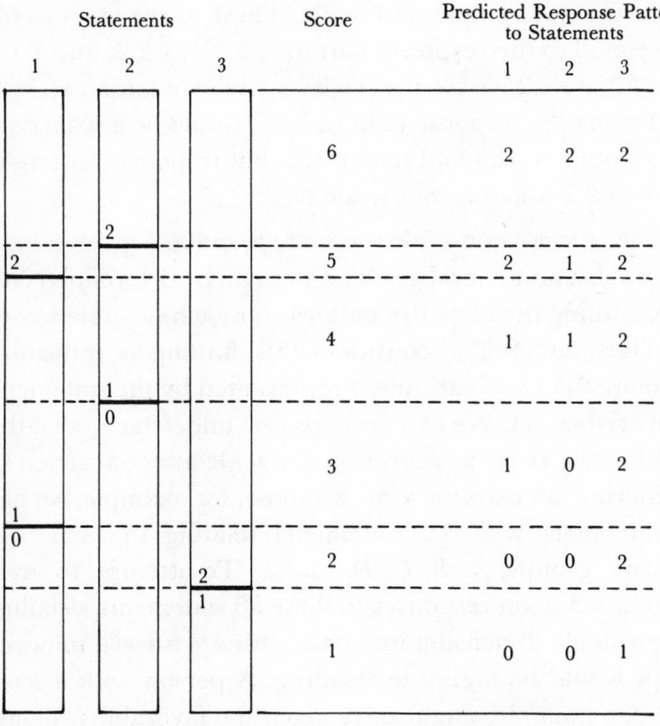

FIG. 7.2—Bar charts for a set of three statements with more than two categories of response. The bar charts are constructed from the data of Table 7.5.

cate the scale types and it is a simple matter to determine the relative frequency of these types for the present sample, assuming perfect scalability. Not all of the seven *possible* scale types need appear in the sample. For example, the scale type corresponding to a score of 0 is missing since no one in the sample fell in the 0 category of Statement 3.

Non-scale types would correspond to possible patterns of response other than those shown in Figure 7.2. For example, there are three ways in which a subject could obtain a score of 5 on the three statement scale. These three ways would correspond to the response patterns: 2 2 1, 1 2 2, and 2 1 2. From Figure 7.2 we see that everyone who obtains a score of 5 by having the response pattern 2 1 2 would be a scale type. Those subjects who had scores of 5, but response patterns of 2 2 1 or 1 2 2 would be non-scale types.

If one or more non-scale types are found in a given sample and in substantial numbers (and this can be determined only by examining the response patterns for each possible score), then Guttman (1947a) considers this finding as indicating that more than one variable is represented by the statements in the original set. We can perhaps best understand what this would mean as far as scores on the scale are concerned by considering an extreme case. Suppose, for example, we had 50 statements with 10 statements relating to each of 5 minority groups, *A*, *B*, *C*, *D*, and *E*. To attempt to treat scores based upon responses to these 50 statements as falling along a single dimension involving attitude toward minority groups would be highly misleading. A person with a score of 20, for example, might have given the favorable response to all of the statements relating to minority groups *A* and *B* and the unfavorable response to the remaining 30 statements relating to minority groups *C*, and *D*, and *E*. Another person with a score of 20 might have given the favorable response to all of the statements relating to groups *D* and *E* and the unfavorable response to all other statements Total scores based upon responses to these 50 statements would be relatively meaningless and definitely not comparable. They would not fall along a single dimension. We would be better off under the above circumstances if we attempted to construct separate scales to measure attitudes toward each of the various minority groups and then found the interrelationships between scores on the separate scales. This, in essence, is what Guttman suggests one should do if one finds that the responses to a given set of statements indicate that more than one variable is represented by the statements. If that is the case, then attempts may be made to develop new scales to measure each of the variables. This would mean, of course, that the universe of content as originally defined is not itself scalable, but that it might be broken up into subuniverses which are scalable (Guttman, 1947a). It is important to note that Guttman (1945) believes the content of the subuniverses must be defined in such a way as to clearly indicate the separation of the sets of statements belonging to each before the separate sets of statements are treated by scale analysis.

QUASI-SCALES

When the patterns of response fail to indicate substantial frequencies for non-scale types, but the coefficient of reproducibility is less than .85, the set of statements is said by Guttman to constitute a quasi-scale.[9] Quasi-scales often have a coefficient of reproducibility that is not much higher than that predicted from the modal categories alone in the manner described previously. In the case of quasi-scales, the scores of subjects are believed to be determined by one major variable and a number of minor variables, the minor

[9] Just what constitutes a "substantial" frequency for a non-scale type is a question that has not as yet been answered. See, for example, Festinger (1947) and Guttman (1945, 1947a).

variables contributing to the error of reproducibility. If the error introduced by the minor variables is random error, then the rank order of the subjects will ordinarily be in terms of the one dominant variable.

QUESTIONS AND PROBLEMS

1. What is meant by a unidimensional scale? How many numbers does it take to locate a person on a unidimensional scale? On a two-dimensional scale? On a three-dimensional scale?

2. Do the methods of scaling described in earlier chapters assume that a unidimensional continuum or scale is involved? Why?

3. If we have five statements with dichotomous scoring, how many possible scale types are there? How many possible scale and non-scale types? If the five statements each had three categories of response, then how many scale types would be possible? How many non-scale types? What is meant by a non-scale type?

4. What does Guttman mean by a cutting point? What rules does he believe must be observed in locating cutting points?

5. What does the coefficient of reproducibility measure?

6. What does Guttman mean by minimal marginal reproducibility?

7. If we have five statements, all with dichotomous response categories, and the proportions of favorable responses for the five statements are .60, .70, .80, .40, and .20, then what are the predicted response patterns for the scale types?

8. What would we expect with a perfect scale of 10 statements, each statement with marginals of .5 and .5? Why do we desire a range of marginals for a Guttman scale?

9. What does Guttman mean by a quasi-scale?

10. Read over the set of 100 statements you used in constructing an equal-appearing interval scale. Select a set of seven statements from this group that you believe to be homogeneous in content. Now, using the data you obtained in developing a summated-rating scale, test the set of seven statements for scalability by means of the Cornell technique.

11. If the reproducibility obtained above is not high, combine response categories and find predicted response patterns using the bar chart method.

REFERENCES AND SUGGESTED READINGS

CLARK, K. E., and KRIEDT, P. H. An application of Guttman's new scaling technique to an attitude questionnaire. *Educ. psychol. Measmt.*, 1948, 8, 215-224.

EDWARDS, A. L. On Guttman's scale analysis. *Educ. psychol. Measmt.*, 1948, 8, 313-318.

————An application of scale analysis in film research. Incidental Report No. 3. Instructional Film Research Program, Pennsylvania State University, 1951.

*————and KILPATRICK, F. P. Scale analysis and the measurement of social attitudes. *Psychometrika*, 1948, 13, 99-114.

*FESTINGER, L. The treatment of qualitative data by "scale analysis." *Psychol. Bull.*, 1947, 44, 149-161.

FORD, R. N. A rapid scoring procedure for scaling attitude questions. *Publ. Opin. Quart.*, 1950, 14, 507-532.

GOODENOUGH, W. H. A technique for scale analysis. *Educ. psychol. Measmt.*, 1944, 4, 179-190.

*GUTTMAN, L. A basis for scaling qualitative data. *Amer. sociol. Rev.*, 1944, 9, 139-150.

————*Questions and answers about scale analysis.* Research Branch, Information and Education Division, Army Service Forces. Report D-2, 1945.

* ————On Festinger's evaluation of scale analysis. *Psychol. Bull.*, 1947a, 44, 451-465.

*———— The Cornell technique for scale and intensity analysis. *Educ. psychol. Measmt.*, 1947b, 7, 247-280.

*————The problem of attitude and opinion measurement. In S. A. Stouffer *et al.*, *Measurement and Prediction*. Princeton, N. J.: Princeton Univ. Press, 1950a. Pp. 46-59.

*————The basis for scalogram analysis. In S. A. Stouffer *et al.*, *Measurement and Prediction*. Princeton, N. J.: Princeton Univ. Press, 1950b. Pp. 60-90.

KAHN, L. H., and BODINE, A. J. Guttman scale analysis by means of IBM equipment. *Educ. psychol. Measmt.*, 1951, 11, 288-314.

LOEVINGER, JANE. The technic of homogeneous tests compared with some aspects of "scale analysis" and factor analysis. *Psychol. Bull.*, 1948, 45, 507-529.

RILEY, MATILDA, W., RILEY, J. W., JR., TOBY, J., *et al. Sociological studies in scale analysis.* New Brunswick, N. J.: Rutgers Univ. Press, 1954.

SUCHMAN, E. A. The scalogram board technique. In S. A. Stouffer *et al., Measurement and Prediction.* Princeton, N. J.: Princeton Univ. Press, 1950. Pp. 91-121.

8

The Scale-Discrimination Technique[1]

One of the troublesome problems confronting an investigator who attempts to construct a scale by following the procedures outlined in Guttman's publications is that of selecting the initial set of statements. Guttman (1945) offers little help at this point, other than to suggest that this is a matter of intuition and experience. This important step, however, should not be left a matter of intuition. On what intuitive basis, for example, did Guttman (1947*b*) select the following 7 statements from the universe of content defined as attitude toward Adamic's book (1945), *A Nation of Nations*, used in one of Guttman's classes?

1. *A Nation of Nations* does a good job of analyzing the ethnic groups in this country.
2. On the whole, *A Nation of Nations* is not as good as most college textbooks.
3. Adamic organizes and presents his material well.
4. As a sociological treatise, Adamic's book does not rate very high.
5. Adamic does not discuss any one group in sufficient detail so that a student can obtain a real insight into problems of ethnic group relations in this country.
6. By providing a panorama of various groups, *A Nation of Nations* lets the student get a good perspective on ethnic group relations in this country.

[1] The following paragraphs are reprinted, with minor changes, from an article by Edwards and Kilpatrick (1948*a*).

201

7. *A Nation of Nations* is good enough to be kept as a textbook for this course.

This set of statements was found to scale. It is conceivable, however, that at least a hundred or more statements could be formulated, all of which would be judged in terms of a priori considerations as belonging to the universe of content as defined by Guttman. To infer, as Guttman (1945, 1947a) would, that *any* set drawn from the universe would scale because this particular set of statements scales is not justifiable. There is no basis for assuming that this particular set is representative of the universe as defined. To argue that these additional statements might be broken up into sets of statements representative of subuniverses, and that these in turn might possibly scale, means also that the universe as originally defined (attitude toward the textbook) is not being tested with the sample set of statements initially selected. The present sample would have to be regarded as a subuniverse from the original universe. And if that is so, then what is the characteristic of the subuniverse at hand that differentiates it from all other possible subuniverses—a characteristic of the subuniverse that Guttman (1945, p. 4) states it must have before it can be tested for scalability? How can this characteristic be defined?

In many respects, it is unfortunate that this problem of initial selection of statements has been relatively ignored. [2] The merits of scalogram analysis, as *a technique for evaluating a set of statements,* are obvious and need no defense. But scalogram analysis can be applied to *any* set of statements, regardless of how the set is selected. It would appear as if the important problem is to be able to select a set of

[2] Later publications by Guttman (1950a, 1950b), than those cited above, indicate that the problem of initial statement selection is still considered to be primarily a matter of intuition.

statements, in advance of applying the technique of scalogram analysis, that one may with some hope count upon to meet the requirements of a Guttman scale. It is true, as Guttman (1945, p. 10) says, "Item analysis is not adequate to test for the existence of scales in the sense of reproducibility from a single variable," but it is also true that scalogram analysis is not adequate for the problem of initial statement selection. Guttman (1947a) has not solved this problem by suggesting that we look for statements with a homogeneous content. Item analysis and the scaling of statements by the method of equal-appearing or successive intervals have something to contribute at this point and scalogram analysis plays its part *after* the initial statement selection.

CUTTING POINTS FOR THURSTONE STATEMENTS

Assume that we have a scale in which the *latent variable* attitude increases in degree of favorability toward some psychological object from left to right as in Figure 8.1. On the vertical axis we have scaled the probability that a response assigned a weight of 1, that is, a favorable response, will be made to a given statement. Then we know that the operating characteristic, if the statement belongs in a set meeting the requirements of a Guttman scale, must be such that the probability of the occurrence of a favorable response is 0 up to a given point on the horizontal scale and then 1 from that point on. This is the model for an ideal statement (*a*) in a perfect or ideal Guttman scale as shown in the figure.

It is not too difficult to believe that, for a given statement, one might find, instead of a jump from 0 probability to a probability of 1, that a favorable response will occur at a given point on the attitude continuum, that the probability

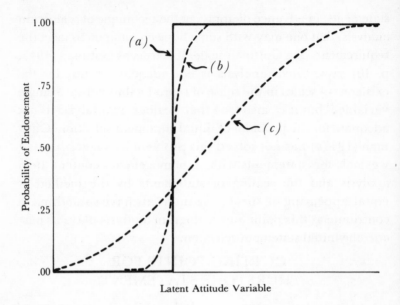

FIG. 8.1—Theoretical operating characteristics of various attitude statements. The operating characteristic for (*a*) represents an ideal statement in a Guttman scale. The operating characteristic for (*b*) shows a sharply increasing probability of endorsement over a narrow interval on the latent attitude continuum and that for (*c*) a gradually increasing probability of endorsement over the entire continuum.

increases sharply but *continuously* within a narrow interval or range on the attitude continuum, as indicated by the curve for a statement such as (*b*) shown in Figure 8.1. Statements with operating characteristics of this kind would, of course, contribute to the error of reproducibility in a scalogram analysis, but not to the extent that a statement such as (*c*) would, with its gradually increasing probability of a favorable response with increasing values of the latent attribute.

Recalling that in the Thurstone technique of scale construction, statements are scaled along a continuum ranging from "extremely unfavorable," through "neutral," to "extremely favorable," it is a logical conclusion that the frequency or probability of endorsement of statements located along the continuum is related to the scale values of the statements, assuming a normal distribution of attitudes. This assumption has nothing to do with the *test of scalability*. The same metric that Guttman uses will apply to these statements, if they prove to be scalable in his sense of the term. It does mean however, that for statements scaled at the two extremes of the continuum, and permitting only an "agree" or "disagree" response, we would expect the modal frequencies of the statements to be high and, as we move in toward the center of the continuum, we would expect the frequencies to be distributed more evenly between the two categories of response. This, if true, would provide us some assurance that we would have a spread of marginals and also, through the inclusion of some statements with a .5 and .5 division of response, a rigorous test of scalability.

There are, however, at least three difficulties with this argument as it stands. One is that if the distribution of attitudes is not normal over the entire Thurstone continuum—if we have a very homogeneous group, for example, one that is strongly opposed to, let us say, capital punishment—then we would expect the majority of the subjects to disagree with statements that are scaled as favorable to capital punishment and the same subjects to agree with statements that are scaled as unfavorable to capital punishment. Thus the modal frequencies for all statements will be quite high and the coefficient of reproducibility might not be much larger than that established as the minimum possible, that is, not much larger than the average of the modal categories of the statements.

A second difficulty is that we would expect the "neutral"

statements to be quite poor, in the sense of not showing clear cutting points. Edwards (1946), for example, has expressed his belief that the "neutral" or middle categories of the Thurstone continuum may function as a kind of catch-all in the judging procedure. He provides evidence to indicate that not only the more ambiguous and irrelevant statements tend to be sorted into the middle categories, but also that statements indicating a state of indifference or apathy and ambivalence tend to be placed there. Using the Thurstone and Chave (1929) criterion of irrelevance, Edwards investigated 20 "neutral" statements from various scales constructed by the method of equal-appearing intervals. The criterion of irrelevance for these 20 statements indicated that for most of them the operating characteristic was that of a straight line with almost zero slope. Thus the probability of endorsement of a Thurstone statement with a "neutral" scale value would seem to be much the same for those with attitudes properly scaled at opposite extremes of the psychological continuum. Because of the probable overlap in the responses to these statements of those with high and those with low rank-order scores, responses to these statements will not be reproducible from the rank-order scores. "Neutral" statements, in other words, may be expected to contribute greatly to error, and the coefficient of reproducibility will be decreased accordingly.

Still a third difficulty is the fact that not all statements with the same scale values on the Thurstone continuum are equally discriminating. We have frequently found that statements falling within the same scale interval and with comparable Q values still differ tremendously in their power to differentiate between high and low criterion groups. The hypothesis that the cutting point of a statement is related to the Thurstone scale value of the statement, within the limitations noted, however, is an interesting one to consider.

AN EMPIRICAL TEST OF THE SCALABILITY OF STATEMENTS IN THURSTONE SCALES

Responses of 44 subjects on the Peterson (1931) scale measuring "Attitude Toward Capital Punishment" and the responses of 55 subjects on the Thurstone (1931) scale measuring "Attitude Toward Communism" were available for a preliminary analysis. Both of these scales were constructed using the method of equal-appearing intervals. Papers for these subjects were rescored, for purposes of scalogram analysis, by scoring "disagree" as 1, "?" as 2, and "agree" as 3 in the case of statements scaled at the favorable end of the continuum and assigning reverse weights for statements at the unfavorable end of the continuum. Only the 12 statements with scale values outside the "neutral" section of the continuum were used in these two tests. When the response categories were dichotomized by successive approximations, the coefficients of reproducibility were .86 for the "Capital Punishment" scale and .91 for the "Communism" scale.

In another test, 10 statements were selected from the "Capital Punishment" scale by taking every second statement in order of their scale values on the psychological continuum. Thus, statements ranging from the lowest scale value, through "neutral," to the highest scale value were used. The papers were rescored in the manner indicated above, but, as might be expected, the "neutral" statements (scale values of 5.3 and 5.7) failed to show any clear relationship to the rank-order scores, and cutting points could not be established for them. When these two "neutral" statements were eliminated, and the papers were rescored and retested by means of scalogram analysis, the coefficient of reproducibility was .91.

On the basis of these preliminary findings, the Thurstone

statements were tested with a new and larger sample. The 12 statements with the most extreme scale values (both high and low) from the "Communism" scale and the 12 statements with extreme scale values from the "Capital Punishment" scale were selected for investigation. These two sets of statements were given to 159 subjects and scores obtained by the method described earlier. The coefficient of reproducibility for the "Capital Punishment" scale was .88 and for the "Communism" scale, the coefficient of reproducibility was .92. The range of the modal frequencies, however, for the "Capital Punishment" scale (all dichotomous statements) was from .65 to .93 with a mean value of .82. The range for the 12 statements from the "Communism" scale was from .81 to .95 with a mean value of .89. Consequently, the obtained coefficients of reproducibility do not represent any great increase over the minimum values set by the modal frequencies. The difficulty here is as pointed out earlier: the subjects were all opposed to communism and capital punishment. We need more statements with lower modal frequencies.

THE SCALABILITY OF STATEMENTS IN SUMMATED-RATING SCALES

Since statements in scales constructed by the method of summated ratings are selected on the basis of their ability to differentiate between individuals with high and individuals with low total scores, it should follow that these statements will tend to minimize overlap between the responses of those with high and those with low rank-order scores. And since it has been established by Ferguson (1941) and Edwards (1946) that Likert-selected statements tend to be those falling outside the "neutral" section of the Thurstone scale continuum, by testing a set of Likert statements in terms of scalogram analysis, we shall essentially be testing a set of Thurstone statements with high and low scale values, and also with proved discriminating power.

The 12 most discriminating statements from a Likert scale designed to measure "Attitude Toward Labor Unions" [3] were rescored for a set of 56 papers and the data recorded in a table for scalogram analysis. The obtained coefficient of reproducibility was .86. The range of the modal categories for the 12 statements, all with but two categories of response was from .50 to .91 with a mean value of .65. The obtained coefficient of reproducibility, .86, represents a substantial increase over the lower limit of .65.[4]

On a second test, the responses of 56 subjects on the 8 most discriminating statements from a 21-statement Likert scale designed to measure "Attitude Toward Radio" [5] were rescored and recorded in a table for scale analysis. The obtained coefficient of reproducibility for these 8 statements was .90. The range of the modal categories for the 8 statements, all with but two categories of response, was from .68 to .95 with a mean of .81. For purposes of comparison, the 8 least discriminating statements from the 21 radio statements were also selected and tested for scalability. This time no discernible pattern appeared even after the categories of response had been reduced to dichotomies. It proved impossible to draw meaningful cutting points for these statements and the coefficient of reproducibility was not computed.

[3] This scale was constructed by Clemans, Knaack, Shenkel, and Sines (1948).

[4] A 22-statement scale constructed by Rundquist and Sletto (1936) using the method of summated ratings was investigated for its scalability by Clark and Kriedt (1948). They report, for dichotomous response categories, coefficients of reproducibility of .79 and .80 for two separate samples. See also the study by Kriedt and Clark (1949) in which they compared reproducibility coefficients for sets of items selected in various ways.

[5] This scale was constructed by Powers, Provo, and Jones (1947).

THE SCALE-DISCRIMINATION TECHNIQUE

On the basis of the preliminary studies described above, Edwards and Kilpatrick (1948*b*) devised a method for constructing attitude scales which they call the scale-discrimination technique. In developing their technique, they proceeded on the assumption that a combination of scaling and item analysis procedures would enable one to select a relatively small set of attitude statements from a larger number of available statements such that the set selected would also have a good chance of meeting the requirements of a Guttman scale.

The initial steps in the scale-discrimination method are similar to those followed in constructing scales by the method of equal-appearing or successive intervals. A large number of attitude statements relating to the psychological object of interest are first collected and then edited in accordance with criteria previously described.

Obtaining Scale and Q Values

The statements are then given to a group of judges with instructions to judge the degree of favorableness of each statement in terms of 9 or 11 intervals or categories Any of the procedures previously described for obtaining equal-appearing or successive interval judgments can be used. Since the validity of the assumption of equal-appearing intervals is not vital to the scale-discrimination technique, the scale values of the various statements can be conveniently obtained as in the method of equal-appearing intervals. For each statement a Q value is also obtained.

The statements are then plotted in a two-way table according to the scale and Q values, the scale values being plotted on the baseline and the Q values on the vertical axis. The median of the Q values for all statements is found and a horizontal line is drawn through the two-way table at the median Q value. All statements with Q values above this line are rejected and all those below retained for further analysis. This step amounts to eliminating the 50 per cent of the statements that show the greatest degree of spread of judgments on the psychological continuum.

Obtaining Summated-Rating Responses

The remaining 50 per cent of the statements are then prepared in the form of a Likert or method of summated-rating scale. Each statement in this form is followed by various categories of response. Edwards and Kilpatrick used six categories (strongly agree, agree, mildly agree, mildly disagree, disagree, strongly disagree) but fewer categories could also be used. The statements in this form are then given to a new group of 200 to 300 subjects who are asked to use the response categories provided to indicate their own agreement or disagreement with each of the statements.

The responses of the subjects are scored in terms of the method of summated ratings, with weights of 0 through 5 being assigned to the six response categories. These weights are assigned to the response categories so that the largest weight is always given to the response category that indicates the most favorable attitude. The direction of the weights for each statement can be determined easily from the location of the statements on the Thurstone equal-appearing interval continuum. For each subject, a total score is obtained, based upon his responses to all of the statements.

Each statement is now subjected to some form of item analysis. Edwards and Kilpatrick selected the top and bottom 27 per cent of the subjects in terms of total scores on the statements. We can call the top group a "high" group and the bottom group a "low" group in terms of total scores. For each statement a distribution is obtained showing the frequency for each response category for the high and low groups. In Table 8.1 we show such a distribution for a low group of 100 subjects and a high group of 100 subjects.

TABLE 8.1

The distribution of responses to an attitude statement for a low group and a high group

RESPONSE CATEGORIES	WEIGHTS	LOW GROUP	HIGH GROUP
		f	f
Strongly agree	5	3	38
Agree	4	5	42
Mildly agree	3	8	15
Mildly disagree	2	26	2
Disagree	1	36	2
Strongly disagree	0	22	1
n		100	100

Dichotomizing Response Categories

Edwards and Kilpatrick believed that it would eventually be necessary to dichotomize the response categories of statements, regardless of the particular set of statements they selected to test by means of scalogram analysis. In order to avoid some of the difficulties encountered in combining categories at the time one actually is involved with a scalogram analysis, [6] they proceeded to dichotomize the response categories at this stage in the procedure. The particular response categories to be combined can easily be determined from the statement distributions as shown in Table 8.1.

The rule followed in combining response categories at this

---

[6] See, for example, the study by Clark and Kriedt (1948).

stage is to draw a line between the response categories, as shown in Table 8.1, so as to *minimize the total number of subjects in the low group above the line and the number of subjects in the high group below the line.* For example, if the line were drawn between response categories 5 and 4, we would have 3 subjects in the low group above the line and $42 + 15 + 2 + 2 + 1 = 62$ subjects in the high group below the line, giving a total of 65. If the line were drawn between response categories 4 and 3, then we would have $3 + 5 = 8$ subjects in the low group above the line and $15 + 2 + 2 + 1 = 20$ subjects in the high group below the line, giving a total of 28. Moving the line down between response categories 3 and 2 would give $3 + 5 + 8 = 16$ subjects in the low group above the line and $2 + 2 + 1 = 5$ subjects in the high group below the line, for a total of 21. It is obvious, from the table, that moving the line down between response categories 2 and 1 or between 1 and 0 would give us a larger total than 21. For this particular statement, then, the line would be drawn between response categories 2 and 3. This means that *if this statement is retained in the set to be tested for scalability,* the scoring weights would be 1 for response categories previously weighted 5, 4, and 3, and 0 for response categories previously weighted 2, 1, and 0.

In the same manner the response categories for all other statements are dichotomized. The entire procedure can be summarized in terms of Table 8.2. We say that regardless of how many response categories we have to begin with, the horizontal line should be drawn in Table 8.2 so as to minimize the frequencies in cells $a + d$ of the table.

Finding the Discriminating Power of the Statements

We now require, for each statement, a coefficient that will represent the discriminating power of the statement. Edwards

TABLE 8.2

Schematic representation for dichotomizing response categories when more than two categories of response are permitted

Response Categories	Low Group	High Group	Total
	a	b	$a + b$
	c	d	$c + d$
Total	$a + c$	$b + d$	

and Kilpatrick used, primarily because of its simplicity, the *phi coefficient*. Calculation of the phi coefficient $r\phi$ can be expressed in terms of the notation of Table 8.2. Thus

$$r\phi = \frac{bc - ad}{\sqrt{(a + b)\ (b + d)\ (a + c)\ (c + d)}} \tag{8.1}$$

Substituting in the above formula with the data from Table 8.1, we obtain

$$r\phi = \frac{(95)\ (84) - (16)\ (5)}{\sqrt{(111)\ (100)\ (100)\ (89)}} = .79$$

It is not actually necessary to make the calculations shown in formula (8.1) for the phi coefficient. The nomographs prepared by Guilford (1941) or the tables prepared by Jurgensen (1947) enable one to obtain values of the phi coefficient very quickly and conveniently without detailed calculations.

Selection of Statements for the Scale

Once phi coefficients have been obtained for each statement, the statements are then plotted in a new two-way table in which the Thurstone scale values are on the horizontal axis and the values of the phi coefficient on the vertical axis. Edwards and Kilpatrick divided the nine-interval Thurstone continuum into half-scale intervals. Only 7 of these half-intervals contained statements and Edwards and Kilpatrick selected the 4 statements with the highest phi coefficients from each of these half-scale intervals, obtaining a total of 28 statements. [7] It would of course be possible to divide the Thurstone scale continuum into larger or smaller intervals and to select statements with the highest phi values from within these intervals. The widths of the intervals to be used will depend, in any particular case, upon the distribution of Thurstone scale values of the statements, upon the number of available statements, and upon the number of statements desired for the attitude scale.

The 28 statements were then arranged in rank order of their Thurstone scale values, from most to least favorable, and two forms of an attitude scale devised by assigning statements with alternate scale values to the two forms. These scales thus consisted of 14 statements each. For Forms A and B, respectively, the mean scale values of the 14 statements were 3.85 and 3.91; the mean Q values were .90 and .92. The phi coefficients for the statements in Form A ranged from .58 to .78, with a median value of .65. For Form B the range of the phi coefficients was from .58 to .76, with a median value of .66.

The two forms of the scale were then given to a new group of subjects. These subjects were instructed to indicate

[7] The intervals actually involved were those from .5 to 2.5 and from 6.5 to 8.0 on the Thurstone continuum. The interval 4.0 to 5.0 contained statements, but none were selected from this interval for reasons which were relevant to the particular research of Edwards and Kilpatrick but which are not pertinent to the procedure described here.

their agreement or disagreement with each statement in terms of the original six response categories. Scores on these scales were obtained using the dichotomized response categories with weights of 0 and 1 established previously. Applying scalogram analysis separately to each of the two sets of 14 statements, a coefficient of reproducibility of .875 was obtained for Form A and a coefficient of reproducibility of .872 for Form B. The range of the modal response categories for the 14 statements in Form A was from .51 to .82, with a mean value of .57. For Form B, the range of the modal response categories was from .52 to .67 with a mean value of .57.

ADVANTAGES CLAIMED FOR THE SCALE-DISCRIMINATION TECHNIQUE

In summarizing their research, Edwards and Kilpatrick (1948*b*, pp. 382-383) state:

The method of scale construction described in this paper has been called the scale-discrimination method because it makes use of Thurstone's scaling procedure and retains Likert's procedure for evaluating the discriminatory power of the individual items. Furthermore, the items selected by the scale-discrimination method have been shown, in the case described, to yield satisfactory coefficients of reproducibility and to meet the requirements of Guttman's scale analysis. The scale-discrimination method is essentially a synthesis of the methods of item evaluation of Thurstone, Likert, and Guttman. It also possesses certain advantages which are not present in any of these methods considered separately.

The scale-discrimination method, for example, eliminates the least discriminating items in a large sample, which Thurstone's method alone fails to do. The unsolved problem in the Thurstone procedure is to select from within each scale interval the most discriminating items. Items within any one scale interval may show a high degree of variability with respect to a measure of discrimination. For example, we found within a single interval, items with phi values ranging from .24 to .78. That Thurstone's criterion of Q does not aid materially in the matter of selecting discriminating items is indicated by the plot of phi values against Q values, *after* the 50 per cent of the items with the highest Q values had already been rejected. Under this condition, items with Q values from 1.00 to 1.09 had phi coefficients ranging from .32 to .76. Thurstone's method also, by the inclusion of "neutral" items, tends to lower reliability and to decrease reproducibility of the set of items finally selected.

Thus when selecting items by Thurstone's technique alone, we have no basis for making a choice between items with comparable scale and Q values, and yet these items are not equally valuable in the measurement of attitude. By having available some measure of the discriminatory power of the items, the choice becomes objective as well as advantageous as far as the scale itself is concerned.

The advantage of the scale-discrimination method over the Guttman procedure lies essentially in the fact that we have provided an objective basis for the selection of a set of items which are then tested for scalability. It may happen that the scale-discrimination method will not always yield a set of items with a satisfactory coefficient of reproducibility. But this is not an objection to the technique any more than the fact that not always will a set of intuitively selected items scale. Rather, it seems that the scale-discrimination method offers greater assurance of scalability than any intuitive technique such as applied by Guttman. Furthermore, the set of items selected by the scale discrimination technique provides a wider range of content than do the intuitive Guttman items. In the scale-discrimination method, we obtain items which are not essentially multiple phrasings of the same question as is often true when the selection of a set of items to be tested for scalability is left to the experience of the investigator (Festinger, 1947).[8]

QUESTIONS AND PROBLEMS

1. Using the data previously obtained by the method of equal-appearing intervals and the method of summated ratings for your 100 attitude statements, construct a scale of 12 items using the scale-discrimination technique. Give this scale to a new group of 100

---

[8] Since publication of this article by Edwards and Kilpatrick, the scale-discrimination technique has been used in constructing scales to measure attitude toward local government and also attitude toward compulsory health insurance. In both cases, satisfactory coefficients of reproducibility were obtained for the statements selected by the procedures described.

subjects and test the statements for scalability. Find the coefficient of reproducibility and the minimal marginal reproducibility.

2. Why might we expect difficulty in locating cutting points for statements falling in the "neutral" section of the equal-appearing interval continuum?

3. What arguments might be advanced in favor of the hypothesis that the cutting point of a statement is related to the scale value of the statement on the equal-appearing interval continuum? What arguments might be advanced against this hypothesis?

4. What are the advantages claimed by Edwards and Kilpatrick for the scale-discrimination technique of constructing attitude scales?

5. In general, what might we expect to be true with respect to the equal-appearing interval scale values of statements included in a scale constructed by the method of summated ratings?

6. Why might we expect that statements found to discriminate between groups with favorable and unfavorable attitudes would tend to have relatively little error of reproducibility compared with statements that fail to differentiate between the two groups?

REFERENCES AND SUGGESTED READINGS

ADAMIC, L. *A nation of nations*. New York: Harper, 1945.

*CLARK, K. E., and KRIEDT, P. H. An application of Guttman's new scaling techniques to an attitude questionnaire. *Educ. psychol. Measmt.*, 1948, 8, 215-224.

CLEMANS, W., KNAACK, W., SHENKEL, W., and SINES, H. *Attitude toward labor unions*. Seattle: Univ. of Washington, 1948.

EDWARDS, A. L. A critique of "neutral items" in attitude scales constructed by the method of equal-appearing intervals. *Psychol. Rev.*, 1946, 53, 159-169.

―――― and KILPATRICK, F. P. Scale analysis and the measurement of social attitudes. *Psychometrika*, 1948a, 13, 99-114.

*―――― and KILPATRICK, F. P. A technique for the construction of attitude scales. *J. appl. Psychol.*, 1948b, 32, 374-384.

FERGUSON, L. W. A study of the Likert technique of attitude scale construction *J. soc. Psychol.*, 1941, 13, 51-57.

FESTINGER, L. The treatment of qualitative data by "scale analysis." *Psychol. Bull.*, 1947, 44, 149-161.

GUILFORD, J. P. The phi coefficient and chi square as indices of item validity. *Psychometrika*, 1941, 6, 11-19.

GUTTMAN, L. *Questions and answers about scale analysis.* Research Branch, Information and Education Division, Army Service Forces. Report D-2, 1945.

GUTTMAN, L. On Festinger's evaluation of scale analysis. *Psychol. Bull.,* 1947a, 44, 451-465.

—— The Cornell technique for scale and intensity analysis. *Educ. psychol. Measmt.,* 1947b, 7, 247-280.

—— The problem of attitude and opinion measurement. In S. A. Stouffer *et al., Measurement and prediction.* Princeton, N. J.: Princeton Univ. Press, 1950a, 46-59.

—— The basis for scalogram analysis. In S. A. Stouffer *et al., Measurement and prediction.* Princeton, N. J.: Princeton Univ. Press, 1950b, 60-90.

JURGENSEN, C. E. Table for determining phi coefficients. *Psychometrika,* 1947, 2, 17-29.

*KRIEDT, P. H., and CLARK, K. E. "Item analysis" versus "scale analysis." *J. appl.Psychol.,* 1949, 33, 114-121.

PETERSON, RUTH C. *Attitude toward capital punishment.* Chicago: Univ. Chicago Press, 1931.

POWERS, PATRICIA, PROVO, F., and JONES, L. V. *Attitude toward radio.* Seattle: Univ. Washington, 1947.

9

The Improvement of Cumulative Scales

The scale-discrimination technique, described in the previous chapter, had as its objective the selection of a relatively small set of statements from a much larger number of available statements in such a way that the set selected would meet the requirements of a Guttman scale. As was pointed out at the time this technique was described, it cannot provide definite assurance that the obtained set of statements will, in fact, meet the test of scalability. Suppose, for example, we have obtained a set of 10 statements and that the observed coefficient of reproducibility is only 80. Is there any way in which we might improve the scalability of this set of statements?

One procedure that suggests itself is to examine the individual statements to determine whether error of reproducibility is due primarily to only one or a few statements. If these statements are eliminated, we might expect improvement in the coefficient of reproducibility. This improvement, of course, would be obtained at the expense of reducing the number of possible scale types or scores. We might, however, be more satisfied with a smaller number of scores on a scale that better meets the requirements of a cumulative scale than a larger number of scores from a scale that is somewhat less than perfect in this respect.

It should be emphasized that if the set of statements

selected by the scale-discrimination technique to be tested for scalability is relatively large, then some attention must be given to the spacing of the marginals, that is, the proportions giving the favorable response to the various statements. We can see why this is so by examining the marginals for a given pair of statements.

MARGINALS AND THE STABILITY OF RESPONSE PATTERNS

Suppose that we have two statements with dichotomous response categories. For the first statement, we have the proportion giving the favorable or 1 response in a sample of 100 as .50 and for the second statement the proportion giving the favorable or 1 response is .55. We know that the predicted response pattern for a score of 2 will have to be 1 1 and for a score of 0 it will have to be 0 0, since that is the only way in which these two scores can occur. It is the predicted response pattern for a score of 1 that is of interest and we know that this score could occur with a response pattern of either 0 1 or 1 0 to the statements. The bar charts of Figure 9.1 indicate that we should predict a response pattern of 0 1 for everyone with a score of 1. How confident can we be that this is the true scale pattern for a score of 1? If, for example, we were to take another sample of 100 subjects, do we have any assurance that the predicted response pattern obtained from this sample would also be 0 1 rather than 1 0 for those with a score of 1?

Let us assume that in the first sample we have 5 individuals with the response pattern 1 0. In Table 9.1 we have a two-way table showing the frequency corresponding to each of the possible response patterns. Knowing that the cell entry corresponding to response pattern 1 0 is 5, the other cell

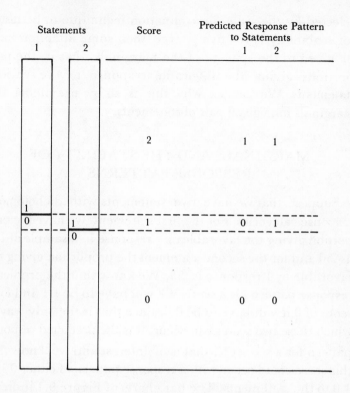

FIG. 9.1—Predicted response patterns for two statements with .50 of the subjects giving the favorable response to Statement 1 and .55 giving the favorable response to Statement 2.

entries can then be obtained by subtraction from the marginal totals. Now, if in a second sample the pattern 0 1 for those with a score of 1 is not to be reversed, then it will also have to be true that the proportion giving the 1 response to Statement 2 will have to be greater than the proportion giving the 1 response to Statement 1. If this is not the case, then it is obvious from an examination of the bar charts of Figure 9.1 that the predicted response pattern for those with a score of

1 would now be 1 0 for this second sample rather than 0 1 as we observed with the first sample.

We can use a χ^2 test to determine the significance of the difference between the frequency of favorable responses to Statement 1 and Statement 2.[1] Thus

$$\chi^2 = \frac{(|d - a| - 1)^2}{d + a} \qquad (9.1)$$

where $d =$ the frequency with the response pattern 0 1 and

TABLE 9.1

A 2×2 table with the cell entries showing the frequency with which each of four possible patterns of response occur for two attitude statements. $N = 100$

STATEMENT 1		STATEMENT 2 WEIGHTS		TOTAL
		0	1	
Weights	1	5	45	50
	0	40	10	50
Total		45	55	100

$a =$ the frequency with the response pattern 1 0. These frequencies are given in Table 9.1.

Substituting in the above formula with the data of Table 9.1, we have

$$\chi^2 = \frac{(|10 - 5| - 1)^2}{10 + 5} = 1.1$$

with 1 degree of freedom. This is not a significant value and

[1] The χ^2 test appropriate for the data of Table 9.1 is discussed in detail by Edwards (1950, pp. 89-90).

the null hypothesis that the frequency of favorable responses given to the two statements is not significantly different would be regarded as tenable. Thus we have no reliable evidence to indicate that in subsequent samples we can expect the number of favorable responses to Statement 2 to exceed those to Statement 1. This, in turn, means that we would have little confidence in regarding the pattern of response 0 1 as the true pattern corresponding to scale types with scores of 1 on the two statements.

Let us suppose now that in the first sample the frequency of favorable responses was 70 instead of 50 to Statement 2, and that we still have 5 subjects with response patterns of 1 0.

TABLE 9.2

A 2 × 2 table with the cell entries showing the frequency with which each of four possible patterns of response occur for two attitude statements. $N = 100$

STATEMENT 1		STATEMENT 2		TOTAL
		WEIGHTS		
		0	1	
WEIGHTS	1	5	45	50
	0	25	25	50
Total		30	70	100

Then the two-way table for these data would be as shown in Table 9.2. If we now compute χ^2, as given by formula (9.1), we have

$$\chi^2 = \frac{(|25 - 5| - 1)^2}{25 + 5} = 12.0$$

and this is a highly significant value for 1 degree of freedom. With these data we have a great deal of confidence that the proportion giving the favorable response to Statement 2 is greater than the proportion giving the favorable response to Statement 1 and that this result will not be reversed in subsequent samples.

We consider still a third case. Let us suppose that the proportions giving the favorable response to the two statements remain the same as in Table 9.1, but that we test the two statements for scalability with a sample of 200 instead of 100 subjects. We again assume that the frequency for response pattern 1 0 is 5. The two-way table for the data would be as shown in Table 9.3. Substituting in the formula for χ^2 with the data of Table 9.3, we obtain

$$\chi^2 = \frac{(|15 - 5| - 1)^2}{15 + 5} = 4.0$$

and this is a significant value ($P < .05$) for 1 degree of freedom. In this instance also we would have good reason to believe that the proportion of favorable responses to Statement 2 would exceed the proportion of favorable responses to Statement 1 in subsequent samples.

These rather simple cases illustrate several important points with respect to scalogram analysis. The data of Table 9.1 and our χ^2 test indicate that if the difference in the proportion of favorable responses to the two statements is not large, and if we use only 100 subjects to test for scalability, then we can have little confidence that the scoring pattern may not be reversed in subsequent samples. Similarly, the χ^2 test for the data of Table 9.2 indicates that large differences in the proportion of favorable responses will tend to give stable predicted response patterns, that is, that the predicted response pattern may be expected to remain the same with subsequent samplings.

If relatively small differences in the proportion of favorable responses to two statements are observed, then Table 9.3 and the χ^2 test for the data of this table indicate that we shall have to use a much larger number of subjects than the usual 100 in order to have confidence that the predicted response pattern will not shift in subsequent samples.

TABLE 9.3

A 2 × 2 table with the cell entries showing the frequency with which each of four possible patterns of response occur for two attitude statements. $N = 200$

STATEMENT 1		STATEMENT 2 WEIGHTS		TOTAL
		1	0	
Weights	1	5	95	100
	0	85	15	100
Total		90	110	200

Evidently, then, in testing a set of statements for scalability, we desire not only a range of marginals, but also that, insofar as possible, the marginals, or proportions giving the favorable response, be widely spaced. Obviously, however, as we increase the number of statements, the spacings or differences in the proportion of favorable responses to the statements must of necessity decrease, since we have only a limited scale from, say, .10 to .90 for the proportions. With nine statements, equally spaced, so that the proportions of favorable responses are .9, .8, .7, .6, .5, .4, .3, .2, and .1, the difference in the proportion of favorable responses between any two adjacent statements would be .1. This, of course, would be an ideal case, and it is not likely that for any sample set of statements we would find the marginals so nicely spaced. Yet, as we have seen, the closer together two marginals are, that is, the smaller the difference in the proportion of favorable responses to two statements, the less confidence we can have in the stability of the predicted response pattern to these statements. And, as we increase the number of statements in the set to be tested for scalability, it is inevitable that the differences in the marginals will decrease. In this situation, a much larger number of subjects than the usual 100 will be necessary in order to determine stable response patterns for the scale types. If we do use only 100 subjects in the test for scalability, then the predicted response patterns should be checked with a second sample to determine whether or not the results we first obtained can be considered stable.

H-TECHNIQUE [2]

It is clear from the above discussion that if we are to use a relatively small number of subjects in testing a set of statements for scalability, and if we are to guard against possible reversals in the scoring patterns for scale types, then the marginals should be widely spaced. And yet, if the marginals are to be widely spaced, then we, in turn, must be limited to a relatively small number of statements, and a consequent reduction in the number of scale types. On the other hand, if we have responses to a larger number of statements available, it might be desirable to find some way

[2] It is believed that the procedure to be described was called H-technique because those responsible for the development of the technique were located at Harvard University. For the same reason, the Cornell technique of scalogram analysis, described in Chapter 7, is sometimes referred to as C-technique.

in which we can utilize this information. Could we not, for example, reduce the number of scale patterns without the necessity of discarding statements? H-technique, as developed by Stouffer, Borgatta, Hays, and Henry (1952), was devised to solve this particular problem. [3]

Instead of necessarily eliminating statements, H-technique converts the responses to two or more statements into a response to a "new" statement that is called a *contrived* statement. Thus, for example, the responses to a set of 12 statements might be combined in such a way as to yield a smaller number of new responses to a set of contrived statements. If the set of 12 statements results in only 4 contrived statements, then we have a corresponding reduction in the possible number of scale types from 13 to 5, but with perhaps a substantial improvement in the scalability of the contrived statements over the original set.

We shall describe the steps in H-technique, showing the method by which contrived statements are formed, using illustrative data from Stouffer, Borgatta, Hays, and Henry (1952). These investigators gave an 11-statement scale to 633 Air Force officers. The scale was designed to measure "sensitivity to sanctions." Four response categories were used with each statement, with weights of 1, 2, 3, and 4. The 1 weight was assigned to the response category indicating "the most independence from pressure," and the 4 weight to that indicating the least. [4]

Using a method of summated-rating scoring system, total scores were obtained for each subject by summing the weights assigned to the responses to the individual statements. The

---

[3] The article by Stouffer, Borgatta, Hays, and Henry (1952) is also reprinted in Riley, Riley, and Toby (1954).

[4] Weights of 0, 1, 2, and 3, could, of course, have been used instead of weights of 1, 2, 3, and 4.

possible range of scores was thus from 11 to 44. A frequency distribution for these total scores was then obtained and the distribution was divided into class intervals such that approximately 10 per cent of the subjects fell within each class interval.

CUTTING POINTS

The distribution of the total scores was then obtained separately for each statement and for each of the four response categories of the statement. The distribution for Statement 1 is shown in Table 9.4. We now consider all possible dichoto-

TABLE 9.4

Response to Statement 1 as related to total scores*

| | RESPONSE CATEGORIES | | | | |
TOTAL SCORES	1	2	3	4	TOTAL
43 - 44				46	46
39 - 42			18	23	41
35 - 38	1	4	38	29	72
33 - 34		3	59	7	69
30 - 32		25	42	5	72
28 - 29		43	25	1	69
26 - 27	4	40	21	2	67
24 - 25	3	48	6	1	58
21 - 23	11	59	4		74
11 - 20	33	30	2		65
Total	52	252	215	114	633

*Reproduced from Stouffer, Borgatta, Hays, and Henry (1952), Table 4, p. 286.

mous combinations of the adjacent response categories for this statement. Thus, for Table 9.4, we could have (1) (2, 3, 4), (1, 2) (3, 4), and (1, 2, 3) (4), and similar combinations could be formed for all other statements.

We consider for the moment only the combination (1)

TABLE 9.5

A 2 × 2 table for the data of Table 9.4 with response categories 2, 3, and 4 combined and with a cutting point located between scores 20 and 21

| TOTAL SCORES | RESPONSE CATEGORIES | | TOTAL |
	(1)	(2, 3, 4)	
21 and above	19	549	568
20 and below	33	32	65
Total	52	581	633

(2, 3, 4). Can we now draw a line (a *cutting point*) in the distribution of total scores to form a 2 x 2 table such that *neither "error" cell has a higher frequency than the smaller of the two frequencies on the principal diagonal?* The "error" cells are the upper-left and the lower-right cells of the 2 x 2 table. The

TABLE 9.6

A 2 × 2 table for the data of Table 9.4 with response categories 1 and 2 combined and response categories 3 and 4 combined and with a cutting point located between scores 29 and 30

| TOTAL SCORES | RESPONSE CATEGORIES | | TOTAL |
	(1, 2)	(3, 4)	
30 and above	33	267	300
29 and below	271	62	333
Total	304	329	633

cells on the principal diagonal are the lower-left and the upper-right cells of the 2 x 2 table. We see that if the cutting point is drawn between the class intervals 11-20 and 21-23, we obtain the 2 x 2 table shown in Table 9.5. Since the smaller of the two frequencies of the cells on the principal diagonal is 33 and the frequencies of the two error cells are

TABLE 9.7

A 2 × 2 table for the data of Table 9.4 with response categories 1, 2, and 3 combined and with a cutting point located between scores 38 and 39

| TOTAL SCORES | RESPONSE CATEGORIES | | TOTAL |
	(1, 2, 3)	(4)	
39 and above	18	69	87
38 and below	501	45	546
Total	519	114	633

19 and 32, this table barely meets the minimum requirements of the rule that no error cell should have a larger frequency than the smaller of the two frequencies on the principal diagonal.

We now consider the combination (1, 2) (3, 4). Again, we attempt to form a 2 x 2 table by drawing a line or cutting point in the distribution of total scores such that the rule regarding the error cells is observed. If we put the cutting point between the class intervals 28-29 and 30-32, we obtain the 2 x 2 table shown in Table 9.6. This table also meets the criterion and is judged acceptable.

Table 9.7 is formed by taking the combination (1, 2, 3) (4). By placing the cutting point in the distribution of total scores between the class intervals 35-38 and 39-42, we obtain the frequencies shown in the cells of Table 9.7. This table is also judged acceptable, in terms of our rule regarding the error cells.

A second rule that is to be observed with respect to the 2 x 2 tables formed from combining response categories to a single statement is that *the sum of the frequencies in the two error cells should be less than 20 per cent of the total frequency*. For the present example we have a total frequency of 633, and 20 per cent of 633 is approximately 127. It may be observed that in all three of the 2 x 2 tables formed from the responses to Statement 1, the sum of the two error cells is less than 127. The three cutting points for Statement 1, thus, also meet the requirements of the second rule.

Table 9.8 shows the distribution of total scores in terms of the response categories of the second statement in the 11-statement scale given to the Air Force officers. The three

TABLE 9.8

Response to Statement 2 as related to total scores*

Total Scores	Response Categories				Total
	1	2	3	4	
43 - 44			3	43	46
39 - 42			9	32	41
35 - 38	2	3	16	51	72
33 - 34	1	2	36	30	69
30 - 32	2	6	37	27	72
28 - 29	1	5	53	10	69
26 - 27		11	42	14	67
24 - 25	2	14	37	5	58
21 - 23		22	49	3	74
11 - 20	7	28	28	2	65
Total	15	91	310	217	633

*Reproduced from Stouffer, Borgatta, Hays, and Henry (1952), Table 4, p. 286.

2 x 2 tables formed by combining response categories for this statement are shown in Table 9.9. It may be observed that two of the 2 x 2 tables formed by combining the response categories, (1) (2, 3, 4) and (1, 2) (3, 4), are judged unsatisfactory in that for each of these tables, the error cells have a larger frequency than the smaller of the two frequencies on the principal diagonal. It is also true, in the case of (1, 2) (3, 4), that we have a frequency of $49 + 82 = 131$ in

TABLE 9.9

The three 2 × 2 tables for the data of Table 9.8

| TOTAL SCORES | RESPONSE CATEGORIES | | TOTAL |
	(1)	(2, 3, 4)	
21 and above	8	560	568
20 and below	7	58	65
Total	15	618	633

| TOTAL SCORES | RESPONSE CATEGORIES | | TOTAL |
	(1, 2)	(3, 4)	
24 and above	49	445	494
23 and below	57	82	139
Total	106	527	633

| TOTAL SCORES | RESPONSE CATEGORIES | | TOTAL |
	(1, 2, 3)	(4)	
35 and above	33	126	159
34 and below	383	91	474
Total	416	217	633

the two error cells and this frequency exceeds 127 or 20 per cent of the total frequency.[5]

In the same manner described above, the three 2 x 2 tables are formed for each of the various statements and each table is tested to determine whether or not it meets the two rules stated. When this step is completed, the cutting points of the 2 x 2 tables can then be arranged in order from the largest frequency of favorable responses to the smallest. The frequen-

[5] Stouffer, Borgatta, Hays, and Henry (1952) point out that an occasional exception to the 20 per cent rule may be made, but that ordinarily a cutting point failing to meet this requirement should be discarded.

TABLE 9.10

Statements and cutting points used in the construction of the contrived statements†

STATEMENTS	RESPONSE CATEGORY WEIGHTS		FREQUENCY FAVORABLE	CONTRIVED STATEMENT IN WHICH THE ORIGINAL STATEMENT IS USED
	0	1		
10	1	2,3,4	620	*
2	1	2,3,4	618	*
5	1	2,3,4	608	*
7	1	2,3,4	601	*
3	1	2,3,4	590	*
1	1	2,3,4	581	**
9	1	2,3,4	580	**
11	1	2,3,4	577	**
8	1	2,3,4	568	*
2	1,2	3,4	527	*
6	1	2,3,4	507	I
10	1,2	3,4	496	I
4	1	2,3,4	489	I
5	1,2	3,4	418	**
9	1,2	3,4	371	II
7	1,2	3,4	370	**
3	1,2	3,4	363	II
11	1,2	3,4	360	II
8	1,2	3,4	349	**
1	1,2	3,4	329	**
4	1,2	3,4	230	III
6	1,2	3,4	220	III
2	1,2,3	4	217	III
10	1,2,3	4	200	**
5	1,2,3	4	134	IV
11	1,2,3	4	134	**
9	1,2,3	4	131	**
3	1,2,3	4	126	**
8	1,2,3	4	125	IV
7	1,2,3	4	119	**
1	1,2,3	4	114	IV
4	1,2,3	4	86	**
6	1,2,3	4	78	**

*Statement with this cutting point has error cell with greater frequency than the smaller of the two frequencies on the principal diagonal.

**Statement with this cutting point satisfies the error rule, but was not used in forming the Contrived Statements.

†Reproduced from Stouffer, Borgatta, Hays, and Henry (1952), Table 5, p. 289.

cy of favorable responses for the three cutting points of Statement 1 are 581, 329, and 114. For Statement 2, the frequencies are 618, 527, and 217. The ordering of the cutting points for the 2 x 2 tables obtained from the complete 11-statement scale is shown in Table 9.10.

CONTRIVED STATEMENTS

Stouffer, Borgatta, Hays, and Henry used Table 9.10 to select triplets to make up four contrived statements. Roman numerals are used to indicate the triplets making up a contrived statement. For example, Contrived Statement I, is made up of original Statements 4 and 6 (with categories 2, 3, and 4 treated as favorable) and original Statement 10 (with categories 3 and 4 treated as favorable).

In selecting triplets to make up a contrived statement, one should seek three cutting points with approximately the same frequency of favorable responses. For example, for Contrived Statement I, we see that these frequencies are 507, 496, and 489. In addition, the different triplets should be spaced as evenly as possible over the entire range of favorable frequencies. [6]

It may be observed that all but one (Statement 7) of the original 11 statements are used in forming the contrived statements.

SCORING CONTRIVED STATEMENTS

The new scale thus obtained from Table 9.10 consists of 10

[6] Stouffer, Borgatta, Hays, and Henry (1952, p. 288) point out that several cutting points which met the test of their two rules were not used. These are designated by the double asterisk in Table 9.10. These cuts were not used for two reasons: "(1) Cutting points so close so the end of the scale were not desired; and (2) it was preferred to use two of the same items (with different cuts) in forming Contrived Item II."

statements making up four contrived statements. This set of 10 statements can then be given to a new group of subjects and scores assigned on the basis of responses not to the individual statements but rather to the contrived statements. The scoring system used for the contrived statements is to give an individual a weight of 1 if his responses on two *or* three of the triplets making up the contrived statement are such that they would also be weighted 1. For example, we may consider the scoring for Contrived Statement I, of Table 9.10.

A person would be given a weight of 1 in response to Statement 6, if his response fell in categories 2, 3, or 4. He would also be given a weight of 1 if his response fell in either category 3 or 4 to Statement 10. On Statement 4, he would receive a weight of 1 if his response fell in categories 2, 3, or 4. If his weights on this triplet were all 1, then he would receive a weight of 1 on Contrived Statement I. A person would also be given a weight of 1 on this contrived statement if any two of his responses to the triplet received a weight of 1. Thus a subject might give a favorable response (categories 2, 3, or 4) to Statement 6 and also a favorable response to either Statement 10 (categories 3 or 4) or a favorable response to Statement 4 (categories 2, 3, or 4). Or he might give a favorable response to Statement 10 (categories 3 or 4) and a favorable response to Statement 4 (categories 2, 3, or 4). Any of these patterns of response to the triplet would also be assigned a weight of 1 on Contrived Statement I. If only one or none of the responses to the triplet fall in the favorable categories, the subject is assigned a score of 0 on the contrived statement.

REPRODUCIBILITY OF RESPONSES

With four contrived statements, each with dichotomous scoring of 1 or 0, the number of possible patterns of response is $2^4 = 16$. Of these 16 possible patterns of response, only 5 would be scale types and the other 11 would be non-scale types. For the 633 Air Force officers the distribution of scale and non-scale types was obtained. This distribution is shown in Table 9.11, with the non-scale types marked by an asterisk.

TABLE 9.11

Frequency of response patterns on the scale of four Contrived Statements†

Response Pattern	Frequency	Score	Error	$f \times$ Error
1 1 1 1	92	4	0	0
1 1 1 0*	1	3	2	2
1 1 0 1*	1	3	2	2
1 0 1 1*	22	3	2	44
0 1 1 1	103	3	0	0
0 1 1 0*	0	2	0	0
0 1 0 1*	8	2	2	16
0 0 1 1	157	2	0	0
0 0 0 1	106	1	0	0
0 0 1 0*	12	1	2	24
1 0 0 1*	0	2	0	0
0 0 0 0	130	0	0	0
0 1 0 0*	0	1	0	0
1 0 0 0*	0	1	0	0
1 1 0 0*	0	2	0	0
1 0 1 0*	1	2	2	2
	633			90

*Indicates non-scale pattern of response
†Reproduced from Stouffer, Borgatta, Hays, and Henry (1952), Table 6, p. 291.

It may be observed that only 45 out of the 633 subjects, or approximately 7 per cent, have non-scale patterns of response to the set of contrived statements.

Using the predicted response patterns corresponding to the scale types of Table 9.11, the errors of prediction for each of the non-scale types can be obtained. With a total of 90 errors out of $(4)(633) = 2,532$ responses, the coefficient of reproducibility would be approximately .96 for the scale of four contrived statements.

Stouffer, Borgatta, Hays, and Henry report that the rank order of the marginals for contrived statements, if they are relatively widely spaced, tends to remain invariant from sample to sample. As evidenced in support of this contention, they report that a scale based upon five contrived statements given to 25 different groups of subjects resulted in only four cases where there was a reversal of rank order of adjacent contrived statements out of 100 possibilities. In addition, the coefficients of reproducibility obtained from the various groups were all above .95.[7]

The use of H-technique for improving cumulative scales would thus seem to be a procedure worth considering if a set of 10 or more statements fails to have satisfactorily spaced cutting points and yet approximates a Guttman scale in the original test of the individual statements for scalability.

W-TECHNIQUE

Edwards (1956) has devised another technique, which might be called W-technique, for improving cumulative scales. He first scales a set of N attitude statements about some psychological object by the method of equal-appearing or successive intervals, so that a scale value representing the degree of favorability of each statement is obtained. From the initial set of N statements, a smaller set of n statements is selected in such a way that the scale separations of the statements are approximately equal.

Each of the n statements is then paired with every other

---

[7]Thistlewaite and Kamenetzky (1955) have used H-technique in the construction of a scale designed to measure attitude toward the Korean War. They report coefficients of reproducibility ranging from .96 to .99 for four samples.

statement, as in the method of paired comparisons. In each pair of statements, one will have a higher, or more favorable, scale value than the other. The statement with the higher scale value in each pair may be designated as A and the statement with the lower scale value as B. These pairs of statements are then presented to subjects with instructions to choose the statement, A or B, in each pair that best indicates how they feel about the psychological object under consideration. A score for each subject is obtained by counting the number of times that he has chosen the more favorable or A statement in the set of $n(n-1)/2$ paired comparisons.

Edwards hypothesizes that a subject's choice in each of the AB pairs will be a function of the subject's own position on the latent attitude continuum. He will choose, in other words, that statement in each pair that is closer to his own position. The subject's own position on the latent attitude continuum is, of course, unknown and must be determined from the choices he makes when confronted with the AB pairs of statements. If a subject falls exactly half-way between the scale values of a given AB pair, then his choice should be a matter of chance and all such choices will contribute to the unreliability of the scores obtained from the scale and also reduce the degree of reproducibility of the statement responses from the scores.

In one test of his method, Edwards selected 9 statements from two forms of an equal-appearing interval scale designed to measure "Attitude Toward the Introductory Course in General Psychology." The scale values of these statements on the equal-appearing interval continuum were: 8.7, 7.8, 6.8, 5.8, 4.9, 4.1, 3.0, 2.0, and 1.0. High scale values correspond to the favorable end of the equal-appearing interval continuum. Each of the 9 statements was paired with every other statement to give $9(9-1)/2 = 36$ pairs of AB statements.

The pairs of statements in the scale were arranged so that for the odd-numbered pairs, the first statement was the A or more favorable statement and in the even-numbered pairs the second statement was the A or more favorable statement. This arrangement was for scoring convenience and Edwards reports that there was no evidence that the students subsequently given the scale were aware of the ordering of the pairs.

Scores on the attitude scale consisting of 36 pairs of statements were obtained for 349 students. Responses of the students to the statements were scored by giving a weight of 1 each time the A or more favorable statement was chosen in a given AB pair. The test papers were also divided into two groups of 175 and 174 by taking alternate papers. All statistical analyses were then done with the first group of 175 papers and the results checked with the second group of 174 papers. Using methods described previously, the proportion of favorable or A responses was obtained for each AB pair of statements. Using these proportions the predicted response patterns for the various scores were determined. The predicted response patterns were then compared with those actually observed.

An error of prediction was counted each time an observed response to a given pair of statements failed to correspond to the predicted response for that pair of statements based upon the total score. Predictions were made for a total of (175) (36) = 6,300 responses, with 711 being in error. The proportion of errors was thus $711/6,300 = .113$ and the coefficient of reproducibility was equal to $1 - .113$ or $.887$. Because of the relatively large number of statements, 36, tested for scalability and the relatively small size of the sample, 175, the results obtained were checked with the hold-out sample of 174 papers.

For each of the papers in this second sample the observed

response patterns were compared with the predicted response patterns based upon the data of the first sample. The errors of prediction for this second sample were thus obtained independently of any consideration of the proportions of favorable responses given by members of the second group. For the second sample the coefficient of reproducibility was $1 - .121$ or .879, a value not substantially different from that obtained with the first sample. [8]

In the test described above, Edwards included statements with "neutral" scale values along the equal-appearing interval continuum. Since, as the study by Edwards and Kilpatrick (1948) cited previously showed, "neutral" statements tend to lower reproducibility more than statements with scale values falling in other than the "neutral" sections of the Thurstone continuum, Edwards believed that it would be worthwhile to investigate the scalability of statements, using W-technique, with "neutral" statements eliminated. He, therefore, eliminated the two statements with scale values of 4.1 and 5.8 from the set of 9 statements.

Using only the $7(7 - 1)/2 = 21$ paired comparisons, the two sets of 175 and 174 papers were rescored. Response patterns and errors of prediction for the first group of 175 papers were obtained as before. The coefficient of reproducibility for this 21-statement scale was, as expected, somewhat higher and equal to .914 for the first sample.

Repeating the analysis with the second set of 174 papers, using the predicted response patterns obtained with the first set, Edwards found the coefficient of reproducibility for this set of papers to be .90. This value is quite similar to that

---

[8] Kuder-Richardson (1937) reliability coefficients were obtained for each sample. For the first set of papers this coefficient was .869 and for the second it was .883.

obtained with the first set of papers and indicates that the stability of the rank ordering of the statements with respect to the frequency of favorable response could not have shifted much from the first to the second sample. [9]

These results would seem to indicate that using the method of paired comparisons in conjunction with a set of attitude statements with known scale values on an equal-appearing or successive-interval continuum has promise as a technique for the construction of attitude scales with a high degree of reproducibility and satisfactory reliability, as does also H-technique.

On the one hand, H-technique, as we have seen, results in the reduction of the number of possible scale types by taking a relatively large number of statements and using these to form a smaller number of contrived items. W-technique, on the other hand, results in an increase in the number of possible scale types by taking a relatively small number of statements in all possible pairs, thus increasing the number of items in the scale.

QUESTIONS AND PROBLEMS

1. Use the summated-rating data obtained previously for the 12-statement scale constructed by the scale-discrimination technique to develop a set of contrived statements following the procedures involved in H-technique. The reproducibility of this scale of contrived statements can then be tested in terms of the responses obtained to the statements when they were scored singly in the previous chapter by the scale-discrimination technique.

2. Equal-appearing interval scale values are known for the 12 statements used in Problem 1. Arrange them in rank order of their equal-appearing interval scale values and take every other statement to obtain a set of 6 statements. From all possible paired comparisons

---

[9] The Kuder-Richardson (1937) coefficients of reliability for these two samples were .829 for the first set of papers and .861 for the second.

in the set of 6 statements and give these pairs to a new group of approximately 100 subjects following the procedure used by Edwards in W-technique. Obtain scores for each subject by giving 1 point each time he chooses the more favorable statement in a given pair. Test the scale for reproducibility.

3. Why, if we have a relatively large number of statements and potentially a relatively large number of scale types, do we need to give some attention to the spacing of the marginals, that is, to the proportions giving the favorable response, and the size of the sample to be used in testing for scalability?

4. What are the rules used in H-technique in regarding a cutting point as satisfactory?

REFERENCES AND SUGGESTED READINGS

EDWARDS, A. L. *Experimental design in psychological research.* New York: Rinehart, 1950.

*———— A technique for increasing the reproducibility of cumulative attitude scales. *J. appl. Psychol.*, 1956, 40, 263-265.

———— and KILPATRICK, F. P. Scale analysis and the measurement of social attitudes, *Psychometrika,* 1948, 13, 99-114.

GREEN, B. F. Attitude measurement. In G. Lindzey (Ed.), *Handbook of social psychology.* Cambridge, Mass.: Addison-Wesley, 1954. Pp. 335-369.

KUDER, G. F., and RICHARDSON, M. W. The theory of the estimation of test reliability. *Psychometrika,* 1937, 2, 151-160.

RILEY, MATILDA W., RILEY, J. W., JR., TOBY, J., et al. *Sociological studies in scale analysis.* New Brunswick, N. J.: Rutgers Univ. Press, 1954.

*STOUFFER, S. A., BORGATTA, E. F., HAYS, D. G., and HENRY, A. F. A technique for improving cumulative scales. *Publ. Opin. Quart.,* 1952, 16, 273-291.

THISTLEWAITE, D. L., and KAMENETZKY, J. Attitude change through refutation and elaboration of audience counterarguments. *J. abnorm. soc. Psychol.,* 1955, 51, 3-12.

Appendix

TABLE I. Table of normal deviates z corresponding to proportions p of a dichotomized unit normal distribution

p	0	1	2	3	4	5	6	7	8	9
.99	2.326	2.366	2.409	2.457	2.512	2.576	2.652	2.748	2.878	3.090
.98	2.054	2.075	2.097	2.120	2.144	2.170	2.197	2.226	2.257	2.290
.97	1.881	1.896	1.911	1.927	1.943	1.960	1.977	1.995	2.014	2.034
.96	1.751	1.762	1.774	1.787	1.799	1.812	1.825	1.838	1.852	1.866
.95	1.645	1.655	1.665	1.675	1.685	1.695	1.706	1.717	1.728	1.739
.94	1.555	1.563	1.572	1.580	1.589	1.598	1.607	1.616	1.626	1.635
.93	1.476	1.483	1.491	1.499	1.506	1.514	1.522	1.530	1.538	1.546
.92	1.405	1.412	1.419	1.426	1.433	1.440	1.447	1.454	1.461	1.468
.91	1.341	1.347	1.353	1.359	1.366	1.372	1.379	1.385	1.392	1.398
.90	1.282	1.287	1.293	1.299	1.305	1.311	1.317	1.323	1.329	1.335
.89	1.227	1.232	1.237	1.243	1.248	1.254	1.259	1.265	1.270	1.276
.88	1.175	1.180	1.185	1.190	1.195	1.200	1.206	1.211	1.216	1.221
.87	1.126	1.131	1.136	1.141	1.146	1.150	1.155	1.160	1.165	1.170
.86	1.080	1.085	1.089	1.094	1.098	1.103	1.108	1.112	1.117	1.122
.85	1.036	1.041	1.045	1.049	1.054	1.058	1.063	1.067	1.071	1.076
.84	.994	.999	1.003	1.007	1.011	1.015	1.019	1.024	1.028	1.032
.83	.954	.958	.962	.966	.970	.974	.978	.982	.986	.990
.82	.915	.919	.923	.927	.931	.935	.938	.942	.946	.950
.81	.878	.882	.885	.889	.893	.896	.900	.904	.908	.912
.80	.842	.845	.849	.852	.856	.860	.863	.867	.871	.874
.79	.806	.810	.813	.817	.820	.824	.827	.831	.834	.838
.78	.772	.776	.779	.782	.786	.789	.793	.796	.800	.803
.77	.739	.742	.745	.749	.752	.755	.759	.762	.765	.769
.76	.706	.710	.713	.716	.719	.722	.726	.729	.732	.736
.75	.674	.678	.681	.684	.687	.690	.693	.697	.700	.703
.74	.643	.646	.650	.653	.656	.659	.662	.665	.668	.671
.73	.613	.616	.619	.622	.625	.628	.631	.634	.637	.640
.72	.583	.586	.589	.592	.595	.598	.601	.604	.607	.610
.71	.553	.556	.559	.562	.565	.568	.571	.574	.577	.580
.70	.524	.527	.530	.533	.536	.539	.542	.545	.548	.550
.69	.496	.499	.502	.504	.507	.510	.513	.516	.519	.522
.68	.468	.470	.473	.476	.479	.482	.485	.487	.490	.493
.67	.440	.443	.445	.448	.451	.454	.457	.459	.462	.465
.66	.412	.415	.418	.421	.423	.426	.429	.432	.434	.437
.65	.385	.388	.391	.393	.396	.399	.402	.404	.407	.410
.64	.358	.361	.364	.366	.369	.372	.375	.377	.380	.383
.63	.332	.335	.337	.340	.342	.345	.348	.350	.353	.356
.62	.305	.308	.311	.313	.316	.319	.321	.324	.327	.329
.61	.279	.282	.285	.287	.290	.292	.295	.298	.300	.303
.60	.253	.256	.259	.261	.264	.266	.269	.272	.274	.277
.59	.228	.230	.233	.235	.238	.240	.243	.246	.248	.251
.58	.202	.204	.207	.210	.212	.215	.217	.220	.222	.225
.57	.176	.179	.181	.184	.187	.189	.192	.194	.197	.199
.56	.151	.154	.156	.159	.161	.164	.166	.169	.171	.174
.55	.126	.128	.131	.133	.136	.138	.141	.143	.146	.148
.54	.100	.103	.105	.108	.111	.113	.116	.118	.121	.123
.53	.075	.078	.080	.083	.085	.088	.090	.093	.095	.098
.52	.050	.053	.055	.058	.060	.063	.065	.068	.070	.073
.51	.025	.028	.030	.033	.035	.038	.040	.043	.045	.048
.50	.000	.003	.005	.008	.010	.013	.015	.018	.020	.023

P	0	1	2	3	4	5	6	7	8	9
.49	− .025	− .023	− .020	− .018	− .015	− .013	− .010	− .008	− .005	− .003
.48	− .050	− .048	− .045	− .043	− .040	− .038	− .035	− .033	− .030	− .028
.47	− .075	− .073	− .070	− .068	− .065	− .063	− .060	− .058	− .055	− .053
.46	− .100	− .098	− .095	− .093	− .090	− .088	− .085	− .083	− .080	− .078
.45	− .126	− .123	− .121	− .118	− .116	− .113	− .111	− .108	− .105	− .103
.44	− .151	− .148	− .146	− .143	− .141	− .138	− .136	− .133	− .131	− .128
.43	− .176	− .174	− .171	− .169	− .166	− .164	− .161	− .159	− .156	− .154
.42	− .202	− .199	− .197	− .194	− .192	− .189	− .187	− .184	− .181	− .179
.41	− .228	− .225	− .222	− .220	− .217	− .215	− .212	− .210	− .207	− .204
.40	− .253	− .251	− .248	− .246	− .243	− .240	− .238	− .235	− .233	− .230
.39	− .279	− .277	− .274	− .272	− .269	− .266	− .264	− .261	− .259	− .256
.38	− .305	− .303	− .300	− .298	− .295	− .292	− .290	− .287	− .285	− .282
.37	− .332	− .329	− .327	− .324	− .321	− .319	− .316	− .313	− .311	− .308
.36	− .358	− .356	− .353	− .350	− .348	− .345	− .342	− .340	− .337	− .335
.35	− .385	− .383	− .380	− .377	− .375	− .372	− .369	− .366	− .364	− .361
.34	− .412	− .410	− .407	− .404	− .402	− .399	− .396	− .393	− .391	− .388
.33	− .440	− .437	− .434	− .432	− .429	− .426	− .423	− .421	− .418	− .415
.32	− .468	− .465	− .462	− .459	− .457	− .454	− .451	− .448	− .445	− .443
.31	− .496	− .493	− .490	− .487	− .485	− .482	− .479	− .476	− .473	− .470
.30	− .524	− .522	− .519	− .516	− .513	− .510	− .507	− .504	− .502	− .499
.29	− .553	− .550	− .548	− .545	− .542	− .539	− .536	− .533	− .530	− .527
.28	− .583	− .580	− .577	− .574	− .571	− .568	− .565	− .562	− .559	− .556
.27	− .613	− .610	− .607	− .604	− .601	− .598	− .595	− .592	− .589	− .586
.26	− .643	− .640	− .637	− .634	− .631	− .628	− .625	− .622	− .619	− .616
.25	− .674	− .671	− .668	− .665	− .662	− .659	− .656	− .653	− .650	− .646
.24	− .706	− .703	− .700	− .697	− .693	− .690	− .687	− .684	− .681	− .678
.23	− .739	− .736	− .732	− .729	− .726	− .722	− .719	− .716	− .713	− .710
.22	− .772	− .769	− .765	− .762	− .759	− .755	− .752	− .749	− .745	− .742
.21	− .806	− .803	− .800	− .796	− .793	− .789	− .786	− .782	− .779	− .776
.20	− .842	− .838	− .834	− .831	− .827	− .824	− .820	− .817	− .813	− .810
.19	− .878	− .874	− .871	− .867	− .863	− .860	− .856	− .852	− .849	− .845
.18	− .915	− .912	− .908	− .904	− .900	− .896	− .893	− .889	− .885	− .882
.17	− .954	− .950	− .946	− .942	− .938	− .935	− .931	− .927	− .923	− .919
.16	− .994	− .990	− .986	− .982	− .978	− .974	− .970	− .966	− .962	− .958
.15	−1.036	−1.032	−1.028	−1.024	−1.019	−1.015	−1.011	−1.007	−1.003	− .999
.14	−1.080	−1.076	−1.071	−1.067	−1.063	−1.058	−1.054	−1.049	−1.045	−1.041
.13	−1.126	−1.122	−1.117	−1.112	−1.108	−1.103	−1.098	−1.094	−1.089	−1.085
.12	−1.175	−1.170	−1.165	−1.160	−1.155	−1.150	−1.146	−1.141	−1.136	−1.131
.11	−1.227	−1.221	−1.216	−1.211	−1.206	−1.200	−1.195	−1.190	−1.185	−1.180
.10	−1.282	−1.276	−1.270	−1.265	−1.259	−1.254	−1.248	−1.243	−1.237	−1.232
.09	−1.341	−1.335	−1.329	−1.323	−1.317	−1.311	−1.305	−1.299	−1.293	−1.287
.08	−1.405	−1.398	−1.392	−1.385	−1.379	−1.372	−1.366	−1.359	−1.353	−1.347
.07	−1.476	−1.468	−1.461	−1.454	−1.447	−1.440	−1.433	−1.426	−1.419	−1.412
.06	−1.555	−1.546	−1.538	−1.530	−1.522	−1.514	−1.506	−1.499	−1.491	−1.483
.05	−1.645	−1.635	−1.626	−1.616	−1.607	−1.598	−1.589	−1.580	−1.572	−1.563
.04	−1.751	−1.739	−1.728	−1.717	−1.706	−1.695	−1.685	−1.675	−1.665	−1.655
.03	−1.881	−1.866	−1.852	−1.838	−1.825	−1.812	−1.799	−1.787	−1.774	−1.762
.02	−2.054	−2.034	−2.014	−1.995	−1.977	−1.960	−1.943	−1.927	−1.911	−1.896
.01	−2.326	−2.290	−2.257	−2.226	−2.197	−2.170	−2.144	−2.120	−2.097	−2.075
.00		−3.090	−2.878	−2.748	−2.652	−2.576	−2.512	−2.457	−2.409	−2.366

TABLE II. Table of the angular transformation of percentages to degrees*

p	0	1	2	3	4	5	6	7	8	9
0.0	0	0.57	0.81	0.99	1.15	1.28	1.40	1.52	1.62	1.72
0.1	1.81	1.90	1.99	2.07	2.14	2.22	2.29	2.36	2.43	2.50
0.2	2.56	2.63	2.69	2.75	2.81	2.87	2.92	2.98	3.03	3.09
0.3	3.14	3.19	3.24	3.29	3.34	3.39	3.44	3.49	3.53	3.58
0.4	3.63	3.67	3.72	3.76	3.80	3.85	3.89	3.93	3.97	4.01
0.5	4.05	4.09	4.13	4.17	4.21	4.25	4.29	4.33	4.37	4.40
0.6	4.44	4.48	4.52	4.55	4.59	4.62	4.66	4.69	4.73	4.76
0.7	4.80	4.83	4.87	4.90	4.93	4.97	5.00	5.03	5.07	5.10
0.8	5.13	5.16	5.20	5.23	5.26	5.29	5.32	5.35	5.38	5.41
0.9	5.44	5.47	5.50	5.53	5.56	5.59	5.62	5.65	5.68	5.71
1	5.74	6.02	6.29	6.55	6.80	7.04	7.27	7.49	7.71	7.92
2	8.13	8.33	8.53	8.72	8.91	9.10	9.28	9.46	9.63	9.81
3	9.98	10.14	10.31	10.47	10.63	10.78	10.94	11.09	11.24	11.39
4	11.54	11.68	11.83	11.97	12.11	12.25	12.39	12.52	12.66	12.79
5	12.92	13.05	13.18	13.31	13.44	13.56	13.69	13.81	13.94	14.06
6	14.18	14.30	14.42	14.54	14.65	14.77	14.89	15.00	15.12	15.23
7	15.34	15.45	15.56	15.68	15.79	15.89	16.00	16.11	16.22	16.32
8	16.43	16.54	16.64	16.74	16.85	16.95	17.05	17.16	17.26	17.36
9	17.46	17.56	17.66	17.76	17.85	17.95	18.05	18.15	18.24	18.34
10	18.44	18.53	18.63	18.72	18.81	18.91	19.00	19.09	19.19	19.28
11	19.37	19.46	19.55	19.64	19.73	19.82	19.91	20.00	20.09	20.18
12	20.27	20.36	20.44	20.53	20.62	20.70	20.79	20.88	20.96	21.05
13	21.13	21.22	21.30	21.39	21.47	21.56	21.64	21.72	21.81	21.89
14	21.97	22.06	22.14	22.22	22.30	22.38	22.46	22.55	22.63	22.71
15	22.79	22.87	22.95	23.03	23.11	23.19	23.26	23.34	23.42	23.50
16	23.58	23.66	23.73	23.81	23.89	23.97	24.04	24.12	24.20	24.27
17	24.35	24.43	24.50	24.58	24.65	24.73	24.80	24.88	24.95	25.03
18	25.10	25.18	25.25	25.33	25.40	25.48	25.55	25.62	25.70	25.77
19	25.84	25.92	25.99	26.06	26.13	26.21	26.28	26.35	26.42	26.49
20	26.56	26.64	26.71	26.78	26.85	26.92	26.99	27.06	27.13	27.20
21	27.28	27.35	27.42	27.49	27.56	27.63	27.69	27.76	27.83	27.90
22	27.97	28.04	28.11	28.18	28.25	28.32	28.38	28.45	28.52	28.59
23	28.66	28.73	28.79	28.86	28.93	29.00	29.06	29.13	29.20	29.27
24	29.33	29.40	29.47	29.53	29.60	29.67	29.73	29.80	29.87	29.93
25	30.00	30.07	30.13	30.20	30.26	30.33	30.40	30.46	30.53	30.59
26	30.66	30.72	30.79	30.85	30.92	30.98	31.05	31.11	31.18	31.24
27	31.31	31.37	31.44	31.50	31.56	31.63	31.69	31.76	31.82	31.88
28	31.95	32.01	32.08	32.14	32.20	32.27	32.33	32.39	32.46	32.52
29	32.58	32.65	32.71	32.77	32.83	32.90	32.96	33.02	33.09	33.15

*Table II is reprinted from Table 11.12.1 of Snedecor: *Statistical Methods*, Iowa State College Press, Ames, Iowa, by permission of the author and his publisher, and by permission of C. I. Bliss, who computed the tabled entries.

p	0	1	2	3	4	5	6	7	8	9
30	33.21	33.27	33.34	33.40	33.46	33.52	33.58	33.65	33.71	33.77
31	33.83	33.89	33.96	34.02	34.08	34.14	34.20	34.27	34.33	34.39
32	34.45	34.51	34.57	34.63	34.70	34.76	34.82	34.88	34.94	35.00
33	35.06	35.12	35.18	35.24	35.30	35.37	35.43	35.49	35.55	35.61
34	35.67	35.73	35.79	35.85	35.91	35.97	36.03	36.09	36.15	36.21
35	36.27	36.33	36.39	36.45	36.51	36.57	36.63	36.69	36.75	36.81
36	36.87	36.93	36.99	37.05	37.11	37.17	37.23	37.29	37.35	37.41
37	37.47	37.52	37.58	37.64	37.70	37.76	37.82	37.88	37.94	38.00
38	38.06	38.12	38.17	38.23	38.29	38.35	38.41	38.47	38.53	38.59
39	38.65	38.70	38.76	38.82	38.88	38.94	39.00	39.06	39.11	39.17
40	39.23	39.29	39.35	39.41	39.47	39.52	39.58	39.64	39.70	39.76
41	39.82	39.87	39.93	39.99	40.05	40.11	40.16	40.22	40.28	40.34
42	40.40	40.46	40.51	40.57	40.63	40.69	40.74	40.80	40.86	40.92
43	40.98	41.03	41.09	41.15	41.21	41.27	41.32	41.38	41.44	41.50
44	41.55	41.61	41.67	41.73	41.78	41.84	41.90	41.96	42.02	42.07
45	42.13	42.19	42.25	42.30	42.36	42.42	42.48	42.53	42.59	42.65
46	42.71	42.76	42.82	42.88	42.94	42.99	43.05	43.11	43.17	43.22
47	43.28	43.34	43.39	43.45	43.51	43.57	43.62	43.68	43.74	43.80
48	43.85	43.91	43.97	44.03	44.08	44.14	44.20	44.25	44.31	44.37
49	44.43	44.48	44.54	44.60	44.66	44.71	44.77	44.83	44.89	44.94
50	45.00	45.06	45.11	45.17	45.23	45.29	45.34	45.40	45.46	45.52
51	45.57	45.63	45.69	45.75	45.80	45.86	45.92	45.97	46.03	46.09
52	46.15	46.20	46.26	46.32	46.38	46.43	46.49	46.55	46.61	46.66
53	46.72	46.78	46.83	46.89	46.95	47.01	47.06	47.12	47.18	47.24
54	47.29	47.35	47.41	47.47	47.52	47.58	47.64	47.70	47.75	47.81
55	47.87	47.93	47.98	48.04	48.10	48.16	48.22	48.27	48.33	48.39
56	48.45	48.50	48.56	48.62	48.68	48.73	48.79	48.85	48.91	48.97
57	49.02	49.08	49.14	49.20	49.26	49.31	49.37	49.43	49.49	49.54
58	49.60	49.66	49.72	49.78	49.84	49.89	49.95	50.01	50.07	50.13
59	50.18	50.24	50.30	50.36	50.42	50.48	50.53	50.59	50.65	50.71
60	50.77	50.83	50.89	50.94	51.00	51.06	51.12	51.18	51.24	51.30
61	51.35	51.41	51.47	51.53	51.59	51.65	51.71	51.77	51.83	51.88
62	51.94	52.00	52.06	52.12	52.18	52.24	52.30	52.36	52.42	52.48
63	52.53	52.59	52.65	52.71	52.77	52.83	52.89	52.95	53.01	53.07
64	53.13	53.19	53.25	53.31	53.37	53.43	53.49	53.55	53.61	53.67
65	53.73	53.79	53.85	53.91	53.97	54.03	54.09	54.15	54.21	54.27
66	54.33	54.39	54.45	54.51	54.57	54.63	54.70	54.76	54.82	54.88
67	54.94	55.00	55.06	55.12	55.18	55.24	55.30	55.37	55.43	55.49
68	55.55	55.61	55.67	55.73	55.80	55.86	55.92	55.98	56.04	56.11
69	56.17	56.23	56.29	56.35	56.42	56.48	56.54	56.60	56.66	56.73

p	0	1	2	3	4	5	6	7	8	9
70	56.79	56.85	56.91	56.98	57.04	57.10	57.17	57.23	57.29	57.35
71	57.42	57.48	57.54	57.61	57.67	57.73	57.80	57.86	57.92	57.99
72	58.05	58.12	58.18	58.24	58.31	58.37	58.44	58.50	58.56	58.63
73	58.69	58.76	58.82	58.89	58.95	59.02	59.08	59.15	59.21	59.28
74	59.34	59.41	59.47	59.54	59.60	59.67	59.74	59.80	59.87	59.93
75	60.00	60.07	60.13	60.20	60.27	60.33	60.40	60.47	60.53	60.60
76	60.67	60.73	60.80	60.87	60.94	61.00	61.07	61.14	61.21	61.27
77	61.34	61.41	61.48	61.55	61.62	61.68	61.75	61.82	61.89	61.96
78	62.03	62.10	62.17	62.24	62.31	62.37	63.44	62.51	62.58	62.65
79	62.72	62.80	62.87	62.94	63.01	63.08	63.15	63.22	63.29	63.36
80	63.44	63.51	63.58	63.65	63.72	63.79	63.87	63.94	64.01	64.08
81	64.16	64.23	64.30	64.38	64.45	64.52	64.60	64.67	64.75	64.82
82	64.90	64.97	65.05	65.12	65.20	65.27	65.35	65.42	65.50	65.57
83	65.65	65.73	65.80	65.88	65.96	66.03	66.11	66.19	66.27	66.34
84	66.42	66.50	66.58	66.66	66.74	66.81	66.89	66.97	67.05	67.13
85	67.21	67.29	67.37	67.45	67.54	67.62	67.70	67.78	67.86	67.94
86	68.03	68.11	68.19	68.28	68.36	68.44	68.53	68.61	68.70	68.78
87	68.87	68.95	69.04	69.12	69.21	69.30	69.38	69.47	69.56	69.64
88	69.73	69.82	69.91	70.00	70.09	70.18	70.27	70.36	70.45	70.54
89	70.63	70.72	70.81	70.91	71.00	71.09	71.19	71.28	71.37	71.47
90	71.56	71.66	71.76	71.85	71.95	72.05	72.15	72.24	72.34	72.44
91	72.54	72.64	72.74	72.84	72.95	73.05	73.15	73.26	73.36	73.46
92	73.57	73.68	73.78	73.89	74.00	74.11	74.21	74.32	74.44	74.55
93	74.66	74.77	74.88	75.00	75.11	75.23	75.35	75.46	75.58	75.70
94	75.82	75.94	76.06	76.19	76.31	76.44	76.56	76.69	76.82	76.95
95	77.08	77.21	77.34	77.48	77.61	77.75	77.89	78.03	78.17	78.32
96	78.46	78.61	78.76	78.91	79.06	79.22	79.37	79.53	79.69	79.86
97	80.02	80.19	80.37	80.54	80.72	80.90	81.09	81.28	81.47	81.67
98	81.87	82.08	82.29	82.51	82.73	82.96	83.20	83.45	83.71	83.98
99.0	84.26	84.29	84.32	84.35	84.38	84.41	84.44	84.47	84.50	84.53
99.1	84.56	84.59	84.62	84.65	84.68	84.71	84.74	84.77	84.80	84.84
99.2	84.87	84.90	84.93	84.97	85.00	85.03	85.07	85.10	85.13	85.17
99.3	85.20	85.24	85.27	85.31	85.34	85.38	85.41	85.45	85.48	85.52
99.4	85.56	85.60	85.63	85.67	85.71	85.75	85.79	85.83	85.87	85.91
99.5	85.95	85.99	86.03	86.07	86.11	86.15	86.20	86.24	86.28	86.33
99.6	86.37	86.42	86.47	86.51	86.56	86.61	86.66	86.71	86.76	86.81
99.7	86.86	86.91	86.97	87.02	87.08	87.13	87.19	87.25	87.31	87.37
99.8	87.44	87.50	87.57	87.64	87.71	87.78	87.86	87.93	88.01	88.10
99.9	88.19	88.28	88.38	88.48	88.60	88.72	88.85	89.01	89.19	89.43
100.0	90.00	—	—	—	—	—	—	—	—	—

TABLE III. Table of χ^2*

Degrees of Freedom	P = .99	.98	.95	.90	.80	.70	.50	.30	.20	.10	.05	.02	.01
1	.000157	.000628	.00393	.0158	.0642	.148	.455	1.074	1.642	2.706	3.841	5.412	6.635
2	.0201	.0404	.103	.211	.446	.713	1.386	2.408	3.219	4.605	5.991	7.824	9.210
3	.115	.185	.352	.584	1.005	1.424	2.366	3.665	4.642	6.251	7.815	9.837	11.341
4	.297	.429	.711	1.064	1.649	2.195	3.357	4.878	5.989	7.779	9.488	11.668	13.277
5	.554	.752	1.145	1.610	2.343	3.000	4.351	6.064	7.289	9.236	11.070	13.388	15.086
6	.872	1.134	1.635	2.204	3.070	3.828	5.348	7.231	8.558	10.645	12.592	15.033	16.812
7	1.239	1.564	2.167	2.833	3.822	4.671	6.346	8.383	9.803	12.017	14.067	16.622	18.475
8	1.646	2.032	2.733	3.490	4.594	5.527	7.344	9.524	11.030	13.362	15.507	18.168	20.090
9	2.088	2.532	3.325	4.168	5.380	6.393	8.343	10.656	12.242	14.684	16.919	19.679	21.666
10	2.558	3.059	3.940	4.865	6.179	7.267	9.342	11.781	13.442	15.987	18.307	21.161	23.209
11	3.053	3.609	4.575	5.578	6.989	8.148	10.341	12.899	14.631	17.275	19.675	22.618	24.725
12	3.571	4.178	5.226	6.304	7.807	9.034	11.340	14.011	15.812	18.549	21.026	24.054	26.217
13	4.107	4.765	5.892	7.042	8.634	9.926	12.340	15.119	16.985	19.812	22.362	25.472	27.688
14	4.660	5.368	6.571	7.790	9.467	10.821	13.339	16.222	18.151	21.064	23.685	26.873	29.141
15	5.229	5.985	7.261	8.547	10.307	11.721	14.339	17.322	19.311	22.307	24.996	28.259	30.578
16	5.812	6.614	7.962	9.312	11.152	12.624	15.338	18.418	20.465	23.542	26.296	29.633	32.000
17	6.408	7.255	8.672	10.085	12.002	13.531	16.338	19.511	21.615	24.769	27.587	30.995	33.409
18	7.015	7.906	9.390	10.865	12.857	14.440	17.338	20.601	22.760	25.989	28.869	32.346	34.805
19	7.633	8.567	10.117	11.651	13.716	15.352	18.338	21.689	23.900	27.204	30.144	33.687	36.191
20	8.260	9.237	10.851	12.443	14.578	16.266	19.337	22.775	25.038	28.412	31.410	35.020	37.566
21	8.897	9.915	11.591	13.240	15.445	17.182	20.337	23.858	26.171	29.615	32.671	36.343	38.932
22	9.542	10.600	12.338	14.041	16.314	18.101	21.337	24.939	27.301	30.813	33.924	37.659	40.289
23	10.196	11.293	13.091	14.848	17.187	19.021	22.337	26.018	28.429	32.007	35.172	38.968	41.638
24	10.856	11.992	13.848	15.659	18.062	19.943	23.337	27.096	29.553	33.196	36.415	40.270	42.980
25	11.524	12.697	14.611	16.473	18.940	20.867	24.337	28.172	30.675	34.382	37.652	41.566	44.314
26	12.198	13.409	15.379	17.292	19.820	21.792	25.336	29.246	31.795	35.563	38.885	42.856	45.642
27	12.879	14.125	16.151	18.114	20.703	22.719	26.336	30.319	32.912	36.741	40.113	44.140	46.963
28	13.565	14.847	16.928	18.939	21.588	23.647	27.336	31.391	34.027	37.916	41.337	45.419	48.278
28	14.256	15.574	17.708	19.768	22.475	24.577	28.336	32.461	35.139	39.087	42.557	46.693	49.588
30	14.953	16.306	18.493	20.599	23.364	25.508	29.336	33.530	36.250	40.256	43.773	47.962	50.892

*Table III is reprinted from Table III of Fisher: *Statistical Methods for Research Workers*, Oliver & Boyd Ltd., Edinburgh, by permission of the author and his publishers.

For larger values of df, the expression $\sqrt{2\chi^2} - \sqrt{2\,(df)} - 1$ may be used as a normal deviate with unit standard error.

Index of Names

252

Index of Subjects